OFF MY ROCKER

one man's tasty, twisted,
star-studded quest for everlasting music

KENNY WEISSBERG

Sandra Jonas Publishing House
BOULDER, CO

Sandra Jonas Publishing House
PO Box 20892
Boulder, CO 80308
www.sandrajonaspublishing.com

Printed in Canada
19 18 17 16 15 14   1 2 3 4 5 6

Book Design by Sandra Jonas

Publisher's Cataloguing-in-Publication Data

Weissberg, Kenny.

Off my rocker : one man's tasty, twisted, star-studded quest for everlasting music / Kenny Weissberg — Boulder, CO : Sandra Jonas Pub. House, 2014.

p. : ill. ; cm.
ISBN: 9780985581565

1. Weissberg, Kenny — Biography. 2. Disc jockeys — United States — Biography. 3. Music journalists — United States — Biography. 4. Rock mu-sicians — United States — Biography. 5. Music publicity — United States — History.

ML429.W45 2013   781.64092 — dc23

2013940054

PHOTOGRAPHY CREDITS:

Samantha Dudley, photography editor, *The Quad News* (257), Sam Gold-berg (27), Gary Heery (198), Dominique Isserman (252), Keith Perry (244), Bill Sevcik (177), Jon Steele (45), Hans Teensma/Bill Warren (115), Bill Warren (112).

For Helen
You are the one. We are the two.

contents

author's note

This memoir is based on information gleaned from my personal journals, research, taped interviews, conversations with people who appear in the book, and my own memory of real events and interactions. I have changed the names and identifying characteristics of certain individuals to preserve their anonymity. In a few instances, I have melded real people into composite characters.

PART I
A Kid from Jersey

I.

december 10, 1967

THE AFTERNOON IT WAS ANNOUNCED that Otis Redding and the Bar-Kays would be performing in Madison, two friends and I cut class and raced to the Factory, where we plunked down three bucks apiece for tickets.

In the weeks leading up to the concert, Steve Kruvant, Rick Kleiner, and I wore out the grooves of Otis's *Live in Europe* LP. From the emcee's introductory cheerleading ("Gimme an O!") to the final horn blasts of "Try a Little Tenderness," it was far and away the most dynamic live album of its time. Throughout the fall of 1967, we browbeat our University of Wisconsin dorm mates with repeated spins and shout-alongs.

I would impersonate Otis, plunging down to my knees and belting out a plaintive version of "I've Been Loving You Too Long," a song I nailed in the confines of my bedroom but butchered mercilessly during an audition for a college musical (I didn't make the callbacks). Kruvant aced Redding's frenetic up-tempo numbers like "Can't Turn You Loose" and "Day Tripper," but Kleiner couldn't carry a tune in a briefcase, so he'd mimic the choreographed horn section.

All of us came from the suburbs. Kruvant and I grew up in the lush village of South Orange, New Jersey, and Kleiner attended the fabled Beverly Hills High. Three white Jewish boys—yet every day, we playacted at being hybrids of Memphis/Motown soul singers.

I was obsessed with Redding's entire catalog, from his 1964 debut *Pain in My Heart* through his more recent duet album with Carla Thomas, *King & Queen*. The wait was interminable and I created an oversized calendar to cross out the days until I'd get to see my idol.

On the afternoon of the concert, we arrived at the Factory three hours early for the 6:30 show. We wanted to be first in line so we could press up against the stage as soon as the doors opened. The temperature was in the low twenties and the icy wind stung our faces, but it didn't matter. We would have stood all day in a raging snowstorm for a chance to see Otis perform.

Our thermos of hot chocolate didn't last long, and we kept warm by jogging in place and chanting the refrain from "Respect." At 5:30, the more casual Otis fans began showing up, and the line grew from three to three hundred.

When the doors hadn't opened by six o'clock, the horde became restless and started staccato clapping. The doors remained closed.

"Has anyone seen the bus pull up?" someone asked Kruvant.

"Let me run around the corner and look. Save my place."

We hadn't heard anything from inside the Factory either, but soundchecks in those days weren't the norm. Our pounding on the door was ignored.

"No bus," Kruvant reported.

At 6:30, word started spreading that Otis was a no-show. There was talk in line that he hadn't fully recovered from his recent throat surgery and wasn't ready to perform.

But he always made his dates.

The crowd began swapping Otis stories. "Did anyone see him at Monterey in June? He and Hendrix blew everyone off the stage."

"Yeah, I was there. I went to see the Byrds and Buffalo Spring-field. I had never even heard of Otis Redding—he kicked ass."

"Well, if he's so great, where the *fuck* is he?"

At 6:45, we got our answer when a stagehand came out the front door holding a placard above his head. Written on it in black marker were words I'll never forget:

OTIS REDDING AND BAR-KAYS HAVE BEEN IN A PLANE CRASH. REFUNDS AT THE BACK DOOR.

The building manager followed behind him and repeated the news into a megaphone. "We apologize for keeping you out here in the cold, but we just received confirmation that Otis Redding and his band have been in a plane crash. We're offering full refunds at the back door, but—"

Before he could finish, the long line of ticket holders dispersed and ran around the corner to reclaim their three-dollar investment. The announcer tried unsuccessfully to stem the tide. "Please be patient, people," he said, screaming at us now. "We're trying to fly in the Chambers Brothers from Boston in time for the 9:00 show. Your 6:30 tickets will be honored then. I repeat . . ."

Kruvant, Kleiner, and I seemed frozen in time. It was almost seven o'clock and it was just the three of us again, by ourselves, in front of the Factory—only now we were crying hysterically. Finally, we began walking the endless mile back to our dorm.

"Hey, wait a minute," I said. "Nobody said anything about Otis dying. Maybe they survived and he's in a hospital."

We sprinted home and turned on Madison's number-one Top 40 station, WISM. We heard the same report over and over for the next two hours, hoping it was wrong, yearning for a correction.

"Soul singer Otis Redding and his band, the Bar-Kays, were killed when their twin-engine Beechcraft crashed into Lake Monona, less than three miles from the Madison airport. Investigators are at the scene but rescue efforts are being hampered by fog, blowing snow, and poor visibility. There are no known survivors at this time." (We later learned that the Bar-Kays trumpeter, Ben Cauley, had miraculously lived.)

It was impossible to sleep that night. Visions of Otis drowning in the icy waters kept flashing through my mind. I put *Dictionary of Soul* on my record player and sobbed some more.

The next morning, still shaken up, I trudged down to Victor Music on State Street to buy the only Otis Redding albums missing from my collection: two Stax/Volt Revue compilations recorded live in London and Paris. Less than a month later, "(Sittin' on) the Dock of the Bay," recorded three days before his death, exploded onto the airwaves and spent four weeks at number one on the pop charts. It was the only Top 20 pop single of Redding's career and still receives significant airplay (and butchered karaoke renderings) forty-plus years after its initial release.

Three posthumous Otis Redding albums hit the shelves in 1968, and ensuing years unearthed more outtakes, rejects, and demos never intended for commercial release. Despite wildly varying quality, even the bad songs were good. Every track conveyed a spirit, soul, and playfulness that have often been imitated but never duplicated by any vocalist.

It was Otis's grit, vocal phrasing, humor, and zest for making music that first made me a fan, then a devotee, and ultimately a zealot. If he had been a cult leader, I would have mopped his floors, driven his tour bus, or lugged his equipment—anything to be part of his inner circle.

Otis's death left a hole in my soul. Over the next couple of years, he would make cameo appearances in my dreams, and I'd have sporadic "conversations" with him. His message was always clear. I needed to sing. I needed to dance. I needed to surround myself with music. I didn't have to become an orthodontist, pediatrician, or corporate lawyer like every kid I grew up with.

I felt in my core that I had to follow the music, but who was I kidding? I had no direction, no game plan, no obsessive drive. I'd never had the self-discipline to go against the grain and listen to my heart.

Yeah, I knew what I wanted—did I have the guts to go after it?

2.

when radio mattered

I GOT MY FIRST TRANSISTOR RADIO when I was seven and slept with it under my pillow. It was 1955 and Bill Haley & His Comets had unofficially ushered in the rock 'n' roll era with "(We're Gonna) Rock Around the Clock." Even though I was a suburban first grader with a crew cut, I didn't identify with this plaid dinner-jacketed front man. But the rockabilly guitar solo in the middle of the song hooked me.

The next year, it all kicked in for me. AM radio in the New York metropolitan area was the mother lode. I'd be glued to the Philco in my bedroom, hog the presets in my parents' Cadillac, and log additional listening hours while pedaling my Huffy Radio Bike. Cousin Brucie was on (770) WABC, Murray "the K" Kaufman on (1010) WINS, Gary Stevens and all the "good guys" on (570) WMCA, and Dandy Dan Daniel, Ron Lundy, Alan Freed, Dan Ingram, B. Mitchell Reed . . . the list of memorable disc jockeys went on and on.

But the radio guy who made the biggest impact on my life was Peter Tripp, the "curly-headed kid in the third row" on (1050) WMGM. Every Wednesday afternoon at five, Tripp would count down the Top 40 in a dramatic fashion that would make the Dick Clarks and

Casey Kasems of ensuing years seem tame and predictable by comparison. As he would climb the ladder from number forty to number one each week, I'd excitedly scribble the results on the back of my mother's discarded stationery. I can remember trying to beat him to the punch by peeking at my sheet from the previous week when he'd introduce the next song with "up three notches to number eight" or "down seven slots to the number twelve position."

I wanted to be like Peter Tripp. At my eighth-birthday party in April 1956, while wolfing down a thick slice of ice cream cake, I announced to my family and friends that I was going to be a disc jockey when I grew up.

That was also the year Elvis Presley emerged from the Deep South and changed the world. I sheepishly admit being more turned on by "Love Me Tender" than "Heartbreak Hotel," although I would get bitten big time by the rock 'n' roll and R&B bugs as the years went by. I started collecting 45s that year, spending my forty-nine-cent allowance on Frankie Lymon & the Teenagers' "Why Do Fools Fall in Love," Gene Vincent's "Be-Bop-A-Lula," Fats Domino's "Blueberry Hill," and every Elvis single.

Radio in the late '50s was a melting pot of diversity. Top 40 stations interspersed homogenized pop with doo-wop, vintage soul with country, and organ-drenched instrumentals with button-down lounge singers. Elvis remained the king, spawning such milquetoast impersonators as Tab Hunter, Pat Boone, and Bobby Rydell. V-neck crooners à la Andy Williams, Perry Como, and Johnny Mathis had hit after hit. Rockabilly artists had their fair share of chart dominance as well, with the likes of Sonny James, Buddy Knox, Jimmie Rodgers, and Charlie Gracie all laying claim to the number one position in 1957 alone.

By the time I was an eleven-year-old fifth grader, the balance in my Howard Savings account had crept to $150. With a generous matching grant from my parents, I purchased a Wollensak 3¾-speed reel-to-reel tape recorder. Not only could I now tape my favorite radio shows, but I could also hone my announcing skills, albeit with a squeaky prepubescent voice.

My friends congregated at my house after school and on the weekends to participate in interviews, skits, and phony phone calls. Occasionally I'd portray a pro-wrestling announcer and my interview foils included faux Haystacks Calhoun and Johnny Valentine. I pretended to hold court with sports icons of the era like Cassius Clay or Y. A. Tittle. But I spent most of my mic time conducting my own Top 40 countdowns.

Raw rock 'n' roll had begun permeating the American psyche. As the Ames Brothers, Frankie Laine, Theresa Brewer, and Patti Page started to fade, Chuck Berry, Jerry Lee Lewis, Little Richard, Fats Domino, and Buddy Holly took control. The remarkable thing about radio was that all musical genres peacefully coexisted. It wasn't unusual for the McGuire Sisters to segue into the Silhouettes or to find Steve Lawrence surrounded by the Dell-Vikings and the Diamonds. Frankly, this diverse programming was downright exhilarating. Even when the dawning of "progressive" or "underground" radio left AM radio in the dust, nothing ever surpassed the '50s and '60s Top 40 in terms of blissful potpourri, aural hodge-podge, or sonic gumbo.

The most unsettling trend was the preference of vanilla over chocolate. Pat Boone should have stuck with "Love Letters in the Sand" and left "Tutti Frutti" to the real architect of rock 'n' roll: Little Richard. Gale Storm actually released "Why Do Fools Fall in Love" before Frankie Lymon & the Teenagers soared past her on the charts. Joey Dee & the Starliters' remake of the Isley Brothers' "Shout" was a much bigger hit than the more potent original. And the Crew Cuts' tame version of "Earth Angel" fared far better on the pop charts than the Penguins' infinitely more soulful reading of the same song.

Racial favoritism continued to plague what could have been the natural order of things on radio, but trailblazing white DJs like Alan Freed, Wolfman Jack, and Murray the K were pivotal in getting independently produced R&B on the airwaves (albeit amid constant payola investigations). By 1959, Sam Cooke, Lloyd Price, Brook Benton, Ray Charles, and Jackie Wilson were side by side with Fabian, James Darren, Bobby Vee, and Frankie Avalon. Doo-wop groups exploded onto the scene with names like the Jive Five, Capris, Danleers, Jarmels, and Marcels. They were black, white, Latino, and interracial. The barriers seemed to be breaking down.

A year later, for every Johnny Tillotson, there was a Jerry Butler. Classic voices of Roy Orbison, the Everly Brothers, Ben E. King, and Dinah Washington were showcased on the same wavelength as the Chipmunks, Percy Faith, Connie Stevens, and Anita Bryant. Next came a barrage of girl groups like the Chiffons, Crystals, Ronnettes, Shirelles, and Shangri-Las. If you closed your eyes, you couldn't tell who was black or white. Not only did race become less of an issue, but it actually behooved vocalists to be black. Motown hit with a fury led by Smokey Robinson & the Miracles, Mary Wells, Gladys Knight & the Pips, and the Marvelettes, followed in the next few years by Marvin Gaye, the Four Tops, the Temptations, and the Supremes.

Of course, the British Invasion began in earnest when the Beatles released "I Want to Hold Your Hand" in the States on January 18, 1964. Two days later, I trudged four miles in a blizzard to Village Records to buy *Meet the Beatles*, becoming the first person in South Orange to own that iconic album. With their appearance on *The Ed Sullivan Show* a few weeks later, the Beatles changed the course of music and pop culture forever, as well as adding more flavors to the smorgasbord of AM radio.

The Beatles had an unbelievable six number one songs in '64 and were joined at the top of the charts by other British imports Manfred Mann, the Animals, and Peter and Gordon. But radio also played the hell out of Louis Armstrong (albeit "Hello, Dolly" only), Dean Martin, Bobby Vinton, and *Bonanza*'s Lorne Greene (whose "Ringo" was not about a mop-top drummer).

While most of my preferred listening took place on the left and center portions of the AM dial, the most off-the-wall vault of soul was located on a low-powered frequency at the far right end of the band—all-black 1600 WWRL.

Just as the Beatles had sent me reeling in 1964, WWRL, with its incredible lineup of jocks playing a nonstop assault of R&B music, shook my foundations from 1966 to 1970. Mornings began with Hal Atkins, a mellow, down-to-earth father figure who clearly loved the sides that he spun. As easy-going as Atkins was, his midday counterpart Al G ("the Master, sockin' it to you!") was conversely frenetic. Afternoons were helmed by the legendary Frankie "Hollywood" Crocker, who remained a force in AM and FM radio in New York until his death in 2000. The suavest of them all was late-nighter Jeffrey Troy ("my mama's favorite son").

It was WWRL that turned me on to Otis Redding, along with Solomon Burke, Wilson Pickett, Peaches & Herb, Peggy Scott & Jo Jo Benson, the Hesitations, and the Mighty Marvelows. It was black radio for a black audience. I felt like a privileged eavesdropper.

For a while, I was a shameless R&B elitist, refusing to listen to anything else. During my freshman and sophomore years at the University of Wisconsin, I played my expanding soul music collection on my stereo and ignored local Madison radio, which had nothing to offer as far as I was concerned. When I returned home to spend summers in New Jersey, my car radio dial was stuck on WWRL.

My fondest memory is when Wilson Pickett's "I'm a Midnight Mover" came out in the summer of '68. The song had an infectious groove that drove Pickett into a propulsive vocal frenzy. I wanted to buy it immediately and hear it again, a feeling obviously shared by Al G. He played it four consecutive times, screaming his enthusiastic approval before, during, and after each spin. I swore that if I ever had a chance to grace the radio airwaves, I'd be equally spontaneous.

Then FM radio exploded on the scene with its stereo signal and freeform programming, and once again, my impressionable mind was boggled. Experimenting with 102.7 FM after succumbing to an aggressive print and television advertising campaign, I discovered the progressive sounds of WNEW. Originally, it had no commercials, a great way to lure listeners. The music echoed the free-love vibe of Haight-Ashbury, and the artists dominating the format eventually became headliners at Woodstock.

Typically in "underground" radio, the music was the message and the disc jockeys were mellow voices that backlisted what they played once every half hour. But almost all the WNEW jocks were conversational, articulate, and informative. There was former Top 40 maven Scott Muni, along with Pete Fornatale, Dennis Elsas, and Alison "the Nightbird" Steele. My favorite was a Sinatraphile-turned-progressive DJ named Jonathan Schwartz (who, nearly forty years later, would launch his own High Standards station on XM Satellite Radio). His style was straightforward and friendly for the most part, but laced with just enough New York persnickety cynicism to give him a bit more edge than his colleagues.

Jonathan's clever turns of phrase had me hanging on every word. I could barely wait for the musical sets to end so I could hear his description of them. He sprinkled his monologues with anecdotes, vignettes, personal reflections, and just enough gossip to make his show a bit tawdry.

He felt like a friend. I was so captivated by him and felt so much kinship that I set out to meet him.

Before radio turned corporate, employing receptionists and security guards to separate the announcers from their audience, it was fairly easy to reach the DJs who often answered their own phones. I surreptitiously got Jonathan Schwartz's inside line from a station volunteer and called him during one of his air shifts.

"Schwartz," he said.

"Hi . . . Jonathan?" I asked.

"Yeah?" It didn't sound like him at all. His voice was much gruffer, his demeanor not nearly as friendly as it was when the mic was turned on.

I introduced myself and proceeded to lie. "I'm a disc jockey in Madison, Wisconsin," I said. I told him I'd been listening to him for years. "I really dig your show. Can I stop by the station and visit you?"

"That's out of the question," he said. "I'm the only one here at night and I can't have intruders."

"How about if I get there before you go on?"

"Impossible. I don't have the time."

"Would you listen to an audition tape if I sent you one?"

"That's Scott Muni's job." He hung up.

I called back immediately to tell him that he didn't have to be so rude, that I understood his time was valuable, and that maybe one weekend I could take him out to lunch. The phone rang twenty-eight times before I gave up—it was the closest I came to meeting my radio role model.

I swore to myself that as a DJ, I would always make time for my audience. I would never shun a listener. Years later, when stalking became part of the human fabric, I understood why Jonathan Schwartz had hung up on me.

3.

hyde park and woodstock

W<small>HEN THE BEATLES HIT OUR</small> shores in February of '64, I ran out and bought a cheap Stella guitar and started taking lessons from Mr. Ross, a fiftyish jazz-oriented stylist unfamiliar with the emerging British Invasion songbook, who taught me rock instrumentals like "Pipeline," "Perfidia," and "Wipe Out." A year later, I upgraded to a Gibson F-25 Cherry Sunburst acoustic with a pickup, and I purchased a used tube amp. My fantasies expanded to include rock star as a future job description.

I hit a major speed bump the week before heading off to college. I had packed my guitar, record player, and LP collection, the indispensable appendages of my life at the time. My mother, who never once encouraged my musicality or understood my passion for rock 'n' roll, announced in her stern, intractable voice that I could either take my guitar or my record collection—but not both. Arguing with her was always futile, so I opted for my records. The fact that I chose listening over playing is therapy fodder to this day.

At Wisconsin, I intended to be a psychology major, but dropped that idea when I got a C in my first class. Switching to communications, I ironically abandoned that path when my first radio course was too boring.

After Otis Redding died during my sophomore year, my heart told me to follow the music to New York City. I had visions of living in Greenwich Village and playing open mic nights at the Bitter End and Gerde's Folk City. It wasn't important that I had never performed before. I wanted to inhabit the same stages that had launched the careers of Bob Dylan, Phil Ochs, and Odetta.

But my head reminded me that dropping out of college would immediately make me eligible for the draft—with Vietnam as my likely destination. So I put my dreams on hold and stayed in school. Lacking a meaningful direction, I enrolled in courses like introductory Italian and meterology. (Today, I can barely pronounce *arrivederci* and have no idea what a high-pressure system is.)

During Christmas vacation in 1968, my parents announced that they were taking the family to Europe the following summer to celebrate my upcoming twenty-first birthday. We'd fly first class, spend a week each in London, Paris, Rome, and Madrid, do all the typical tourist stuff, and eat at the finest restaurants. It was a once-in-a-lifetime opportunity, seemingly brought on by the fact that I was now old enough to drink and vote (twenty-one was the magic number in '69).

My mother assembled my sister, brother, and me for a meeting to lay down the ground rules of the trip. No jeans allowed. Jacket and tie required for dinner. Shaving every day. No beard.

"You're kidding, right?" I asked.

"Absolutely not, mister," she huffed.

"I'm not wearing a tie on vacation. And I'm finally able to grow a beard—and I like it." I looked her straight in the eye, daring her. "That's nonnegotiable."

"Then the trip is off."

And it was. (Our next family trip wasn't until we convened in 1998, spouses and offspring in tow, for an Alaskan cruise celebrating my father's eightieth birthday. We all dressed formally for dinner, although I had to borrow a tie from my father. I have successfully lived a life without ties.)

My parents would still fund a trip to Europe the next summer if I agreed to take along my seventeen-year-old brother, Roger, who would enter Brandeis as a freshman in the fall. He and I had a fantastic relationship, completely devoid of sibling rivalry. We'd gotten into only one fight in our entire lives and that was when I blindsided him with a flying dropkick while we were having a fake wrestling match on my parents' bed. He was furious, but even at age nine, he forgave me an hour later.

Several months before boarding our July 1 chartered flight to London, a full-page ad in the *Village Voice* grabbed my attention. I subscribed to the *Voice* mainly because of the weekly columns by Alexander Cockburn, Nat Hentoff, and Robert Christgau, but also because of the extensive ads and listings for clubs, concerts, stereo gear, and record stores.

The ad trumpeted the Woodstock Music and Art Fair and promised "3 Days of Peace & Music" on August 15–17. The jaw-dropping roster of talent included the Who, Jimi Hendrix, Joan Baez, Richie Havens, the Grateful Dead, and Janis Joplin. The recently formed supergroup of Crosby, Stills & Nash would be appearing for only the second time. The eclectic lineup covered the spectrum from Tim Hardin to Sha Na Na. I splurged for two three-day tickets at $18 a pop, sort of expensive for a 1969 music event, but a savings of $1.50 a day from a single-day ducat.

The tickets arrived about a month later and I stored them in my underwear drawer. Since I'd be returning from my European vagabonding on August 12, I would have to stay in South Orange for just a couple of days before hitting the road again.

Our time in Europe was so riveting that I completely forgot about Woodstock. With our Eurail passes, we took trains to Paris, Amsterdam, Lucerne, Venice, Florence, Rome, Madrid, Barcelona, and Toledo. We splurged on puddle jumpers to Ibiza, Formenterra, and Majorca.

We saw *Hair* in two languages and danced onstage during the encores of both the London and Paris performances. We saw all the masters at the Louvre, the Prado, the Uffizi Gallery, the Tate, and the Rijksmuseum. We walked enough miles on cobblestone roads that the contours of our feet developed serrated edges. We dined on seventy-five-cent combo platters of macaroni, green salad, and red wine with Italian workers at the Ristorante Economico. We scarfed escargot by the dozen in French bistros while snooty Parisian waiters tried in vain to hasten our departure. We engaged Spanish bartenders in conversation about the oppressive Franco regime. (*"No soy politico"* was the common response.)

When we wanted to see astonishing flowers, we took a bus to London's Kew Gardens. When we wanted the intimate company of women, we window-shopped in Amsterdam's Red Light District, where one night we took turns trying to seduce a Swedish playwright named Finica (neither one of us got it up during our separate fifteen-minute encounters with her—she politely asked me if she could keep her fee of $5.40 worth of guilders anyway). When we wanted drugs, we hailed the freakiest longhairs we could find and overcame any and all language barriers, although one Afro-laden expatriate from Detroit sold us a cleverly charred pencil eraser that he said was dynamite Lebanese hash. We usually sought out ethnic food, but when we craved American diner fare, we went to Le Drug Store in Paris for burgers and banana splits.

It was a profound coincidence that the Rolling Stones were playing a free concert in Hyde Park four days after we arrived in London. In spite of the tragic death of their former lead guitarist, Brian Jones, two days before at the age of twenty-seven, the Stones decided to carry on with the concert in Brian's memory (with new guitarist Mick Taylor making his Stones debut).

We woke up at 7 a.m. on July 5, had some eggs 'n' scones and went to Hyde Park to claim our turf. My journal entry that day notes that we got "a good seat on the lawn, seventy-five yards from the stage." I would never describe that as a good seat later in life, but on that day, only 200,000 people were in front of us and 450,000, with worse seats, were behind.

Maybe it was because of our fatigue or lack of binoculars, but the Stones didn't seem very cohesive that day in spite of the enormity of the event. They took the stage at 5:15 p.m. and didn't ignite until an hour into their set with a somewhat satisfying "Satisfaction." For the relatively new "Sympathy for the Devil," which closed the show, an energetic ensemble of African tribal drummers and dancers accompanied the Stones, but it was ultimately a gimmicky and anticlimactic finale. In retrospect, the most intriguing part of their performance was at the outset when Mick Jagger, dressed in white from head to toe, read poetry from Keats and Shelley to eulogize Brian Jones while the stagehands released 20,000 white butterflies, which had the visual effect of reverse confetti.

The musical highlights of the day came from other bands. King Crimson, led by vocalist Greg Lake and guitarist Robert Fripp, made their first public appearance (how many groups can say their debut gig was in front of 650,000 people?), and I immediately knew that they were going to be stars. One of their soon-to-be classic songs, "21st Century Schizoid Man," was scintillating and prophetic, written and released thirty-one years before George W. Bush was elected president of the United States, ushering in the twenty-first century.

Also on the bill was Family, featuring the quirky histrionics of vocalist Roger Chapman. They never really caught on in the States, but the hometown crowd gave them massive support during their forty-five-minute performance.

We left Hyde Park physically drained but psyched. How often would you share a communal musical experience with a half-million people? In my case, it would happen again not more than two months later.

Boarding the BOAC charter back to Newark, I felt waves of depression and remorse. I had never felt as free-spirited as I had during our six-week European continental crisscross. I proclaimed several times during the final days of the trip that I was staying in Europe, quitting college, and continuing life as an adventurous nomad. When Roger reminded me I had only $187 left to my name, it didn't faze me at all.

Sad to say, I caved at the last minute. The fear of draft-dodger status loomed over my head, as did the reality that I'd alienate my parents (who were critical enough of my lack of direction as it was). The flight back to Newark was a blur as I downed five or six mini bottles of cheap pinot noir. I felt a combination of anger and impotence. I needed to go to a gym and punch a heavy bag.

Being back in South Orange was a drag, but when I changed my underwear the next morning and found my Woodstock tickets, I got a jolt of adrenalin. On Friday, August 15, I jumped into my midnight-blue, vinyl-roofed '67 GTO to pick up my sort-of girlfriend in Port Washington, Long Island.

Joan was a trip. A soon-to-be Phi Beta Kappa with a degree in social work, she was somewhat petite except for succulent breasts and big, wild hair. When I met her during my junior year at Wisconsin, she was relatively new to sex, drugs, and rock 'n' roll, but quickly embraced all of them.

Our "3 Days of Peace & Music" got off to a shaky start when she greeted me at her front door. Her trademark wild-woman hair had been shaved off as if she were being treated for lice or about to enlist in the Marines. I was stunned, and not in a good way.

"Whaddya think?" she asked in her typically effusive manner. "Don't I look like Jean Seberg?"

"More like Gene Autry," I said. "Did your gardener get bored with clipping the hedges?"

It didn't set the right tone for the promising weekend that lay ahead, so I quickly apologized and she led me to her bedroom in her parentless home. Joan's enthusiastic writhing provided welcome and necessary relief for my massive case of European blue balls—the result of several almost, but not quite, all-the-way liaisons during my travels.

We had no idea that Woodstock would be the largest campsite in concert history, but since we had made reservations at a local motel, we never became part of the half-a-million-strong sleepover. When I was sixteen, I had befriended Susan Etess, granddaughter of the famed hotelier Jenny Grossinger, on a cross-country teen tour. I hadn't seen or spoken to her in five years, but I called her nonetheless to see if she could put us up at her grandma's historic Borscht Belt resort. She couldn't accommodate us there but used her influence to get us a reasonable rate at a quaint bed-and-breakfast about seven miles from Bethel. Her explicit back-road directions kept us out of the infamous traffic snarls that forced thousands of people to abandon their vehicles and hike to the festival—or turn around and head home.

The inside info we got from Susan separated us from the statistical onslaught of people who slept in the rain and had no food or water. We slept and napped in a comfortable bed, returned to the inn for shower/sex breaks, frequented country stores for groceries (which we bought in bulk and gladly shared with our voracious lawn mates at the concert), and easily navigated back and forth on deserted side streets.

What *didn't* separate us from the rest of the Woodstock community was our opting to stay high for the three days. Our drug of choice was organic mescaline, which I'd purchased in the suburbs. For all we knew it was synthetic strychnine, but it turned out to be both potent and mellow, and we avoided the notoriously sinister brown acid eventually immortalized on film via repeated warnings from the public address announcer.

We parked the GTO in a sparsely populated parking lot (another tip from the invaluable Susan Etess) and walked about a mile and a half to the entrance of the festival. Or, at least, what had originally been designated as entry gates.

We didn't know it at the time, but Woodstock had officially become a free concert. The fences and barriers had come down. There were still uniformed ticket takers, but they just stood there haplessly as the hordes marched by them. I approached one and handed him our two tickets. He looked at me with bemused disbelief, shrugged his shoulders, and put the tickets in the pockets of his cargo pants. Years later, a friend frantically called me up and offered me $2,500 for my unused tickets, which would have completed a scavenger hunt and netted him $25K. I've since seen them offered on eBay for up to ten grand.

It was Friday, August 15, 1969, at 4 p.m. When we reached the crest of the hill overlooking the makeshift venue, we fell to the ground laughing convulsively (and we hadn't even taken our first hit of mescaline). Before us stretched a sea of at least a quarter of a million people, many of whom had been there for an entire week. The ubiquitous PA announcer was lavishing praise on the early arrivals. "We are now the second largest city in New York! The New York State Thruway has just been closed to all traffic! The governor has declared us a disaster area!"

Charismatic folkie Richie Havens was the first to take the stage. At one point during his two-and-a-half-hour solo performance, I wondered if any of the other headliners had arrived yet or if they were all helplessly stuck in traffic. During Havens's opening slot, about a hundred thousand more people arrived.

By the time Havens finished hammering out a passionate "Handsome Johnny," my forty-eight-hour mescaline experience had kicked in. I have only vague memories of Friday night's performances other than Joan Baez offering a chill-inducing a cappella version of "We Shall Overcome," John Sebastian warbling a typically off-key "How

Have You Been," and Arlo Guthrie arousing the crowd with a spirited "Comin' into Los Angeles." The opening-night performance that moved me the most was by an unknown, frizzy-haired, angst-ridden New Yorker named Bert Sommer.

The twenty-year-old had been booked at Woodstock by festival producer Artie Kornfeld (who had also produced Sommer's largely ignored debut album *The Road to Travel*). Amazingly, this was Sommer's first concert appearance and he made the most of it. Song after song of rebellion, suicide notes, failed romance, and Seconal addiction were delivered with an impassioned, plaintive tenor that seemed hopelessly out of place at such a celebratory event. Still, Bert Sommer's performance affected me much more than subsequent sets by Tim Hardin, Sweetwater, and Ravi Shankar. Before reaching the only feel-good portion in the set with his well-chosen Simon & Garfunkel cover "America," Sommer artistically brought us all down with the poignant "A Note That Read," during which the protagonist commits suicide at home and gloats from the afterlife that his death will finally allow his parents to get him the haircut they had long been insisting upon.

Although Sommer's riveting performance in front of 500,000 people momentarily lifted him from the depths of obscurity, he was soon relegated to a life as a local musician in Albany, New York. He died of respiratory failure in 1990 at the age of forty-one.

Day two (Saturday) of Woodstock was transcendent musically, even as the rains came and turned the venue into a six-hundred-acre mud bog. I snoozed through unmemorable sets from Quill and the Keef Hartley Band but was jolted back to life by the unveiling of Santana, an emerging Bay Area phenomenon in the midst of their first East Coast tour.

Talk about making an impact—Carlos Santana justifiably rode the waves of his breakout Woodstock performance for the next four decades. Santana's rhythmic, Latin-jazz-rock fusion had never been heard by mainstream rock audiences before and has been imitated and expanded upon ever since. Santana was only the third band of the day, but I was convinced that no one could put out the fire they ignited that afternoon. I never would have guessed that their set would only be the fifth best of day two.

Ensuing performances by Canned Heat, Mountain, and the Grateful Dead ranged from workmanlike to lackluster. At 9 p.m., when Creedence Clearwater Revival took the stage, we contemplated heading back to our motel room for some respite from the rain. I had written off CCR as a tailored-for-Top-40 band based on their AM hits "Suzie Q" and "Proud Mary." But from the opening fuzz tones of "Born on the Bayou," I knew I'd be mired in the muck until Sunday. Creedence tore through the impossibly funky "Green River," gave new meaning to Wilson Pickett's "Ninety-Nine and a Half (Won't Do)," and pumped out back-to-back barn burners of "Bootleg" and "Commotion." When the hits ("Proud Mary," "Bad Moon Rising") followed, they had a harder edge than their recorded versions, and by the time they delivered ten-minute opuses of "Keep on Chooglin'" and "Suzie Q," I had a new favorite band.

Next up was Janis Joplin, who had recently left Big Brother & the Holding Company to go solo. In my mescaline haze, I scrawled a note on the back of a bank deposit slip that described it as "apoplectic blues-rock shrieking." If you've seen the movie, you know that Janis delivered a soul-wrenching "Ball and Chain." When she closed with the reach-for-the-sky wailing of "Piece of My Heart," every man and woman at the festival wanted to go home with "Pearl" that night. She would die of a heroin overdose less than fourteen months after her triumph at Woodstock.

The intermission between Janis and Sly and the Family Stone was interminable by today's standards, but no one there seemed to mind. Festival audiences were infinitely more patient in 1969. Concertgoers spent the two-plus hours sharing jug wine, joints, and whatever food they could scrape off their mud-encrusted blankets. Over the years, the clichés regarding the communal coming together of Woodstock

Nation have not been exaggerations. It was the ultimate "*mi casa es su casa*" weekend.

Sly time arrived. The furious funk and choreographed octane of the Family Stone's performance has been well documented over the years. A half-million matches and disposable Bics lit the sky at 3 a.m. as Sly took us higher. They played only nine songs, somewhat strung together as one relentless jam of their greatest hits. "M'Lady" into "Sing a Simple Song" became "You Can Make It If You Try" and "Everyday People," which yielded to the trifecta of "Dance to the Music," "Hey Music Lover," and "I Want to Take You Higher." The next two, "Love City" and "Stand," were mild letdowns, but this propulsive hour of music set the standard for all funk rock concerts of the future and spawned such bands as Earth, Wind & Fire and the Red Hot Chili Peppers. Arguably, the rhythm section of Larry Graham and Greg Errico has never been surpassed.

The masses were drained after Sly. That must have been the peak. But then came the Who and the bar kept rising. The year had already been a pivotal one in the careers of Pete Townshend, Roger Daltrey, John Entwistle, and Keith Moon. Two months prior to Woodstock, the Who released *Tommy*, considered by most rock historians to be the first full-length "rock opera." The sweeping saga about a young boy struck deaf, dumb, and blind by a traumatic family murder had never been performed in the U.S. in its entirety.

The Who had booked a week at the Fillmore East in October to debut *Tommy* and hadn't planned on performing it at Woodstock. But just two songs into their set (the rarely performed "Heaven and Hell" and their first hit single "I Can't Explain"), along came *Tommy* in all its bombastic splendor. Woodstock's most cosmic moment occurred when Daltrey reached his spiritually tender "see me, feel me, touch me, heal me" refrain. Those who were still awake (let alone tripping) experienced a multicolored sunrise simultaneously as the fictitious protagonist regained his eyesight.

Creedence, Janis, Sly, and the Who. All mind-boggling. Each

performance was not only spectacular but more incendiary than the one before. Could the Jefferson Airplane, who hit the stage at 8 a.m., possibly keep the momentum going? Not a chance.

Originally scheduled to close Saturday night's proceedings at midnight, the Airplane gave it a go with Grace Slick urging the crowd to rock out instead of heading off to church services. "It's time for some morning maniac music," she screamed before inexplicably beginning the set with the sanguine Fred Neill song "The Other Side of This Life." The Airplane failed to reignite the crowd.

Joan and I looked at our blanket, towels, and rain gear, all of which had been embedded in the landscape, then left them there and took a long walk back to my GTO. Back at the B and B, we spent more than an hour washing cakes of mud off our bodies. Drying each other off and looking longingly at the queen-size bed, feather pillows, and embroidered quilt, I had initial inklings that I might be a yuppie, even though no such subculture existed yet. While hundreds of thousands of others huddled in their tents or pulled their ponchos over their heads to retreat from the rainstorms, we were under the covers in an upscale motel, miles away from the chaos.

When we woke up early Sunday afternoon, it was pouring again. Regardless of how much we wanted to see Crosby, Stills & Nash, Jimi Hendrix, Joe Cocker, the Band, and Blood, Sweat & Tears, we had no adventure left in us (and no mescaline either). We stuffed our dirty clothes into a pillowcase, put our empty suitcases in the trunk, and took the deserted back roads back to Jersey. Traffic jams at Woodstock? What traffic?

I spent Monday night alone at home watching *The Dick Cavett Show*. Guests Joni Mitchell (who had been talked out of playing Woodstock but later wrote an anthem commemorating the experience), the Jefferson Airplane, David Crosby, and Stephen Stills had an impossible time describing what had taken place that weekend. They may have been too stunned or exhausted.

"It was amazing," Crosby said a few times, and he managed to rattle off a couple of witticisms about what it was like descending onto the site via helicopter. "Man, it looked like an encampment of the Macedonian army on a Greek hill, crossed with the biggest batch of gypsies you ever saw," he said to a befuddled Cavett, who seemed more intent on reading his next cue card than crafting a meaningful follow-up question.

Joni Mitchell performed stirring solo renditions of "For Free" and "Willie" on piano. Stills did an abridged version of "4 + 20" on acoustic guitar, and the Airplane again proved they were the most overrated superstars of the hippie era with self-conscious run-throughs of "Somebody to Love," "Volunteers," and "We Can Be Together."

Although feeling jittery from too much mescaline and very uncomfortable in my own home, I was aware that my forty-two hours at Woodstock would have a profound effect on me. Just as my connection to Otis Redding had steered me toward a freer form of expression, Woodstock succeeded in pounding home the truth that my only limitations in life would be self-imposed. I was hesitant about returning to Wisconsin to complete my senior year, but it gave me another nine months of protection from the draft and was only a minor detour on the road to a musical future.

4.

pit stops
on a bumpy road

I ENDED UP MAJORING IN SOCIOLOGY, with a parental push toward
pursuing a career in law. But the day before I was scheduled to
take law boards in the fall of 1969, I swallowed a tab of "white light-
ning" LSD, and the pervasive image that swirled around my head
for the next twelve hours was an endless loop of me going to school
from age four to age twenty-two. I knew that if I did well on the law
boards, I'd be tacking on three more years of studentdom.

I called my parents while completely out of my gourd and announced that I wouldn't be taking the LSATs the next day. In fact,
I needed a one-year hiatus from formal education. The urgency in
my voice must have been apparent because they didn't try to "put
me in my place."

Of course, when I wasn't high, the threat of Vietnam was always
on my mind. If I couldn't figure out how to beat the draft, I'd have
to hang on to my student deferment.

Two months before graduation, I flew to New Jersey for a mandatory draft physical. For six weeks leading up to D-day, I went on
a modified version of the high-protein/low-carb Stillman diet. Since

I was a quasi vegetarian at the time, my daily intake consisted of hardboiled eggs and water.

My normal body weight was 130, pretty skinny but not emaciated. I dropped down to 111, well below the minimum acceptable weight for my height. The morning I faced the music, I compounded my unhealthy appearance by wearing striped bell-bottoms and a plaid lumberjack coat three sizes too big.

Two thousand draft-eligible men crammed into a gymnasium in downtown Newark. We listened to a few lectures from drill sergeants I hoped not to work for and then sat down at long tables to take a written personality assessment. I intentionally gave distorted answers to questions like "Do you think people are always following you?" and "Are you homosexual?"

Based on the results of my test, I was interviewed by the army shrink. His name tag said "Rosenberg"—would a fellow Jew be sympathetic or see through my ruse?

After discussing a few red-flagged disorders with me (paranoia, anxiety, loneliness), he got to the brunt of the army's concern. "You checked yes to 'Are you homosexual?' What does that mean to you?"

I stared at his kneecaps and said nothing for thirty seconds. Finally, in a well-rehearsed effeminate voice, I said, "I've loved only two people in my life. One was a woman and one was a man. Love comes so infrequently, you've got to get it when you can."

Dr. Rosenberg looked at me knowingly. I wasn't a very convincing actor. He scribbled something on a pad, tore off the duplicate copy, and handed it to me. "Take this to the clerk in room 542. Good luck."

I took the elevator to the fifth floor, too scared to read his recommendation. When I finally looked, I had to hold in my scream. His note said, "Unfit for military service. 4-F."

After that, graduating from college became anticlimactic. When the Kent State Massacre took place on May 4, 1970, most universities, including Wisconsin, suspended classes for the rest of the semester and gave students the option to take all their courses pass/fail. I went through the motions during my final month on campus, got my BA, and skipped my graduation ceremony (much to my parents' dismay).

Still, my folks were proud that their number one son had gotten his college diploma. They made the mistake of asking me what I wanted for a graduation gift, and I became the proud owner of a baby-blue Ford Econoline van. Had they known I would replace the rear seats with a queen-size bed and drive back and forth from coast to coast twice during the next nine months, they might have given me a Rolex, a Brooks Brothers wardrobe, and *Encyclopedia Britannica* instead.

After two weeks in New Jersey, I returned to Madison for a month, eventually heading west with my friends Kenny Weinberg, Jeff Fields, Donald and Dotsie Lipski, Tom Delahanty, and Jackie Ochs. We drove through Minnesota up into Canada and contemplated living on Vancouver Island before crossing the border back into Washington, eventually ending up in Berkeley.

By then, our septet had shrunk to Weinberg, Fields, and me, and that trio didn't last much longer. Fields was pressured by his family to return to Wisconsin to finish his senior year, and Weinberg, sensing no immediate pot o' gold in California, rejoined his girlfriend, Lois, in Madison as well.

Feeling abandoned and disoriented, I hooked up with my sister's roommate in Berkeley, an eighteen-year-old named Sara, and drove her to Santa Barbara, where she began her freshman year at UCSB. We had a torrid sexual connection and a love of music in common, making it reason enough for me to bide time in Southern California for a while. After eighteen years in New Jersey followed by four in Wisconsin, I was determined to experience my first non-winter.

On one level, Santa Barbara was a magical elixir. On another, it was akin to a mind-numbing barbiturate. The Edenic aspects included having access to the UCSB campus, where I audited a poetry course and sat in on music theory classes. I took group guitar lessons and formed a short-lived folk duo with a sophomore named Jill

Feldman, who years later became a renowned opera singer in Italy. I also honed my playground basketball skills, finding outdoor pickup games every weekday afternoon.

Every so often, I'd halfheartedly look for jobs in record stores, but basically I felt like an entitled bum. I smoked a lot of pot, drank Olympia Beer with my roommate (a third-grade teacher named Sharon), drove to Lakers games in LA with Sara (whenever they played my beloved New York Knicks), ate Mexican food at El Charro, wolfed down gallons of McConnell's mint-chocolate-chip ice cream, and shunned real-life responsibilities.

This pattern continued for seven months. My time in Santa Barbara had been critically important for developing a sense of independence from family ties and pursuing my own muse. Other than my girlfriend who spent most of her time attending college, I had known no one when I first arrived. I had to learn to create my own reality, make new friends, and fend for myself.

My creative flow and relative peace of mind were severely derailed on January 28 when Sara and I picked up a hitchhiker at midnight. He was so grateful to get a ride at that hour that he whipped out a thick joint we gladly shared. As a gesture of goodwill, we drove a mile beyond our normal freeway exit to take this guy home.

We were too kind.

The blinking red lights appeared in my rearview mirror less than a minute after we dropped off the hitchhiker. Two policemen pulled us over, pointed glaring flashlights in our faces, and asked us to step from the van. The marijuana stench was potent and obvious.

"What did I do, officer?" I asked, trying to be mellow.

"I'm citing you for going through a blinking red light without coming to a full stop," he said, Jack Webb deadpan-like, while studying my license and registration.

"Are you sure, officer? I'm an extremely careful driver and I stop at every red light, stop sign, or blinking red—"

"Breathe on me," he said.

I was alarmed and did as he asked. I was so ripped that he must have gotten a contact high, but he kept his equilibrium.

"We're going to take a look at your vehicle."

He directed Sara and me to the sidewalk while he and his partner ransacked the Econoline. They overturned my mattress, removed the raggedy red carpet, dumped the contents of the ashtray into a Ziploc bag, and went through Sara's purse and my backpack. I'll never know if it was planted or not, but they produced a minuscule roach that was not the remains of the joint we had just smoked.

"You have the right to remain silent," he said. Then he announced he was arresting us for possession of illegal contraband and hauling us off to the station. Although we were only a half mile from our house, he radioed for a tow truck to impound my van.

After we arrived at the station, he called over a young cop as a witness to an eye-dilation exam. Pointing a flashlight toward my right eye, the arresting officer asked, "What do you think—does this look like one centimeter?"

"I guess so," he mumbled.

"Excuse me," I blurted out. "What do you mean 'I guess so'? My freedom's at stake here. Is it one centimeter or isn't it?"

"And the left eye—that looks like one centimeter, don't you agree?" the officer said, ignoring me.

"I suppose so," the rookie said in a near whisper.

"Hey, wait a second," I said. "Is it one centimeter, about one centimeter, less than one centimeter—*what is it?*"

They removed my belt and shoelaces, placed all my belongings in a manila envelope, and let me make my one phone call. Sara had been released on her own recognizance, but I didn't know that, so I called my roommate, Sharon, and asked her to contact a bail bondsman to post the $625 bond. I was placed in the drunk tank, sharing a cell with eight zoned-out winos for the next four hours. The sun was rising by the time I was released and given a court date.

I hadn't planned on informing my family about this, but our

arrest garnered a paragraph with a boldfaced headline in the *Santa Barbara News-Press* the next afternoon (apparently it was a *really* slow news day).

My parents, who were often critical of me for no reason, were always supportive when I was up against a wall. When I was seven and my name wasn't announced at a Cub Scout merit badge awards presentation dinner, my mother stormed the podium to let the scoutmaster know he had erred. When I didn't make the "majors" in Little League in fifth grade, despite having scored the third best tryout in South Orange, my mother called the league president and reamed him for a half hour (I was still relegated to the minors). When I got caught cheating on an eighth-grade Latin exam and was publicly humiliated by my teacher, my mother calmly made an appointment with my guidance counselor to discuss the ramifications of my actions.

I expected harsh reprimands for my Santa Barbara misadventure, but my parents again came to my aid. They wired me money to cover my expenses (lawyer's fee, municipal fine, impound charges for my car) and advised me how to behave during my upcoming court appearance. They also sent me enough money for travel expenses so I could come home to them in New Jersey.

As I put on a borrowed jacket and tie for my day in court, I was fuming at the inequities of the justice system. My lawyer informed me that I had been offered a plea bargain. If I pleaded guilty, the charge of contraband possession, a felony, would be reduced to public intoxication, a misdemeanor that would carry a $250 fine and eighteen months' probation.

"But I would be pleading guilty to something that wasn't the case," I said. "That sucks. I was perfectly sober. I'm sure they planted the roach. Those assholes were just looking to hassle a freak and fill their quota."

"As your attorney, I'm advising you to take the plea. But, of course, you're free to do whatever you choose. Just let me know in advance."

I sat in the courtroom, stewing over my plight and scribbling notes in a loose-leaf notebook. If I was going down, I would go down swinging. On the spot, I composed the following dissertation to the judge:

Your Honor, I would like to address the court for two reasons—one very pressing and specific, the other more universally important that I would like to deal with at greater length.

First and foremost, I would like to make a plea for clemency as far as whatever monetary punishment the court is about to levy on me. I will be paying my way through graduate school for the next four years and paying my lawyer back for at least that duration of time. The fact that I did not qualify to be released on my own recognizance, even though I know several distinguished citizens of Santa Barbara, necessitated my retaining a bail bondsman because I could not have raised the required bail at 2 a.m. To add insult to injury, I had to pay towing charges to get back my impounded vehicle, which the arresting officer had refused to allow me to drive home, only five blocks from the site of the arrest.

Thus I am quite financially crippled and humbly plead for the mercy of the court.

However, my primary concern in addressing Your Honor is of greater significance and hopefully will result in increased understanding for all presently involved. I wish to deal with the broad and frequently discussed topics of youth, the courts, and police.

Like most liberals, I feel that there are heinous inequities in this country as well as threatening repression to personal freedom. Also, like most liberals, I do not resort to violence, crime, or illicit dealings to cope with my frustrations. I am merely a harmless brooder and do what I can to make things better for myself and others.

So what happens to me? It is 12:45 a.m. and I am approaching a blinking red light at an intersection preparing to make a left turn. As I slow down, I notice there are no other cars coming from any of the three adjacent directions and, inadvertently, am possibly a shade short of making a legal full stop. A police car pulls us over, ransacks my van without telling us why we are detained, and takes us to jail. And now you have two completely coherent, stable people who have to pay $500 in fines to have charges dropped to "public intoxication."

Elders, you ask, why is there alienation? Why do so many good people turn bad? Why frustration, suicide, depression, hopelessness . . . ?

I'll tell you why, using my plight as merely a minor example.

I am a rational—perhaps too rational—person and thus will not smash the state after you reprimand me and fine me more money than I can possibly afford to pay.

But others, Judge—other peace-loving, borderline cases who happen to brake only momentarily at a blinking red light and are subsequently burdened with half a thousand dollars of legal fees and fines—they are the ones who explode and join the senseless revolutionary forces who destroy, break windows, and loot innocent merchants, scream, disturb the peace, and yell "right on" as a mimicking chant.

The police state and judicial system drive these peace-loving in-betweens to that obnoxious, irrational consciousness.

I am a scholar. A sympathizer. An accepter. I'm depressed, financially crippled, and bitter, but understand the power of the traditional judiciary. All my situation does is stifle my day-to-day, peace-loving consciousness by making me ask why.

I went through a blinking red light with no cars on the road after only coming to a half stop. A traffic summons, maybe. A probable warning? More likely. But a ninety-minute search of my person and vehicle? What kind of harassment is that? It

produced a stale, smoke-like odor that led to an arrest of two
innocent, peace-loving people.

It didn't have to happen like this, Your Honor. I ask you
for your understanding, the dismissal of these charges and fines,
and a clean slate.

I fidgeted nervously in my seat awaiting my encounter with the judge. It was bad enough to be constrained by a jacket and tie for two hours. I tried memorizing my script for better dramatic effect. When my name was finally called, I walked deliberately toward the podium, knees buckling but ready to do battle.

"Mr. Weissberg, you have been offered a reduced charge of public intoxication. How do you plead?" the judge asked.

"Your Honor, I would like to take just a few minutes to—"

"How do you plead, Mr. Weissberg?"

"But, Your Honor, if I could just address—"

"I'm losing my patience, Mr. Weissberg! Guilty or not guilty?"

I looked at my lawyer, who offered me no support whatsoever. He silently mouthed "guilty."

"Guilty, but—"

"Eighteen months' suspended sentence and a $250 fine. See the bailiff to sign your release. Next case."

Time stood still. My legs felt like Jell-O and my lawyer had to steer me toward the exit. I folded up my notes and put them in my journal. I had never felt so helpless, so utterly defeated.

For all intents and purposes, my life in Santa Barbara was over. I phoned my poetry pals, guitar-playing partners, basketball buddies, and assorted acquaintances to tell them I was leaving. I collected addresses and phone numbers I'd never use, packed my van, got TripTiks and flat-tire insurance from AAA, plotted my trip back to New Jersey, and kissed Sara goodbye.

5.

head east
and westward ho!

THE THREE-THOUSAND-MILE VOYAGE TO SOUTH Orange was arduous and lonely. I stopped briefly in places where familiar faces lived. Donald and Dotsie Lipski had relocated to Boulder, so I crashed with them for a few days. My first impression was that it was a highly appealing college town but Donald warned me that it was very cliquish and hard to break into. My next brief stop was in Lawrence, where one of my college girlfriends was pursuing an MFA at the University of Kansas, and then I headed for Madison, my comfort zone.

The closer I got to New Jersey, the harder it was to put the van in drive. I feared succumbing to the lure of a safe job, a steady paycheck, and parental support. I was obsessed with "finding myself" and making it on my own. So I stayed in Madison for three weeks, hanging out with Weinberg's girlfriend, Lois, and her roommate, a stunning, dark-haired beauty I would have married in a flash had she not already had a boyfriend. Other than arriving on time for daily playground basketball games, I remained unmotivated and directionless.

When my revolving circle of friends got tired of putting me up (and putting up with me), I finally left Madison, stopping overnight to play guitar with an ex-roommate living with his parents in Shaker Heights, Ohio. There was nothing more depressing and desolate than driving across Pennsylvania, especially approaching the New Jersey border, despite the unique beauty of the Delaware Water Gap.

I pulled the van to the bottom of our sloped driveway and tiptoed into the house to avoid waking my parents. It was past midnight but they were waiting up for me. We convened in the big den with the peek-a-boo view of the New York City skyline. My mother sipped Cutty Sark on the rocks.

"Your father has arranged a job interview for you with a major Wall Street brokerage firm," my mother said, almost simultaneously with "hello."

"I just got home, Mom. I'm burned out from the trip and my legal hassles. Let me stay in bed for a few days and then we'll talk about it."

While I caught up on my sleep, my mother rifled through my suitcases and found my journal. She read it in its entirety and suddenly was a scholar on my extensive drug use, sex life, and bumdom. When they called me to the dining room table to have breakfast at 1:30 the following afternoon, the diary was opened to the page that recounted my unsuccessful attempt to invest $350 of their money in a marijuana deal.

It was hard to say which one of us was the most livid. I felt violated and betrayed, whereas they felt I needed more help than they could provide.

"We'll pay for you to see a shrink," my mother said.

I had seen a psychiatrist in college, mainly to get out of the draft. While I was under his supervision, he had prescribed Placidyls, an ethchlorvynol-based hypnotic, to cure my insomnia and tried to encourage me to have sex with my longtime best friend, Kenny Weinberg. Although I never followed his urgings to experiment with homosexuality, I did eventually become addicted to Placidyls (my family doctor kept refilling the prescription), sharing them recreationally with my friends for the next six years. Looking back at my journals, I could tell when I was having a "Dilly come-on": my unusually good (for a guy) handwriting turned into illegible squiggles before I'd nod out.

Without revealing why, I quashed the psychotherapy suggestion. "Not only am I not seeing a shrink on your dime, I'm not interviewing for the Wall Street job."

In retrospect, I might have been looking for an excuse to escape from New Jersey, and the diary pillaging gave me the impetus I needed to truncate my homecoming. Within days, I was looking for land in northern Massachusetts and Vermont with Kenny Weinberg, Sam Goldberg, and Jack Weissman. We found an idyllic farmhouse in a sad state of disrepair for sale in North Bernardston, just south of the Massachusetts-Vermont border, with an asking price of $11,000. Fantasies flowed about converting it into a commune and starting a children's theater troupe, but we abandoned the idea when locals told us that the winter heating bills would far exceed the cost of the property.

Undeterred, I convinced Sam and Jack to uproot with me and head west again. We bandied around assorted scenarios and finally decided to homestead in southern Oregon. After only ten days back in Jersey, I gave my parents a perfunctory kiss goodbye, and my fellow explorers and I drove to the Department of Agriculture in Washington, D.C., to investigate homesteading.

We waited in line for two hours at the DOA, picked up a few instructional pamphlets regarding land use in Oregon, and spent the night at the apartment of a former Wisconsin free spirit named Eileen. She took turns ravaging all of us and we were refreshed and ready to roll the next morning. Unfortunately, the Econoline, which we had parked in a public lot, had been vandalized. My prized eight-track tape deck had been ripped off its hinges.

With no tunes to spur us on, optimism gave way to depression as we hit the monotonous Pennsylvania Turnpike, destination Madison to pick up Sam's and Jack's girlfriends. We then headed through Minnesota and set up camp in a wondrous state park. Later, as I struggled to sleep in the back of the van, the only sounds I heard were my four comrades making love in their respective tents. Loneliness took on a new dimension that night.

Our goal the next day was to make it as far as the Black Hills of South Dakota. The cacophony of lovemaking prevalent the night before had disintegrated into bickering and cat fighting. The bond and chemistry I had felt with these friends were already evaporating.

At the campfire that night, I dropped an unrehearsed bombshell. "I can't go on to Oregon with you," I said, avoiding eye contact with all of them. "I know it's my van and I'm leaving you in the lurch, so let's get out the atlas and I'll drive you anywhere within reason."

After trying to prod me into reconsidering, Sam and Jack realized I was a lost cause. The remoteness and desolate aura of the Black Hills made it difficult to conceive of a mutually desirable destination. Studying the map, I pointed to Boulder, five hundred miles due south.

"We could get there by tomorrow night," I said and no one offered a better solution. It was an out-of-the-way detour for them, but they had no choice.

We arrived at our destination on July 3, 1971. I figured I'd spend a few days there, maybe a week, which would give me time to collect my thoughts and plot my next move. My restlessness was unsettling. What I really longed for was a relationship, a job, and a sense of community—in that order.

I found all that and more in Boulder, Colorado.

6.

circuitous routes

My FIRST FEW MONTHS LIVING in the Rockies were anything but productive. I would sleep until noon, then head to the park on Canyon Boulevard for some pickup basketball. After two hours of hoops, I'd grab some takeout barbecue from Uncle Joe's or a substandard rare roast beef sandwich from a restaurant that had the audacity to call itself the New York Deli.

I spent most evenings at Tulagi, a 350-seat, 3.2-beer nightclub that presented an ambitious and tasty lineup of live music. On any given night, you could see Doc & Merle Watson, Taj Mahal, John Lee Hooker, Tim Buckley, the Flying Burrito Brothers, or Muddy Waters.

Not knowing many people in Boulder, I circulated as much as possible, looking for a job, new friends, and one-night flings. At Tulagi one Friday evening in September, I struck up a conversation with Jason Sherman, the morning DJ at Boulder's underground FM station KRNW. A Jewish Vietnam vet from St. Louis, Jason regaled me with real-life war stories about his days as a disc jockey in the DMZ, playing a steady stream of Hendrix, Joplin, Sly, and the Doors while bombs and grenades exploded within earshot. We had an immediate rapport and I told him I'd kill to get a part-time gig at KRNW.

"Do you have any radio experience?" he asked.

"Well, only four years of college radio," I said. We were deep into our second pitcher of beer, and I began fabricating tales about my radio days in radical Madison and my volunteer shifts on the campus station in Santa Barbara. The truth is that I'd never even been inside a radio station.

"Hell, that's plenty," he said, seemingly impressed. "Drop by my show on Monday morning and I'll introduce you to the owner of the station. There's a long list of substitute DJs but you have more experience than any of them."

"I'll be there," I said, wondering if I would even remember our conversation.

I woke up energized on Monday, eager to follow up the momentum of Jason's invitation. I was introduced to Bob Wilkinson, the pudgy, prematurely gray and balding forty-eight-year-old owner (he looked sixty-five) of KRNW. Bob turned out to be one of the most eccentric people I've ever met. He had inherited the station from his father, and when the classical format he instituted didn't garner an audience or revenue, Bob let a bunch of rebel hippie radio veterans talk him into switching to freeform, a non-format that gives the disc jockey complete control over selections, regardless of musical genre.

The station's sound was borderline schizophrenic. Jason kicked things off in the morning from 6 to 10 with a comfort food blend of what would later be called classic rock. Day after day, he'd pump out a mix of Beatles, Stones, Steppenwolf, Airplane, the Dead, and Creedence. Following Jason until 2 p.m. was Rick Morse, a tall, skinny son of a banker from Boston with a Mike Bloomfield Afro. His show featured a grating mix of Black Sabbath, Humble Pie, Alice Cooper, and Yes, an aurally damaging mixture at any hour, but especially late mornings in the Rockies.

Dave Nettles, who wore the same tie-dyed shirt and bandana

to work *every* day, stayed true to his San Francisco roots in the afternoons with lots of Quicksilver, Stoneground, Joy of Cooking, New Riders, and anything endorsed by Wavy Gravy. Bob Wilkinson insisted on programming classical music from 6 to 10 p.m. and usually manned the board himself, occasionally turning over the reins to a gentle, alcoholic Eskimo named Russ. At 10 p.m. Michael Kinnicutt, a very wealthy trust-fund technophile from Connecticut, spaced people out with lengthy sets of Pink Floyd, Hawkwind, Can, and Gentle Giant. A hashish enthusiast named Mike James, whose radio moniker was Krispy Kritter, helmed overnights and tracked whatever loud, abrasive album sides he could find. Captain Beefheart, you have a home!

"I need to post your third-class operator's license at the station," Wilkinson said to me, motioning to the clipboard behind the reel-to-reel deck.

"All my belongings are in Santa Barbara and I'm having them shipped to me," I lied.

"Get it down here when it comes," he said. "I can't let you on the air without it. I'm in enough trouble with the FCC as it is."

I was so excited at the possibility of being on the radio that I couldn't hold my food down, let alone sleep that night. I drove to the FCC in Denver the next morning, picked up a study manual, and crammed on the front steps of the building for three hours. The test was obtuse, all about translating sine waves to kilohertz and other unnecessary equations, but I breezed through it. My heart sank when the proctor informed me that the results would be mailed to me in six weeks. I refused to wait that long.

When I got back to Boulder, I called the FCC office and told the receptionist I had a job offer that would be withdrawn if I didn't produce a third-class license. She couldn't help me, she said. But when I added that my continued state of unemployment would force me to move back to New Jersey, I struck the right chord. She had left New Jersey five years before and hated the Garden State. She promised to locate my test and rush the license to me if I passed. Amazingly, the document was in my mailbox two days later.

I bolted over to KRNW to post my license. I explained to Wilkinson that the FCC in Denver had issued me a duplicate when I told them mine was lost.

"This isn't a duplicate," he snarled, pointing to his own license on his desk that was clearly stamped "DUPLICATE" in boldfaced thirty-six-point type.

"Um . . . well . . . I couldn't wait for my stuff to be sent from Santa Barbara, so I just took the test again," I said, turning a sprain into a compound fracture.

Grabbing my license and wedging it under a pile about twelve deep, Wilkinson mumbled, "Maybe we'll give you a call." He walked away without shaking hands or saying goodbye. My ruse had gotten me to third base with a head of steam but I was tagged out sliding into home plate. I figured that was as close as I'd ever get to being on the radio.

PART 2

Behind the Mic

7.

me on the air?

J OE GARAGIOLA WAS RECYCLING A trite anecdote during Saturday's
Major League Baseball *Game of the Week* when the phone rang.

"Didn't anyone tell you that you were supposed to take over for
me at noon?" the crotchety voice asked. It had been only three days
since Bob Wilkinson buried my license on the bottom of the substitute stack.

"N-n-no . . . this is the first I've heard of it."

"Well, get down here. Your show started three minutes ago."

I was stunned but had enough wits about me to guzzle the last
half of the sixteen-ounce brew I had been sipping leisurely. I raced
the Econoline to Pearl Street and was face-to-face with Wilk by 12:10.

He methodically ran down the responsibilities for my six-hour
shift. "The commercials are on reel-to-reel. Run two live PSAs an
hour. Don't pot up the vocal mic past two o'clock or you'll overmodu-
late. Log meter readings now and at the end of your shift. Give legal
IDs at the top and bottom of every hour and keep your language
within FCC standards. This pot operates turntable one. This is for
turntable two. This is the preview headphone jack so you can listen

to the records in cue. Remember to back up the albums a third of a revolution for the best segues and you answer the phone too. If I get any calls, I'm out of town until next Friday. Any questions?"

"Nope, I'm all set," I said, feigning supreme confidence. Again without saying goodbye, Wilkinson turned and descended the thirty stairs that separated the second-floor studio from the street. He had left a Tom Paxton album tracking and I estimated it had about fifteen minutes to go.

Everything he'd just said might as well have been in Portuguese. I had no idea what to do next. I surveyed the room with its ten thousand vinyl LPs surrounding a console with dozens of toggle switches, mute buttons, knobs, and directional arrows. I skimmed through a fat operations manual but I was no cryptographer and couldn't decipher any of the codes. I stared in disbelief at the archaic tape recorders mounted on a steel chassis behind the announcer's chair. I hadn't threaded a reel-to-reel since my Wollensak days in fifth grade.

Ready or not, I was about to begin my radio career. I felt a confusing combination of giddiness and panic. My childhood dream of becoming a disc jockey had come true, but I had to learn to fly without a copilot.

As the Tom Paxton disc came perilously close to ending, I had to decide what to follow it with. Hmmm . . . Paxton, Greenwich Village folkie, protest singer . . . Dylan! I thumbed through the *D* section of the alphabetized walls and found *Blonde on Blonde*. The first song I ever played on the radio became "Stuck Inside of Mobile with the Memphis Blues Again." To keep things simple, I segued to "Rainy Day Women #12 & 35" and then went to side four of the double album for the 11:19 opus "Sad Eyed Lady of the Lowlands." That bought me some time to collect my thoughts, leaf through the album stacks, and program the final five hours of the show. I mixed in some Byrds and Burrito Brothers' renditions of Dylan songs and finally mustered up the courage to speak to the listeners.

"This is KRNW at 97.3 on your FM dial in Boulder, Colorado,"

I said with confidence. Then I backlisted the songs I had played, sprinkling in some relevant anecdotes in a laid-back style that became my on-air signature over the years.

As the afternoon progressed, I adjusted to the technical demands and nuances, steering the boat into safe waters. Feeling that my first show might also be my last, I was determined to get my favorite artists into the rotation. Poco, Leo Kottke, Kris Kristofferson, the Beatles, Spirit, Love, the Band, and Eric Clapton all made appearances. I capped things off with a five-song set of Otis Redding songs.

The phone didn't exactly ring off the hook but I received at least a dozen flattering assessments of my musical taste and several requests from sexy female voices. The overall feedback was very positive and I left the station feeling euphoric. I proceeded to call everyone I knew around the country, sharing my triumph. My concave chest was bursting with pride and I'm glad Skype hadn't been invented yet, because I could sense the goofiness of my shit-eating grin.

Over the next few weeks, I hung out at KRNW constantly. At staff meetings, I may have been the peripheral newcomer, but I contributed input as if I were a grizzled underground radio veteran.

Then Jason Sherman called me late on a Thursday night, just two weeks after my Saturday afternoon kamikaze debut, to tell me that he had accepted an offer to go to Denver's KFML, where he'd be joining Colorado freeform stalwarts Bill Ashford, Jerry Mills, Harry Tuft, Thom Trunnell, and Sandi Phelps.

"I met with Wilkinson and convinced him you should replace me doing mornings," Sherman said. "He wants to talk to you tomorrow. You wanna do it?"

Although I slept sporadically that night and was slightly hung over from a combination of weed and Courvoisier, I was calm and clearheaded when I drove to Wilk's house the next morning.

"Hi, Bob," I said with a smile, trying to mask my enthusiasm. As he unlocked the torn screen door, I extended my hand and received the first of thousands of fish-wrist handshakes I would endure over the next six years. Looking down at the ground, he gestured for me to come in.

The dank smell of stale cat urine permeated his living room. Hundreds of 78s and LPs were strewn jacketless all over the floor. Also dotting the landscape were vintage microphones, assorted Victrolas, receivers, and radio memorabilia, mostly circa 1930.

"Jason speaks highly of you," he said, dispensing with any small talk. "Can you start Monday morning?"

"Absolutely. You won't be sorry you made this decision. I am knowledgeable, dedicated, dependable . . ."

My words trailed off as I realized he was preoccupied with stroking the fattest of his seven cats. He cooed at her, roughed her up affectionately, and displayed a paternal affection, completely oblivious to the fact that I was answering his question.

"Do you like big bands?" he asked.

"I like all kinds of music," I said, not admitting that my big-band affection at that time was limited to Glenn Miller's "In the Mood."

"C'mon in here." He motioned toward a room that would have served as a second or third bedroom in a family home. Since Wilkinson was a lifelong bachelor, it was yet another storage room for his antiques.

All but a few square feet of the room was covered with records. The arrangement seemed haphazard, but he pinpointed five specific collections. "These are the complete Smithsonian recordings of Jelly Roll Morton," he said with a nonchalance that belied his obvious pride. "And this is the entire library of Bix Beiderbecke recordings from 1924 to 1930. Original pressings. Here are Jimmy Dorsey's first sides. I like him more than Tommy, but I have all of Tommy's sides too . . ."

For the next half hour, Wilkinson regaled me with stories of his heroes. How Beiderbecke, the best cornet player of his era, had died of alcohol poisoning at age twenty-eight. How Louis Armstrong had apprenticed under Joe "King" Oliver. How Lionel Hampton had insisted that Illinois Jacquet switch from drums to tenor saxophone before hiring him in his band. The stories kept on coming, and every time I would get down on Wilk in the future, I'd try to visualize the passionate, music-loving side of him.

After thanking him for the tour of his museum, historical lectures included, I returned to the subject of my employment.

"So, uh, what's my starting salary?" I asked.

"You know, you'll never get rich in radio," he said. "I pay the others two bucks an hour, but I start people at a dollar sixty. On-air talent never makes money. The only way to make money in radio is in sales. If you do a good job, I'll raise you to two an hour in a few months."

I would have paid him for the opportunity to do morning drive at a freeform station in a town like Boulder, so I didn't try my hand at negotiation.

"I'll be there at 5:45 Monday morning."

I actually arrived at 5:15. The 1400 block of Pearl Street was deserted with the exception of the donut shop below the station that would start doing a brisk business in a couple of hours. I became their first customer every day with the same order of coffee (cream and sugar) and two glazed donuts to go.

As I climbed the steep stairwell to the second floor, a cockroach whizzed by me at eye level on the wall. The light bulb outside the studio was burned out (and wouldn't be replaced for about six months until one of the jocks spent his own money for a new one). The front door had no sign, just a homemade business card taped to the window.

These were merely a few telltale clues to the way this radio station was operated. Instead of having a strategically located transmitter site, KRNW's antenna hung limply out the back window. The broadcast range was about five miles to the east, a mile to the west, and three miles north and south. Once you descended from the scenic overlook on the way to Denver, the signal quickly disappeared. If you headed up Boulder Canyon toward the quaint mountain town of Nederland, the station veered in and out depending on the direction of the winding turns. Since I lived only nine blocks from the station, where the reception was ideal, I never knew about this until I worked there.

The spirit of the station was what made it great and I intended to enhance KRNW's legacy. I spent hours poring through thousands of LPs, preparing specials, and making notes on bands, vocal groups, instrumentalists, and solo artists. I boned up on all genres of music, including folk, rock, R&B, blues, jazz, bluegrass, and international music.

The best part was the sense of discovery, when I found obscure gems getting no record company push or airplay and exposed the public to them. During my six years at KRNW, my playlists included Uncle Jim's Music, Fraser & DeBolt, Blue Jug, Goose Creek Symphony, Frummox, Brinsley Schwarz, Mason Proffit, Horslips, Big Wha-Koo, Julie Driscoll, Plainsong, and Melvin Van Peebles.

Not all my selections would eventually gather dust in cutout bins. I'm pretty sure that I was the first disc jockey in Colorado to play David Bowie, Joan Armatrading, Elvis Costello, Kiss, the Cars, the Eagles, Devo, the Sex Pistols, Graham Parker and the Rumour, the English Beat, Emmylou Harris, Mott the Hoople, Tom Waits, Joe Jackson, the Jam, and the New York Dolls.

My radio show caught on fast and improved my social life dramatically. Lacking a receptionist at KRNW, the disc jockeys answered their own phones. Since there was only one phone line, we could indulge in lengthy calls if we were so inclined or keep the phone off the hook if we felt like concentrating on the program. I began to recognize the voices of repeat callers and started inviting people down to hang out.

The women showed up in droves and they were all beautiful (it was Boulder in 1971, after all). If I had a cold or was coming down with the flu, I'd mention it on the air and before my shift was over, I'd be deluged with herbal cures, gift baskets, and nursing care. Other women just stopped by on a lark, and I ended up having friendships and liaisons with quite a few of them.

Occasionally I'd even get laid on the job. I'll never forget the time a gourmet chef named Wendy appeared with a sexual itch that needed some scratching. I locked the door, slapped on Taj Mahal's eighteen-minute version of "You Ain't No Street Walker Mama, Honey But I Do Love the Way You Strut Your Stuff," and proceeded to give the woman what she wanted. I came at the seventeen-and-a-half-minute mark and jumped back into my chair, stark naked and dripping, in time to backlist the songs I had played and to read three live commercials.

As I got more comfortable on the job, I accepted Krispy Kritter's hashish offerings at 5:45 a.m. before my show began. My slow, deep voice became even more relaxed and my announcing breaks became freeform rambles that either endeared me to the community or irritated those wanting to hear only music. I also started dumping airline-size bottles of Kahlua into my coffee to give me additional wake-up energy.

Unknowingly, I became a surrogate conscience for the mini-masses. On snowy days, I encouraged people to stay in bed, telling them it just wasn't worth it to deal with the elements. I wasn't seeking guru status by any means, but I loved to pontificate on my favorite album of the moment, my novel du jour, or a must-see movie. A notable local record store even set up small displays highlighting my recommendations.

Narcissism and first-person monologues became the norm. I

talked glowingly about my college days at Wisconsin and derisively about growing up in New Jersey. I spewed out stories about the famous and not-so-famous musicians, athletes, and authors I had met. I was simultaneously folksy and self-indulgent. I never really questioned the implications of my personal on-air discourses—but one outrageous remark led me indirectly to the woman I would spend the rest of my life with.

8.

if at flirt
you don't succeed

W HAT TURNED ME ON THE most about the FM radio revolution was the freedom DJs had. Freedom to play whatever songs they wanted to. Freedom to take phone calls on the air and do interviews. Freedom to bare their souls to their audience.

One morning I was particularly depressed. I had been evicted from my attic apartment the day before for playing my records too loud and for "parading girls" in and out of the house past the disapproving gaze of the elderly, church-going landlord couple who lived in the main house below.

I related my tale of woe to the listeners and ended with an off-the-cuff zinger. "You know how uplifting my shows are . . . well, until I find a place to live, I'm going to play four hours of Leonard Cohen every morning!" I was kidding, of course, but the phone rang less than a minute later. A regular listener named Les said he had a small cottage to rent on Arapahoe Avenue near the foothills. I told him I'd be over when my shift ended at ten.

The four-room house was smaller than tiny: a bedroom, a living room, a kitchenette, and an enclosed rear porch. I would have to share the bathroom with Les and his best friend, Steve, both of whom were living out back in a garage and converted storage shed. The house had no interior doors, which presented privacy issues (I ended up hanging sheets and blankets in the doorways). But it came with a water bed and I had no other viable options, so I wrote a check for eighty dollars to cover the first month's rent and moved in the next day.

My new abode at 526 Arapahoe sat across the street from Boulder Creek, on a block mixed with quaint cottages and stately Victorians, many in disrepair. My toiletmates, Les and Steve, were strange eggs but we shared a love of music and basketball, so we had enough common ground. They were both paperboys for the *Denver Post*, but Les cleverly supplemented his income by buying a pound of pot before beginning his route, dividing it into one-ounce baggies, and turning them all over before finishing his deliveries every day. At nineteen, he had earned enough money to buy two adjacent cottages on a half acre of land and was the youngest homeowner I'd ever known.

The tenants next door were Laura, a fiftyish earth mama, her daughter, Jessica, and Jessica's political activist boyfriend, George. Their volatile personalities clashed, often violently, and I heard a constant soundscape of screaming, crashing dishes, and slamming doors. Yet when we'd bump into each other in the backyard, we always exchanged smiles and warm hellos.

One afternoon, I was alone in the living room teaching myself how to fingerpick the Beatles' "Blackbird" when I heard a rustling near my back door. I figured it was Les or Steve coming in for a whiz, but when the door didn't open, I peeked outside and saw a little girl and boy playing, picking flowers, and exploring.

Peanut M&Ms in hand, I introduced myself and offered them some. If I did that today, I'd be branded a pedophile and featured on every neighborhood watch database, but 1972 was different. Nicole (age seven) and Paul (six) told me they lived two doors down in the "big red house," a Victorian with exotic sculptures strewn throughout the garden. The kids were adorable and I became curious about their parents.

A few days later, as I helped Laura unload groceries from her VW Beetle, I picked her brain for information. "Hey, tell me about the family next door."

"Oh, they're fascinating people," she said. "Jacques is a French professor at CU and his wife, Helen, is a fantastic artist. Their children go to Flatirons Elementary. Lovely family."

"Introduce me when you get a chance."

That afternoon, as I got into my Econoline for a quick trip to McGuckin's Hardware, I noticed a woman at the red Victorian weeding her garden. She had long brown hair and wore a revealing orange terry-cloth outfit, but what I noticed most were the alluring ass cheeks peeking out of her short shorts. I will never forget that first glimpse of Helen.

The next morning, returning home from a radio show I had done with very little sleep the night before, I was heading straight for bed when I was intercepted with Laura's "yoo-hoo" from across the backyard. "Come over here and meet Helen."

I straggled over. Laura's massive frame was spread out against a log, and Helen, barefoot in jeans, a white T-shirt, and a purple headband, sat next to her.

I plopped down on the lawn in front of them and shook Helen's hand. "I'm your new neighbor," I said, wondering if I was just imagining the accompanying electrical charge. "I've met your kids a few times. They're so cute."

"Thanks . . . they're quite a handful," she said with an infectious giggle.

We had a friendly three-way coffee-klatch conversation. Laura was unnerved by the tempestuous relationship between Jessica and George. I told them about my radio show and a project that would involve Boulder's senior community in a series of live interviews. Helen described an upcoming exhibit of her paintings and enlisted my help to save the Highland School, a condemned, historic elementary school that was scheduled for demolition unless enough funds could be raised to stave off the wrecking ball.

Just then, a Peugeot pulled up in Helen's driveway, and a short, balding man got out and bolted by us. "What is this, a women's lib meeting?" he muttered, no trace of humor in his voice.

Helen looked at me and laughed under her breath. "That's my husband, Jacques. I guess he didn't look at you too closely."

"I take it as a compliment," I said, smiling. After all, Jacques's cameo appearance and gruff one-liner had given Helen another reason to look at me, talk to me, and giggle again. She got up to follow her husband into the house but made a point of telling me to keep in touch. "Let's save the Highland School," she said.

I promised I'd work with her on the project. (We eventually raised enough money to preserve the building and reclaim its historical designation from the city. Today it's a tastefully refurbished office building that has managed to retain its 1890s charm.)

As Laura and I walked back to our respective homes, I hit her with a barrage of questions. How old was Helen? Was she happily married? What kind of art did she do? How old was Jacques? Had she been his student? Did the kids get along with each other?

"Why do you want to know all this stuff?" Laura asked. Her answers were vague and, I found out later, inaccurate.

"I'm fucking blown away by her. She's an incredible woman."

The next day, Laura told Helen everything I had said, prefacing her narrative with words that puzzled Helen: "You've made a conquest."

9.

let's do it . . .
let's fall in love

THE FATEFUL MOVE TO 526 ARAPAHOE worked out well for me. It wasn't the physical structure that was memorable, but the neighborhood that contained it. There were scads of scenic hiking trails and serene parks within walking distance and a convenience store/laundromat a block away.

All waking hours not devoted to my radio show were spent juggling time with my expansive harem. I was crazy about Jeannie, a tall, slender beauty who was an art student at the University of Colorado (CU) and the daughter of wealthy Long Island socialites. Roberta was a voluptuous blonde hippie-chick who designed custom cowboy shirts for Co-Tangent, Boulder's ultrahip clothing emporium. Celeste, an athletic Jewish hard body, was a pre-law student who made a living driving a tractor for the city's Parks and Recreation Department. Faith was an earthy intellectual who wrote a food column for Denver's *Straight Creek Journal*. Lisette was a dark-haired Cincinnati expatriate who plied me with Quaaludes and barked sexual instructions in a movie director's tone. Naomi was a gifted modern dancer who occasionally popped in unannounced to see if I was available

for a "workout." I remember little about Christie, a local street ur-
chin, other than her dirty feet and my insistence that we remain on
top of the covers.

In this mercifully pre-AIDS era, I was in perpetual coital motion. All the women were younger than me, single and available. It
was highly illogical that a friendship with a married neighbor eight
years my senior would take precedence over everyone else.

Every few days, Helen dropped off new fliers announcing a meeting of the "Save the Highland School" committee. I had signed on to
procure and coordinate the volunteer services of a half-dozen bands
to play at an Independence Day fundraiser on the school's grounds
by Boulder Creek. Helen held weekly planning sessions, usually at
her house.

Although things between us were innocent and friendly, there
were early hints that something deeper might be fomenting. One afternoon, Helen took me on a tour of Highland School. Her daughter, Nicole, had gone to kindergarten there before the building was
proclaimed a safety hazard and shut down by the city. We sat in the
deserted building on the lip of the auditorium stage, our shoulders
touching the whole time Helen briefed me on the school's distinguished history.

A few days later, I had the audacity to ask her if I could use her
washer and dryer so I could save a few bucks. She stopped short of
folding my briefs for me, but I gave her a quick thank-you peck on
the cheek before lugging my bag of clean clothes back home.

Another time I slashed my elbow on a jutting piece of steel in
my shower. Blood gushed as I applied a makeshift tourniquet to the
wound. When I couldn't find a bandage in the medicine cabinet, I
ran over to Helen's to ask for one.

"Do you want me to put it on?" she asked, sincerely concerned.

"If you want to play nurse," I quipped. I was openly flirtatious
with her, but I felt more like her kid brother than the guy next door.
When I first met Helen, Laura told me she was forty. That would

have made her sixteen years older than me. I couldn't believe it—she looked to be in her midtwenties. Even when I found out she was only thirty-two, that was still considerably older than my other friends.

Saturday, May 27, 1972, was an ordinary day of weekend unwinding. I was hanging at the cottage, smoking joints with Steve, and listening to the new Dr. John album. I heard a tentative knock on the screen door.

"Hey, Helen, come in," I said, without moving to get up. She was in shorts, sandals, and a white pocket tee. I was sort of embarrassed that the place reeked of dope, but she seemed oblivious to it. Actually, she seemed nervous.

"Is anything wrong?" I asked.

"No . . . not really," she said, putting a stack of "Save Highland School" posters on the wagon-wheel table.

"Smoke a joint?" Steve asked. That was usually the extent of his dialogue.

"No thanks. I don't do that."

"Just have a few hits," I coaxed. "It'll relax you."

A bit of gentle prodding led to acquiescence. Helen sat cross-legged on the floor and we passed the J around. It was a mellow blend of Colombian and Michoacán and it took the edge off despite Helen's teeny tokes.

"So what's the matter?" I asked.

"I don't want to talk about it," she said.

"Come on . . . you'll feel better. You're among friends," I said, taking my twentieth hit.

"Well . . ." She paused. "A year ago Jacques had a sabbatical and we took the kids to France. When we came back, there were suddenly lots of young men living in the neighborhood and I've become friends with all of you."

She was talking about Les, Steve, George, and me.

"So?"

"I guess he's jealous."

"How can he be jealous? Aren't you allowed to have male friends?" I asked, somewhat incredulously. This was the era of peace, love, beads, incense, and marijuana. Jealousy was an anachronism.

She sighed. "That's just the way he is."

"That doesn't make any sense. How can he possibly be jealous if your feelings toward us are platonic?"

An uncomfortable silence hung in the air. Then Helen looked in my direction and said in a near whisper, "Well, not all of my feelings are platonic . . . especially toward you."

Stunned or not, I pounced on that opening. "Well, I love you!" I blurted out, shocking Helen, Steve, and myself.

Time moved in ultraslow motion as I dropped from my chair to the floor. Helen and I crawled toward each other, met with a clinging embrace, and started kissing each other passionately. I looked over at Steve, who was furiously rolling another joint, and gave him the eye and a head bob. He got the message and bolted out the back door.

I was in a twilight state, a mixture of euphoria and disbelief. I nibbled at Helen's ear, stuck my hand up her shirt, and caressed her angular, writhing, braless body. Before things heated beyond the boiling point, we stopped each other.

"There is nothing in the world I'd rather do than make love with you," I said, breathless. "But I don't want you to do this unless you're absolutely sure this is what you want."

"I know what you mean."

We hugged, kissed, and talked for a while. It turned out that her marriage wasn't so happy after all. She had met Jacques when she was nineteen, married at twenty, and had children shortly thereafter. They shared a love of university life, world travel, and their kids, but a seventeen-year age difference, combined with Helen's spiritual restlessness, sent them veering in opposite directions.

"Listen . . . go home and sleep on it," I said, kissing her repeatedly as I walked her to the door. "If you wake up tomorrow and want to pursue this, I'll be the happiest person alive."

I spent the rest of the afternoon walking around in circles. I had a hard time grasping what had happened. I had never had a dalliance with either a married woman *or* an older one. The modicum of guilt I felt was dwarfed by my ecstatic feelings of love and lust.

Steve and Les came strolling in an hour later.

"Did you fuck her?" Steve asked, he of few syllables.

"Absolutely not," I said. "This is a complex situation."

"Well, if you're not gonna fuck her, I'll fuck her."

I laughed, somewhat derisively. "I don't think it works that way. I don't know what's going to happen."

I was scheduled to do my regular Saturday night radio show from ten to two. My nighttime radio persona was a different animal from my laid-back, early-morning guise. I employed a harder-edged musical palette, interspersing John Lee Hooker, Mountain, Hendrix, John Mayall, and Spooky Tooth with Motown and Stax/Volt dance sets. The late-night audience consisted of drug- and alcohol-induced partiers, an entirely different breed from my morning following.

My near-tryst with Helen was a vague memory when Lisette, my friend John, and a few other stragglers paraded in at 12:30 a.m.

"I have a present for you that you're really gonna like," Lisette announced, sitting on my lap and throwing her arms around me. She reached into her backpack and handed me a pill that looked like a Bufferin. "It's a Soper, direct from the manufacturer in Ohio."

"What's a Soper?" I asked.

"Don't ask questions—just do one."

"But I have another hour and a half on the air. Is this an upper or a downer?"

"It is the mellowest, horniest, grooviest downer in the world. Do it!"

I rarely passed on an offer of free narcotics, but I wanted to be cautious because I took my job seriously. "Okay, but break it in half."

"Pussy," she said, slicing one at the seam with her long pinky fingernail.

Swallowing my first Soper was a bad mistake. Within minutes, I was floating in an ether-like haze. I became a functional illiterate and couldn't properly cue up records. The songs would hit the airwaves with a warped whirr, cutting off several seconds of each intro.

I also had a lapse of judgment when I attempted to do a station ID, backlist a set of songs, and read a few late-night commercials. "Yoor lishnin to KRN-dubelloo, nine-ee sheven point free megahersh in Boulder . . . thish ish Kenny until two inna mornin . . . I am soooooo fugged up . . ."

I turned off the microphone and started falling out of my chair. John caught me and I told him to take over and start playing records. He didn't know the first thing about cueing up records, so most of the songs started in the middle.

I was saved when Krispy Kritter showed up a few minutes early and immediately began his overnight shift. Even though he was rarely coherent himself, he was at least capable of taking the helm. A few loyal listeners who had heard me slurring my words and violating FCC language regulations called the station to express their concern about my condition.

I have no recollection of what happened next. Apparently, Lisette took me home, undressed me, deposited me under the covers, and crawled in with me. The only thing I remember is waking up alone at noon on Sunday.

I found a love note from Lisette telling me how funny I'd been and she added some lewd commentary suggesting that I still had enough sexual energy to respond to her overtures. I swore never to do downers again—at least on the job.

A stiff headwind woke me up as I walked down to Pearl Street to retrieve my car. When I came home, the phone was ringing.

"Hello . . ."

"I can see how long you waited for me to come over. The same day you tell me you love me, you go to bed with someone else."

"What?"

It was Helen. Unable to sleep all night, she had snuck out of her house at six in the morning. She'd made up her mind. "I was about to get in bed with you when I realized that you weren't alone." Her demeanor was calm, yet standoffish. She was clearly miffed.

I begged her forgiveness and offered one lame excuse after another. Nothing I said provided any consolation. I fucked up. I had sworn my love to her at two o'clock on Saturday afternoon and twelve hours later, I was shacked up with the Queen of Sopers.

"Listen, you have no reason to believe me, but I promise I will never be with another woman until it's you . . . if you'll still have me. I blew it and I'm asking you to give me another chance. I swear—"

"We'll see," she cut me off with a voice that was tinged with sarcasm, but sympathetic nonetheless. "I'm not sure this is such a good idea anyway. I have to go. The kids just came in."

I hung up the phone with a queasy pit in my stomach. How could I have blown this opportunity before it had begun? What a moron. I was an asshole. A fuckin' jerkoff. A loser. A dick.

I spent the afternoon alone, prepared for Monday's radio show, and smoked countless bowls of pot. I was furious at myself and cursed my thoughtlessness.

Whenever the phone rang the next day, I picked it up hoping it would be Helen. It wasn't—until the tenth call.

"Will you be home tonight?" she asked.

"If you want me to be."

"I told Jacques that I'm going to a women's group with some friends. I'll see you at eight."

I made certain that Les and Steve knew that the house, bathroom, and refrigerator were off-limits that night. They gladly complied. After all, they had harbored fantasies of their own about their beautiful neighbor and had no fondness for her condescending husband. They'd be vicarious allies in this potential affair.

When Helen arrived, we started making out immediately and were naked beneath the sheets of my water bed within minutes. We sloshed around for hours, making love intermittently. I was as nervous as I was excited, losing my hard-on when amorousness was thwarted by doomsday visions of Jacques bursting in on us.

When it was time for her to go home, Helen kissed me on the forehead and told me not to walk her to the door. I set my alarm for five and drifted off into a deep sleep.

I stumbled into the radio station a few minutes before six on Tuesday morning and immediately began playing a sentimental mix of love songs, both happy and unrequited. The Beatles' "All You Need Is Love." Tom Rush's "No Regrets." Jesse Winchester's "Yankee Lady." Poco's "A Good Feeling to Know."

A couple of hours later, Helen walked in. She told me that she was in love with me and willing to venture down our path to parts unknown. We shared a brief embrace and she left me to my daily freedom of musical expression. I was aroused but scared shitless.

A small, gift-wrapped box was waiting for me at my front door. I opened it slowly and found a three-volume set of Anaïs Nin's diaries with a brief note from Helen. Nin was an icon of creativity and sexual liberation. I read the first few entries and suddenly had a stronger sense of the kind of woman I had flipped for.

We sneaked some stolen moments over the next few days before Helen took her kids (sans husband) to see their grandparents in Miami Beach. I was convinced our relationship was doomed, but I was feeling true love for the first time and was willing to endure the eventual pain of losing it just to savor the experience of having it, however abbreviated our time together might be.

Intellectually, Helen and I knew it wasn't our destiny to walk off into the sunset. Emotionally, we kept turning up the heat.

Late one night about a month into our affair, Jacques accused Helen of infidelity. When she owned up to the truth, he stormed over to my cottage and angrily confronted me. Helen intervened before it got violent, and the three of us spent the next hour discussing our dilemma over shots of scotch.

"If you and Helen decide to work on your marriage, I promise never to see her again," I said, simultaneously sad and upset.

But after two weeks of adhering to that resolution, Helen told Jacques she needed to see me on occasion. He responded by initiating divorce proceedings. I moved in with Helen, Nicole, and Paul the following year.

Four decades later, Helen and I still shake our heads in disbelief that we followed our gut instincts against ridiculous odds and became partners for life.

IO.

i begin asking questions

SHORTLY INTO MY STINT AS a DJ, I noticed an auxiliary micro-phone across the console from me. Since none of the KRNW staff was doing interviews, I didn't think much about it. We were all just playing long sets of music and dishing out accompanying mono-logues of various lengths. But that would soon change.

At Tulagi, my second home, I befriended the club's manager and talent buyer, Chuck Morris, a manic mid-twentyish New Yorker who had abandoned his pursuit of a PhD in political science to become a concert producer. Chuck was a consummate promoter, doing end-less market research and picking the brains of music business profes-sionals before compiling his concert lineup. I was just one member of his coterie of informal advisors, and he called me ten times a day asking for my opinions.

As the leaves began changing colors during the fall of '71, Chuck regularly hounded me to do radio interviews with Tulagi acts upon their arrival in Boulder for multiple-night engagements. In those days, bands would establish "residencies" and perform three to six nights depending on their drawing power.

My first radio interview should have convinced me not to do a second. Legendary blues guitarist Aaron "T-Bone" Walker came down to the station with his manager to plug his Tulagi shows. Walker was sixty-two at the time, but looked much older. I was thrilled to meet this electric guitar pioneer, but kept a calm veneer as if it were just another day, another show.

We talked about his signature songs "Call It Stormy Monday (But Tuesday Is Just as Bad)" and "T-Bone Shuffle" and about his primary mentor, Blind Lemon Jefferson. We moved on to Walker's unique guitar style and broke down the differences between Texas and Chicago blues. I had prepared for this interview and felt that my questions were provocative and well informed. Walker's answers were deliberate, terse, and, unfortunately, much shorter than my questions. I was so captivated by his drawl that I didn't notice his voice tailing off and his eyes closing.

When I asked him about the origin of the nickname T-Bone, he seemed to get a bit more animated, explaining that it was originally T-Bow, which was the phonetic pronunciation of his middle name Thibeaux. Suddenly his voice started to slur and he never finished the anecdote. I quickly changed the subject, asking about his early forays into electric guitar but got no answer whatsoever.

The dead air lingered, so I fired off another question. Again, no answer. Then I heard snoring in my headphones. T-Bone Walker had fallen asleep less than ten minutes into the interview. I quickly cued up his version of "She's the No Sleepin'est Woman," an unintentionally appropriate selection. His manager apologized, woke up his charge, and quickly left the station. I couldn't have asked for a more humbling slice of on-the-job training.

The next few weeks found me sitting face-to-face with blues innovator Willie Dixon, jazz guitar virtuoso Larry Coryell, religious country rockers Mason Proffit, and ex-Flying Burrito Brother Bernie Leadon, in Boulder to woodshed with his new band called Eagle (they changed their name to the Eagles before releasing their debut album in 1972). I enjoyed these intimate interactions immensely and peppered the interviews with personal, penetrating questions about their lifestyles, disciplines, excesses, and instrumental techniques.

I never imagined that people were out there paying attention to these dialogues, but they were. By early 1972, two editors of local publications had contacted me, both encouraging me to try my hand at print journalism. I didn't even own a typewriter at the time, but it made sense to me that I could transcribe my radio interviews into articles and make a few extra bucks in the process.

The first call came from Wayne Robins, who would go on to a distinguished career in rock journalism that included tenures at *Creem* and *Newsday*, was the entertainment editor of the *Colorado Daily* and a regular listener to my morning show. We shared an affinity for vintage rock and doo-wop and both avidly followed the newest strains of music. One day he flipped out when I played the Mighty Marvelows' "In the Morning" and came down to the station. We bonded instantly. He assigned me to review a John Fahey concert that night, which launched my adjunct career as a journalist.

Fahey came down to KRNW at nine in the morning, played live, and gave a charmingly quirky interview. That night I saw his show and accepted his invitation to go to an after-party at a farmhouse in east Boulder. While most of the guests mingled in the living room, Fahey took me aside into one of the bedrooms and taught me seven modal tunings on guitar, remembering that I had specifically asked about them during the morning's radio show. He proceeded to perform three new compositions to a startled audience of one.

I had enough of a story churning in my head that combined all the elements of the day—the interview, the concert, the after-party's private session—when he put his guitar away and asked me if I had ever experimented with homosexuality. Talk about unexpected segues. Letting him know that I had not and wasn't about to, I successfully changed the subject by asking him to give me a condensed account about traveling to Mississippi in search of Bukka White.

He laconically related the story but was more interested in offering me a few doses of Ritalin. I begged off and headed home. Omitting the part about the late-night come-on, I typed up the concert review on my roommate's Olivetti Underwood, slept for two hours, did my radio show, and raced to the *Colorado Daily* to hand in the first of the nearly one thousand articles I would write over the next decade.

Just a few days later, the second editor called. Stephen Foehr, also a fan of KRNW, helmed Denver's weekly underground rag, the *Straight Creek Journal*. He asked me to write record and concert reviews, interviews, thought pieces, and alternative sports stories, and report on counterculture trends.

I basked in the pinball effect that resulted from merging my passions for radio and print journalism. Throughout those years, I took part in countless conversations with both the profound and the profane.

JIM CROCE

I reluctantly agreed to interview Croce as a favor to Chuck Morris in February 1973. All I knew about this rising singer-songwriter was that he had an annoying (to me, anyway) AM hit called "You Don't Mess Around with Jim." I was an FM snob at the time and thought my credibility would suffer if I started interviewing any hack with a hit.

When Croce arrived at the station with his second guitarist/harmony vocalist Maury Muehleisen, I apologized in advance for having just a few minutes to give them to promote their upcoming concert and asked them to pick one song to sing on the air. They played "Operator."

The intricate guitar parts and the poignancy of the song gave me chills. Nearly speechless, I asked them to play one more song. They launched into the soon-to-be released "Bad, Bad Leroy Brown," which included driving, percussive guitar parts that accompanied the humorous story. I became an instant fan and friend and wouldn't let them leave until they had played for an hour. They were as gracious as they were good.

During the interview, I admitted that I had had preconceived negative notions about having Croce on my show and that their transcendent performance was a life lesson for me. I would always be open to exploring someone's depth and not make premature flash judgments, especially based on record companies' force-fed singles. I invited them back to the radio station when they returned to play in Boulder in October.

Sadly, I never got the chance to build on our nascent friendship. A small chartered plane carrying Croce and Muehleisen from Natchitoches, Louisiana, to Sherman, Texas, on September 20 crashed shortly after takeoff, killing everyone on board.

GRAM PARSONS

Talk about eerie coincidences. The same week I interviewed Jim Croce, I had been unable to set up an in-studio session with Gram Parsons, who was scheduled to do a three-night stint at Edison Electric, a small club in Boulder. He abhorred doing press of any kind. The afternoon before opening night, angry creditors shuttered and padlocked Edison Electric, forcing Parsons and his band, the Fallen Angels, to move their gig on the fly to the Pioneer Inn in Nederland. He needed to get the word out regarding the venue change, so he had little choice but to come down to my show for an interview.

It was a frigid afternoon (I was doing the 2–6 p.m. shift at the time), and a bundled-up Parsons stumbled into the station accompanied by his gorgeous backup singer, an unknown named Emmylou Harris. Since he showed up sans guitar, I played some tracks from his new solo LP, interspersing announcements about the new location of his concerts.

I began the interview by timidly asking him if he would talk about his sudden departure from the Byrds in 1968, when he refused to play on a South African tour due to that country's apartheid policies.

"NO!" he screamed. "All I want to talk about is the Pioneer Inn!" He was swigging Annie Greensprings grape rosé from a bottle concealed in a brown paper bag. A calm Emmylou Harris, who was sitting on the floor crocheting pink booties for her infant daughter, seemed accustomed to his drunken hostility.

"After you left the Byrds, you and Chris Hillman formed the Flying Burrito Brothers," I continued, attempting to regain control of the conversation. "Is it true that you tried to convince Roger McGuinn to dissolve the Byrds and join the Burritos?"

"I JUST WANT TO TALK ABOUT THE PIONEER INN!" he shouted, pinning the needle of the modulation meter. "PIONEER INN, PIONEER INN, PIONEER INN . . ."

While raving, Parsons grabbed the flexible gooseneck mic stand and broke it in half. Hearing the commotion, Bob Wilkinson raced in from the adjoining office and stared in shock at the damaged equipment. "What the hell's going on," he hissed, shushing when he realized we were on the air.

I quickly cued up "Streets of Baltimore," potted down the live microphones, and said goodbye to Gram Parsons. He guzzled the remaining swill, flung the brown-bagged bottle into the trash can, and stumbled shakily out the front door. Emmylou shrugged apologetically and followed her leader.

"I shoulda thrown that motherfucker down the stairs," Wilkinson said, gathering the broken parts.

I carried on with my show, stunned and dismayed that one of my favorite singer-songwriters seemed to be on an irreversible downward spiral. Less than six months later, Parsons was found dead of a drug overdose in a motel room in Joshua Tree, California.

In August 1973, *Rolling Stone* magazine called Chuck Morris, who had moved to Denver to operate Ebbets Field, a fantastic new 230-seat club. *RS* was looking for a local writer to cover Dan Hicks's solo concert debut there. It was his first performance after many years of fronting the Hot Licks. Chuck put the magazine in touch with me and I wrote an eight-hundred-word review. The article was accepted and I viewed it as my breakthrough into the big leagues. When the October 15 issue hit the stands, I frantically leafed through it in search of my byline. The article wasn't there.

I called the magazine and left a message for editor Ben Fong-Torres. He never returned the call, but a few days later I got my edited original back in the mail with a polite cover letter from Fong-Torres. He said they were ready to run the review but had to bump it at the last minute to make room for two unexpected obituaries: Jim Croce and Gram Parsons.

TOM WAITS

When I first interviewed Tom Waits in 1973, there were only scant hints that he'd turn into one of the most influential and imitated musicians of our time. His debut LP *Closing Time* had recently been released, he was pigeonholed as a mellow Asylum Records singer-songwriter, and you could detect just a tinge of rasp in a voice that would eventually make Satchmo seem like Nat King Cole in comparison.

Waits had become an opening-act fixture at Denver's Ebbets Field, warming up for the likes of Roger McGuinn, John Stewart, and Gene Clark. Looking like a cross between a beatnik and a hobo, he played most of his songs seated at a piano à la Randy Newman with little of the poetic patter that would soon become his trademark.

"I wonder if it's a blessing or a curse for an artist to get recognition," he told me over coffee at the Oxford Hotel. "I've gotten a little exposure, but not enough to make my head spin and I'm glad about that. I did a three-week East Coast tour opening for Frank Zappa in front of three to four thousand people a night. I got a lot of produce thrown at me, but I did it to challenge myself."

Born in 1949, Waits grew up in Whittier, California, the son of a high school Spanish teacher who had assorted stringed instruments around the house. "My dad had a beat-up Mexican guitar and a ukulele and that's what I learned on. He taught me Mexican folk songs—ranchera and romantica."

After moving to San Diego as a teenager, Waits began playing a St. George electric guitar in a surf band covering songs by the Beach Boys, Surfaris, and Ventures. "I went to O'Farrell Junior High, an all-black school, and started listening to Marvin Gaye, Tammi Terrell, the Supremes, and James Brown. I saw James Brown at Balboa Stadium and some people fainted when he sang 'Please, Please, Please.'"

Waits supported himself between the ages of fifteen and twenty as a utility man at Napoleone Pizza in National City, where he worked as a cook, dishwasher, plumber, janitor, and maintenance man. When he turned twenty, he discovered the Heritage, a coffeehouse/folk club that occupied a one-story cinder block building on the clogged main artery of Mission Beach, a bohemian enclave fifteen miles north of his home.

The Heritage had first opened for business near the end of the folk boom during the early '60s, and for the next several years, it would serve as a venue for traditional music, including string band music, balladeers, and bluegrass. Although the Heritage showcased local performers on hoot nights, it also presented touring artists ranging from Big Joe Williams to Chris Hillman and the Gosdin Brothers.

By the time Waits discovered the Heritage in 1968, the club's offerings had morphed into an eclectic mix of folk, rock, jazz, blues, country, and singer-songwriters. He became an avid patron and regularly participated in the hoots, playing songs by Mississippi John Hurt, Reverend Gary Davis, and Elvis Presley.

As Waits became more closely associated with the Heritage,

he would do fill-in work as the club's doorman, ticket-taker, and bouncer. One night, after hearing an amateur perform a set of original songs, Waits dedicated himself to his own muse and developed an enthusiastic following. In November 1970 he secured his first paid gig at the Heritage, receiving twenty-five dollars to open for a folk-pop duo. During his two years there, he traveled to LA every Monday for hoot night at the Troubadour, the renowned West Hollywood nightclub.

"I took the bus to LA, the 94 local to Doheny, and lined up at 6 p.m. to do three or four songs. It was a slave market. People sold their souls to play there. They came from Georgia, New York City, all over the country."

It eventually paid off for Waits, who was discovered and signed by Herb Cohen, the manager of Tim Buckley, Frank Zappa, and Fred Neil. "I met Herb at the Troub and he asked if I wanted to make a record. I'm a lot more secure with a record deal. A first album is like a diploma, a BA," Waits told me, adding that he had dropped out of college due to "lack of discipline."

Waits was soft-spoken and modest throughout the interview. He was pleased that Tim Buckley and Lee Hazelwood had each recorded "Martha" on their latest albums and was happy that the Eagles, his labelmates, had recorded "Ol' 55" for their upcoming release.

Our next interview took place two years later at the very same table in the Oxford Hotel coffee shop in Denver. Waits was touring in support of his second LP, *The Heart of Saturday Night*, and he'd just finished recording a new record, the soon-to-be-released *Nighthawks at the Diner*, in front of a live studio audience. After opening shows nine times at Ebbets Field over the previous two years, he had graduated to headlining status.

Waits was road tested and infinitely more self-assured when I pushed the record button this time around. He barely said hello before launching into a spoken-word monologue, all from memory.

I rode into town on a boa constrictor with a rattlesnake as
my whip.
Now when I tell you a little more about myself, I know you're
gonna flip.
But I ain't too bad . . . you should see my brother.
Now I go to the land of the jungle and I lay up in the shade.
And I take my daily swims in the Florida Everglades.
I ain't bad . . . you should see my brother.
I go to the land of the cobra and some folks say I ain't got a
chance.
But I make the cobra blow the whistle while I have my dance.
But I ain't bad, I ain't bad . . . you should see my brother.
Some call me the hackshaw, the devil's son-in-law, the high
sheriff of hell.
Cuz I made the devil put in a watercooler and an air condi-
tioner, so it'd be a nice place to dwell.
I ain't bad, no I ain't bad . . . you should see my brother.
Well now here come my brother now.

Waits continued his highly entertaining, nonstop assault for three razor-sharp minutes. When I realized it was okay for me to talk, I asked him if he had dictated these seemingly drug-fueled ramblings into a tape recorder.

"I've never taken any narcotics in my life . . . I just drink beer. I don't talk into a tape recorder. I take notes, just like you." Without needing a cue, he spit out an epilogue.

I go down to the 20 Grand Club, dressed up in a serious seer-
sucker Saturday evening accoutrement ensemble and a
flaming café Nehru.

The Soul and Inspirations are playing a long version of "Har-
lem Nocturne" and I get inspired.
Take two Darvon and drive on.

This had already turned into the kind of interview I loved, where I hardly had to say a word. In 1973, I had to extract teeth when we talked, but since then, Tom Waits had traveled the world. He was finding his voice and becoming much more than a hipster poet of his generation (and he was still five years away from marrying his soul mate, Kathleen Brennan, who would have an even greater effect on his lyrical and musical output).

I asked him if he was currently identifying more with poets or musicians. Even his unscripted answers had a unique timbre.

"Most people have a preconceived idea of what poetry is," he said. "They still think of *Ode to a Grecian Urn*. At the same time, contemporary poets who do have a social conscience are separated from the rest of the world. They don't play nightclubs, they don't play concerts, they're not on the radio, they're not in newspapers or music magazines. It's a very small literary community that is highly competitive, cut-throat, and cold-blooded, with nothing at stake."

The interview became more traditional when I asked him who he most admired these days.

Without skipping a beat, he said, "Charles Bukowski, Rudy Ray Moore, Lord Buckley, Ken Nordine, Randy Newman, Ray Charles, Dr. John, Captain Beefheart, Benny Boulder, and Chuck E. Weiss." The last two were iconic Denverites.

His favorite double bill?

"I just opened for Proctor and Bergman at the Bottom Line."

Weirdest double bills?

"Opening for Martha and the Vandellas in Detroit and for Billy Preston in Phoenix."

Favorite modern-day musician?

"Have you ever seen Bruce Springsteen?" Six months later, I'd lose my Bruce virginity at C. W. Post College in Long Island and become a lifelong fan, but I was only marginally into the pre–*Born to Run* Springsteen. "Onstage, he's fucking magic. All it takes is seeing him one time to make you a believer."

How would Waits describe his own songwriting?

"I write inebriational travelogues and improvisational adventures into the bowels of the metropolitan region. Nocturnal emissions. Please pay when served."

What's his typical breakfast?

"Two eggs looking at me, wheat toast, well-done hash browns, and a cup of coffee that's strong enough to defend itself. Easy on the 30 weight on the blue plate. I like to walk out of a restaurant with enough gas to open up a Mobil station."

Most profound concert experience?

"Seeing Richard Pryor open for Miles Davis."

He didn't want to talk about sex or groupies on the road, but threw out a Waitsian bon mot for good measure. "I'm hornier than a chained-up dog with two dicks."

Before thanking him and saying hasta la vista, I asked him what project he'd be working on next.

"I'm writing a story for *Crawdaddy!* called 'Putnam County,'" he said. "It's written on the corner of Fifth and Vermouth under a Thunderbird moon in a Muscatel sky. I attempted to consolidate all my weekly rendezvous into one low monthly payment."

In 1978, the location changed to a coffee shop in South Boulder. The Tom Waits who met me was now five albums deep into his oeuvre (the latest was *Foreign Affairs*), and he sold out the 2,500-seat Macky Auditorium on the CU campus.

His voice had gained appreciably in gravel and his demeanor was guarded, bordering on aloof. As opposed to greeting me as a familiar ally and a journalist who had been firmly in his corner since his days as a little-known folksinger, I sensed from the start that he just wanted to get the interview over with.

Of course, I didn't help things when right off the bat, I asked him if he was worried that his voice was ravaged and wouldn't stand the test of time.

"No, my voice is just getting to where I like it," he said. I noticed that he was no longer chain-smoking unfiltered Chesterfields.

When I brought up his burgeoning foray into acting, he shrugged it off (this was before he'd become a favorite of Jarmusch, Coppola, and Altman). "Sly Stallone came to see me in a club and asked me to be in *Paradise Alley*, and I'm friends with Martin Mull and he said I could just act like myself in *Fernwood Tonight*." The extended answers and prolonged verbal riffing of our 1975 get-together were MIA.

He got a bit professorial when I asked him to describe "Potter's Field," one of his new epic songs.

"Potter's Field is the cheapest part of every cemetery. This potter's field is an island in the middle of the Bronx River in New York City. It's across from Riker's Island, a maximum-security prison. You get a fifty-dollar burial in a pine box if you die without any visible means of support. So this [song] is like *Odd Man Out*, the James Mason film about a stool pigeon, a hit man, and a convict. The song's got a little Rod Serling and Damon Runyon in it . . . and I recorded it in a studio with a full orchestra, which was a challenge to me."

The only time Waits perked up was when I asked if he had any fantasy projects on the back burner.

"I'm thinking of recording a Nat King Cole–style album with twelve ballads strung together called *Music to Seduce a Divorced Waitress By*."

Sadly, that album remained an unfulfilled idea.

I ran into Tom one more time in May of 1982 outside the Holiday Inn in Boulder. He and his new wife, Kathleen Brennan, were waiting for a taxi to the airport, and I was on my way to the bar to interview John Hiatt.

I had written a flattering article calling Waits one of America's greatest songwriters and plugged his upcoming concert. When I reintroduced myself to him, he looked away and seemed annoyed that I had approached him.

Kathleen had read my story and said, "Tom, this is the guy who wrote that wonderful article. Aren't you going to thank him?" Waits shrugged, nodded at me, and hopped into the cab.

BILL MURRAY

In 1977, I had a high profile in Boulder. I wrote a weekly music column called Hot Licks and Rhetoric for the *Boulder Daily Camera* and hosted a six-hour Sunday night music/talk show on KBCO-FM, the station that KRNW morphed into shortly after Bob Wilkinson sold his heritage 97.3 FM frequency to Iowans Bob and Diane Greenlee. I was deluged with phone messages at both media outlets from people who wanted to either meet me or assault me. Somewhat selective about returning the calls, I typically called back all the women.

One day I got two messages from a Mickey Kelley. Assuming it was a man, I almost didn't return the call, but I'm glad I did. Mickey was a transplant from New York City who had been a television producer, and when her stressful career turned sour, she escaped to Boulder. In one fell swoop, she had gone from producing Howard Cosell's weekly show on ABC to selling mail-order woks from her kitchen. She was calling me to see if I would give her an overview of the local entertainment scene so she could somehow stay involved in the business.

We met for lunch at Herbie's Deli, next door to Tulagi, and hit it off before the lox and bagels arrived at our table. She told me that her boyfriend was coming out from New York City for vacation the following week and I invited them both over for cocktails. Her boyfriend (eventually husband and father of her two children) was Bill Murray, and he was on a two-week hiatus from *Saturday Night Live*.

When Bill and Mickey arrived at our house, Paul greeted them at the front door. "Hey, I know you," he said, pointing at Murray. "Aren't you the guy who played the Secret Service agent at Amy Carter's elementary school?"

"Yeah, that was me," Murray responded, clearly delighted to have an eleven-year-old fan in Boulder. In pure Bill Murray style, he started bantering with Paul and Nicole and had them laughing in seconds.

I led Murray to my music room and he let out a "holy shit!" as soon as he saw my record collection. He gravitated toward the wall of stacked orange crates and started leafing through the albums. "Do you have any Buddy Guy? Any Stylistics? Any Ronstadt?"

Before Helen finished mixing the gin and tonics, Murray agreed to be a guest on my radio show that weekend if I'd let him choose the music. He subsequently became my dream cohost on several visits to Colorado.

For one particularly entertaining show in January 1978, Murray walked into the studio with Mickey, my KBCO colleague Jon Steele, and a twelve-pack of Olympia Beer. He was very forthcoming as an interview subject, providing a fascinating personal history.

The fifth of nine children from Wilmette, Illinois, Murray apprenticed at the Second City workshop for two years, joined the touring company, and finally got paid to be a regular cast member. He moved to New York City to work on *The National Lampoon Radio Hour* and landed a featured role in the National Lampoon Off-Broadway show. From there he moved on to the short-lived Howard Cosell TV variety show as a member of the Prime Time Players along with his brother, Brian Doyle Murray, and Christopher Guest.

"The Cosell show lasted only eighteen weeks," Murray said, "and we were on eleven times. It was in the old Ed Sullivan Theater and there were good things about the experience . . . I got to meet Andy Williams, Lynn Anderson, and Alan King." He then launched into an a cappella impression of Williams doing "MacArthur Park" that included a limp, anticlimactic final note, deflating his soaring approach. It was the first of many times I cracked up during the interview.

Murray's career path took a brief detour to LA for a stint on TVTV that included covering Super Bowl X in Miami. Then came an emergency call from *Saturday Night Live* producer Lorne Michaels.

"Michaels told me that Belushi had broken his leg," Murray said, "and they needed me in New York, so I moved east and joined the cast."

After the biographical part of the interview, Murray played DJ, spinning sides such as the Spinners' "Mighty Love," Ray Charles's "Unchain My Heart," Linda Ronstadt's version of "Blue Bayou," and Otis Redding's "Try a Little Tenderness." He also assumed my role as matchmaker during *The KBCO Communal Bathtub*, a weekly feature I created based on *The Dating Game*. The idea was to have a woman call in, answer questions about herself, and be put on hold while a guy called up attempting to land a date with her.

I usually asked harmless questions regarding age, height, weight, profession, and hobbies. But Murray dove deeper into hilarity by asking what kind of car the person drove (year, make, and model), what mileage they got (city and highway), who would pick up the check, if they skied, and if they were native Coloradoans. He was a natural interviewer and seemed to know tidbits and minutia about everyone's hometown (a local burger place that had shut down, the strip mall that had just opened), vehicles ("They don't make Karmann Ghias anymore, do they? That's a classic."), and occupations (which this night ranged from air-quality specialist to airplane mechanic).

Murray succeeded in fixing up Sandy, a twenty-eight-year-old feminist Mountain Bell employee who drove a '73 Plymouth Duster that got 16 mpg, with Tom, a thirty-three-year-old electronics equipment salesman who said he'd take her to the Walrus (a trendy Boulder restaurant) and pick up the check. Sandy passed on Jack, Kai, Paul, Pete, Jim, and Mike before settling on Tom. I know of two couples who met on *The Communal Bathtub* and later got married, but I never had a follow-up call from Sandy or Tom.

I took the reins back from Murray and kick-started another matchmaking episode. The next caller was Robin, twenty-one, five foot nine, with long dark hair, majoring in speech therapy at CU. I quickly brushed through the first two suitors and uncharacteristically discouraged Robin from selecting them. That's because contestant number three was Bill Murray calling from the phone in the KBCO production studio.

"My name's Jerry. I'm six foot one, 175 pounds, in pretty good shape, drive a Volvo . . . I get decent mileage." He spoke with a slight speech impediment and mentioned that since Robin was into speech therapy, he'd be very interested in meeting her. "Robin, come to me," he pleaded and I almost convulsed on the air. It took all my willpower to keep my composure and not expose the ruse. "I'll take you to a nice dinner. I'll take you to a club afterwards so I can show you off. I'll give you the world."

It was clear that Robin wasn't going to select "Jerry" from the outset, so Murray continued to lay on the schmaltz. When Robin politely declined, Murray became contentious and asked for another chance, trying to convince her that she was making the biggest mistake of her life. I began to feel like I was abusing the airwaves by allowing Robin's torment to continue, but Murray gradually lightened up, started talking in his real voice, revealed his identity, apologized, and said, "The joke's on you." Fortunately Robin was a great sport. (When I saw *Caddyshack* two years later, I was sure I'd heard the voice of Bill Murray's character before. I dug out the tape of our interview, and "Jerry" had been the prototype for greenskeeper/gopher hunter Carl Spackler.)

Murray's three-hour in-studio visit was capped by a lengthy discussion with audience participation about the pride of Colorado, the

Denver Broncos. They had just concluded the best season in their seventeen-year history, winning two playoff games, and were two weeks away from their first Super Bowl appearance. Broncomania was rampant throughout the Rocky Mountains.

"What's wrong with our Broncos?" Murray asked as we opened the phone lines. At first the callers were startled, but they quickly caught on to the tongue in cheek. Although Murray was a lifelong Chicago Bears fan, he was extremely knowledgeable about the Broncos' roster and made a series of fictitious, salacious observations. Quarterback Craig Morton was gay and too distracted by accusations of tax evasion to be an effective leader. Wide receiver Haven Moses was a cough-syrup addict. The Pony Express (Broncos' cheerleaders) was about to be implicated in a sex scandal. And, perhaps most blasphemous, Murray blasted the defensive team's nickname, Orange Crush, saying he preferred tweed to orange.

In my many years of taking phone calls, I'd never had all five lines blinking at once for such a long time. When the last Olympia Beer had been drained, Murray motioned to me to wrap it up. I played the Ramones' "Rockaway Beach" and asked Murray if he wanted to delve into any other topics. I had an hour left in the show. But he was spent, like an athlete who had given his all and badly needed a Jacuzzi and a rubdown. I thanked him for the most memorable interaction of my radio career.

A few days later, Murray invited me to hang out with him at his Hotel Boulderado suite. Joining me were Mickey, Jon Steele, and local music critic Mark Bliesener (one of Murray's high school classmates). We quickly became a captive audience of four.

Murray hospitably laid out thick lines of coke, rolled fat joints that Mickey suggested we avoid due to the potency of the blend, and asked us to make ourselves comfortable as he launched into a twenty-minute monologue. His assortment of voices, impressions, multi-character dialogue, and rat-a-tat delivery had us (literally) gasping for air with bellowing laughter.

Despite how high Murray must have been, whenever a certain bon mot or inflection got a significant response, he would stop on a dime, write notes on pieces of hotel stationery, and push-pin them into the wall. By the end of his "performance," the room was covered with new wallpaper. It was a revealing gaze into one artist's methodology.

Just as Murray knew when to end our radio collaboration, he thanked us for visiting and for our rapt attention and said he had business to attend to. Although I never saw him again (except in his movies), I felt a true connection to him in Boulder.

Mickey moved back to New York City a few months later and started working for an upstart cable network called Home Box Office. When I visited her there in 1979, no one had any idea how innovative, powerful, and revolutionary that company would become.

ELVIS COSTELLO

In late 1977, Elvis Costello's initial stateside reputation painted him as surly, controversial, and irascible. Dressed in stovepipe slacks, a wrinkled sports coat, and his signature (at the time) Buddy Holly glasses, he was an angry punk rocker aggressively promoting his debut album *My Aim Is True*.

Yet in February 1978, when he first walked into the KBCO studio accompanied by his manager Jake Riviera, Costello was soft-spoken, cooperative, and (dare I say it?) gentle. He was in Boulder to perform at the Glenn Miller Ballroom on the University of Colorado campus. The show in the 1,200-seat venue sold out way in advance, thanks to the overwhelming buzz generated by the Columbia Records hype machine and the superb quality of Costello's music.

I asked him if he would pick some songs and play guest DJ. He seemed eager to please and asked if we had any Ian Matthews in the library. We did and Costello chose "Poor Ditching Boy," a Richard Thompson composition. He also asked for Johnny Paycheck's "Take This Job and Shove It," a country hit that seemed out of character in all aspects except the vitriol. Costello said he was also amenable to taking phone calls from the listeners. I had heard that he was a nightmare to deal with, so I was relieved when just the opposite was the case.

But then I turned on the microphone.

I introduced him to the on-air audience, played "Alison" and "(The Angels Wanna Wear My) Red Shoes," and started the interview.

Noting that his album had charted higher in the UK than in the States, I asked, "How would you compare the response your music gets in England to the response it gets from American audiences?"

"That's the stupidest question I've ever heard in my life," he snarled.

I was momentarily stunned but also aware that his punk persona was a marketing invention. Next!

"On this tour, so far, what's been your favorite American city?"

"Dallas," he responded immediately, "because that's where they have the best shots." He didn't mean snifters of bourbon, but people who expertly wielded assault rifles with telescopic lenses.

I laughed nervously and decided to take phone calls with the intent of deflecting his animosity toward the listeners.

"What do you think of the United States?"

"I don't think anything about them."

"Is it true that you used to be a computer programmer?"

"No. I was a terminal operator . . . as in ending your life."

"Are you punk or new wave?"

"We're psychoholic—a cross between psychedelic and alcoholic."

"Elvis—I think you're universally untalented and a complete hype."

"Oh yeah, who the hell are you? How do you know?"

Riviera, a quiet observer up until that point, leaned into the microphone. "Come down here to the radio station and we'll kick your ass!"

When the listeners started screaming and belching, calling Elvis a dumb limey and saying his music sucked, I cut off the phone calls and resumed my role as moderator. Costello came across as annoyed and agitated but his constant smile belied his character's pose. He calmed down a bit, talked lovingly about his Fender Jazzmaster and Jaguar guitars, and anecdotally related that he had written "Watching the Detectives" after viewing an episode of *Starsky & Hutch*.

Riviera nudged him and gave him a "don't be so friendly" look and Costello nodded.

"What do you think of the University of Colorado proclaiming today Elvis Costello Day?" I asked. "They've never done that for a musician in its history."

"If they're serious, then it's just as dumb as Independence Day or Empire Day, which we used to have in England. If it's just a bit of fun, an excuse for a few people to go out and get pissed, then it doesn't bother me that much."

"I think it's time to let you play DJ. When you came in today, you asked if we had any Ian Matthews LPs. Why do you have an affinity for his music?"

"I have none! I hate his guts! I think he's useless . . . a complete limey wimp. That's why I'm playing his record. I'm trying to lower myself to the music programming of most of the stations we've been to. The only reason I'm playing this is because Richard Thompson wrote the song."

The recorded music couldn't come fast enough. I decided to conclude the interview at the end of the song, plug the live cast of that evening's concert, thank Elvis for stopping by, and play "Mystery Dance" as an outro. Before we went back on the air, Elvis timidly reminded me to play the Johnny Paycheck song and asked if he could stay in the studio to listen to it. Off the air, he was effusive with his thanks, polite as he had been ornery, and gratefully accepted my offer to give him and Riviera a ride to his soundcheck. It would save them the five-dollar cab fare.

During the ten-minute drive, we talked about music, politics, the roster of musicians who had recorded at Caribou Ranch (fifteen miles west of Boulder), and the pros and cons of record companies.

Elvis hopped out of the car, sprinted to the venue, gave a stunning performance a few hours later, and proceeded to have an extraordinary life and career.

II.

kenny & the kritix

BEING A MUSIC CRITIC CAN put you in harm's way, especially when you live in a small community like Boulder where it is virtually impossible to remain anonymous.

I wrote newspaper and magazine articles from 1972 to 1983, many of them about Colorado musicians for various Boulder and Denver publications. Although I largely supported the Boulder music community, I wasn't a cheerleader. If a band's output was mediocre or lazy, I would call them on it. If a folk-rock band suddenly tried capitalizing on the disco craze, I wasn't polite when taking them to task. While I wouldn't describe my tone as vicious, I gave few free passes.

One of the biggest bands to break out of Boulder in the 1970s was Firefall, a pop-rock sextet that included accomplished rock veterans Mark Andes (Spirit, Jo Jo Gunne), Rick Roberts (Flying Burrito Brothers), Michael Clarke (the Byrds, Flying Burrito Brothers), and Jock Bartley (Gram Parsons). Firefall was the most commercially successful project any of them had been involved with, but the music was safe, glossily produced AM radio pablum lacking any semblance of risk. Melodic, hook laden, and well crafted, but inconsequential.

In an otherwise flattering feature story I wrote about bassist Mark Andes, I asked him, "How can you go from having played such sophisticated, multidimensional, other-worldly music with Spirit to being satisfied with the radio-friendly pop pap you play with Firefall?"

The night that article hit the stands, I was cornered in a club by a furious Michael Clarke, an intimidating figure when he was high (which was almost always). Clarke was no stranger to brilliant music during his tenures with the Byrds and the Flying Burrito Brothers, and he was not thrilled with my less-than-complimentary assessment of Firefall. Grabbing my shirt in his fist and backing me into a wall, he screamed, "How can you write such negative shit?" Slowly relaxing his grip, he smiled and said, "By the way, you're right."

Too many other times while walking down the street, I would run into a musician I had recently criticized in print. More than once, I was confronted with "I'd like to see what you could do onstage." I took that to heart and often wondered myself how I'd fare in front of an audience. After losing or quitting a series of jobs and finding myself minimally employed during the summer of 1980, friends started asking me what I was going to do next. For no apparent reason, I told them, "I'm gonna put a band together." Although I had futzed around on guitar since seeing the Beatles on *Ed Sullivan* in 1964 (like everyone else), I had never taken music making seriously, played with other musicians, or performed onstage. Despite having no game plan, no musicians in mind, no set list—nothing—I kept repeating, "I'm putting a band together."

Mark Andes became the first original member of Firefall to quit that group in September 1980. It was big news in Boulder, so I devoted a column to it. At the end of the interview at his ranch house east of town, we broke open a few Heinekens, and Andes, having heard of my recent job shake-ups, asked me what I would be doing next. Like the knee-jerk I had become, I said, "I'm putting a band together."

He pressed me for details and I told him that my vision was to put together a band for a series of performances that would include a high-energy, Springsteenesque rock approach, theatrical skits with scripted audio collages, costume changes, obscure cover songs, and material I hadn't written yet.

"Do you need a bass player?" he asked.

I wouldn't have been surprised if spittle started drooling from the sides of my mouth. Ever since his days with the band Spirit, Andes had been one of my favorite musicians. At six foot three with a surfer's build and impossibly beautiful long blonde hair, not only did Mark Andes personify an angelic rock god onstage, he played brilliantly with a searing intensity that rocked hard, provided jazzy undertones when appropriate, and transformed ordinary drummers into great ones.

To this day, the original Spirit remains the best rock 'n' roll band I have ever seen. You can't mention Spirit without reflecting on all five musicians. The visual focus was always on center stage and the spectacular drum setup of Ed "Cass" Cassidy. There were the core members of the band up front, all of them longhaired kids, and this black-clad, head-shaved drummer more than twice their age on a regal drum throne behind them, doing complex solos with his bare hands.

Randy California would be decked out in a turban and floor-length kaftan, playing liquid lead guitar every bit as fluidly as his friend and mentor Jimi Hendrix. Jay Ferguson, with a patent on mic-stand histrionics long before Steven Tyler or Jon Bon Jovi, may be one of the most underrated front men in rock history. John Locke was a mad professor on keyboards, adding a jazz element unfamiliar in rock 'n' roll at that time (check out the breaks in "Fresh Garbage" and "New Dope in Town," not to mention the six-minute instrumental opus "Ice").

And then there was Mark Andes. Onstage, he was usually stationary, but his riffs were thunderous during the hard rockers and subtly supportive when the band drifted into its ethereal cosmos. Even though Andes rarely sang (except on the infectious "Uncle Jack") and avoided the spotlight, it was impossible to take your eyes off him.

And now, without skipping a beat, one of rock 'n' roll's most distinctive musicians was asking me if I wanted him to play bass in my band. I had never even sung into a microphone, except in my daydreams.

"Are you serious?" I asked.

"Well, I'm between gigs . . ."

Suddenly my modest game plan changed. Having Mark Andes on board gave me the cachet to attract the best players in Boulder. The first person I called was Sam Broussard, a supernatural guitarist with such past employers as Jimmy Buffett and Michael Murphey on his résumé. Although I had taken a few guitar lessons from Sam, I didn't know him that well. He was caught off guard and a bit hesitant, but when I mentioned that Andes was the bassist, he signed on immediately.

Chain reaction kicked in. Andes wanted to play with drummer Brian Brown, who had been the original drummer in Firefall before making a full-time commitment (ultimately a career boner) to join country-swingers Dusty Drapes and the Dusters. I had known Brian for years and he gladly supported my maiden voyage.

Next, I turned to my good friend Jamie Kibben, a fantastic piano player, who not only joined the band but also taped the first shows on four-track audiotape and convinced me to hire a videographer to document a rehearsal in case this was the only band I'd ever have. To round out the group, we recruited guitarist Michael Reese (who would later perform in Tommy Bolin tribute bands—he was *that* good) and his bandleader at the time, harmonica dynamo Judy Rudin.

These names might not have meant much outside a thirty-mile radius, but they were all phenoms on their respective instruments. All had achieved iconic status in Boulder. Andes and I christened the band Kenny & the Kritix (he suggested "critics" to emphasize my local identity, and I came up with the alliterative new-wave spelling). I booked a two-night engagement at Boulder's premier club, the Blue Note, for Wednesday and Thursday, December 3 and 4, 1980. Most local bands had to pay their dues in smaller dives for years before landing a slot at the Blue Note, but I had reviewed dozens of national acts at the club, so management threw me a bone.

Now that I had a band and a gig lined up, I needed to learn how to sing. I could carry a tune fairly well but lacked any sense of control or dynamics. The Gillaspie sisters (Gaile and MaryLynn) of the vocal quartet Rare Silk recommended University of Colorado opera professor Barbara Kinsey Sable, so I signed up for a series of lessons.

Before my first one, I wrote a quick note to Barbara explaining that I needed a crash course—my stage debut was less than two months away. She suggested coming in twice a week and she would do her best to whip me into shape. I brought in a tape of the songs I would be singing, and even though she realized I'd be singing rock and R&B, she insisted we do it her way and start with "Edelweiss." What could I say?

Simple vocal exercises came first, mostly major triads, followed by minor, diminished, and augmented scales. I had some difficulties with modulation, but Barbara claimed I was a good student and absorbed her instruction at an impressive clip. I had very little confidence in my singing ability thanks to my fifth-grade teacher, Miss Crisson, the most sadistic teacher in my lifetime, who had permanently scarred me by banning me from the choir when nearly every other kid in the class got in. Still, I did my homework for Barbara and sang scales while pretending to lift the grand piano (her technique, not mine).

After four sessions, I was psychologically prepared to rehearse with the band. Scouring my record collection, I came up with a set list that could comfortably accommodate my limited vocal range.

I scheduled a band meeting at my house on October 21, and the six of us sat around our antique circular claw-foot dining room table. I distributed ninety-minute audio cassettes with suggested songs,

DECEMBER 3-4, 1980/BLUE NOTE	
Don't Let Them Push You Around	Iron City Houserockers
High School Confidential	Jerry Lee Lewis
Wild in the Streets	Garland Jeffreys
Fire	Jimi Hendrix
I'm Bored	Iggy Pop
I'm a Rocker	Bruce Springsteen
The Hard Way	The Kinks
Yo Adrian	Kenny Weissberg
Living a Little, Laughing a Little	Spinners
Claudette	Everly Brothers
Party Doll	Buddy Knox
You Ain't Nothin' But Fine	Rockpile
People Who Died	The Jim Carroll Band
Crying	Roy Orbison
Runnin' Scared	Iron City Houserockers

musical charts, and skinny ties (I was also the designated wardrobe director) and gave each band member a fifty-dollar check to cover five rehearsals.

"You're waaaay too serious," Brian said. "This is all about having fun. Relax."

He was right, but I wanted to set the tone for rigorous preparation. I was a complete novice at this and needed these guys to concentrate and elevate me from quicksand to solid ground. As I began to go over the meeting's agenda, the boys interrupted me with a barrage of off-color jokes targeting musicians, gays, Jews, Mexicans, and ditzy blondes. It was all in fun and what musicians do to unwind, but we had just six weeks until we took the stage and I hadn't budgeted any time for frivolity.

I rented rehearsal space at a studio in North Boulder. We had our initial practice on October 29, and even though it was early afternoon, I came armed with a case of Michelob and a concealed vial of cocaine just in case the troops lost focus or started nodding out.

Walking in with trepidation, I first spotted Mark Andes, rig already in place, wiping down his bass strings. Seeing him took me back to the fall of 1969, when I had flown from Madison, Wisconsin, to New York City to see Spirit/the Kinks/the Bonzo Dog Band play two nights at the Fillmore East. Those concerts were mind-bending experiences for me. Twelve years later, I was in a North Boulder warehouse about to start rehearsing with Spirit's bass player.

Jamie Kibben had set up my vocal mic, and Sparky Nielsen, an ace knob turner who would go on to mix sound for the Everly Brothers, Robert Cray, and Dr. John, was tweaking the mixing board to make sure it all worked. I felt thoroughly supported in my nascent effort, but before the first chord was strummed, Brian Brown started cracking jokes about my premature bald spot and the other musicians piled on. The ribbing actually calmed my jagged nerves and we had a productive rehearsal.

Most of the songs were straight-ahead rockers, three-chord chooglers that didn't seriously challenge the band. I wanted to run through every song a dozen times but that strategy was unanimously vetoed. The only song scrapped from the playlist was Roy Orbison's "Crying." Eyes rolled as my vocals failed to soar to the requisite crescendos.

"One more time?" I cajoled, really wanting to nail the song.

"NO!" the band shouted in unison.

I hung my head but it was less than a minor defeat on our road to the promised land.

Next up, I recited the lyrics of my first original, a pseudo-novelty song about oppression in Boulder called "Yo Adrian."

So you think you found Nirvana in Boulder
So-called land of opportunity

It's the only place that as you get older
You'll find yourself begging to work for free

Why hire him? He wants three bucks an hour
Surely there's some scab who will shine my shoes
Don't they understand that if you want to live in Boulder
When you're fifty, you'll still be paying dues

(Chorus) *So I pull out my hair and punch the fuckin'*
   wall
When I reach into my pockets I find nothing at all
I may be poor and I may be a jerk
But there's someone I can lean on when I come home
   from work
YO ADRIAN! YO ADRIAN!
I can always yell YO ADRIAN!

The oppressors had a luncheon at the Broker Inn
To teach the bosses how to run a tight ship
Since most of you children are living in sin
You should be grateful to be working for tips

You spend thirty thousand dollars on a college education
To sell solar quilts to yachting execs
And you pawn your education at the Used Book Store
To keep yourself from bouncing those checks

(Repeat chorus)

I've tried real estate, computers, tea bags, and drugs
You know none of it really works for me
But when I turn to Naropa, the radio, or hot tubs
They tell me that they'll pay me in prestige

So I'm moving to Broomfield to regain my self-respect
Me and Adrian will raise our children there
In Boulder I'm a mental and a physical wreck
And besides . . . I have nothing left to wear

(Repeat chorus, ending with a second "Yo Adrian" refrain)

I had no idea how to write music, but the band quickly made it into a reggae song featuring a clucky guitar/electric keyboard intro that set both a humorous and spa-resort mood. Bob Marley meets Spike Jones? (When we finally took the stage in December, I sang the song dressed in Everlast shorts, boxing gloves, and a padded sparring helmet).

That first week of rehearsals was exhilarating. I proved to everyone (myself included) that I could both sing with and lead a band. I wasn't much of a taskmaster but when the time-out breaks between songs got too long, I whined effectively enough to get the Kritix back to work. I was also thrilled that the band's chemistry live was as good as it looked on paper. These musicians all knew one another but had never played together before.

Even though the practice sessions weren't long enough to satisfy me on any level, by the fourth rehearsal, I had lost my voice and was the one who wanted to go home early. This was a drag for me because we wouldn't be rehearsing again until after Thanksgiving and we weren't close to being ready to face an audience. Don't worry, my bandmates said, the shows will be great. Later, they all admitted being skeptical that we could pull it off.

November was filled with uncertainty. I was left alone to sing with taped rhythm tracks while the Kritix returned to their respective real-life bands. The instant feedback and camaraderie were gone. My insecurity level was somewhere in between "proceed with caution" and "extremely dangerous."

I'd wake up every day determined to follow a strict regimen.

Vocal exercises for an hour. Script writing and tweaking for an hour. Lunch. Singing with the rhythm tracks for at least an hour. Running a mile or two to build up my endurance. Practice the few songs I'd play on guitar for an hour. Dinner, sleep, and repeat.

My struggles with discipline were ongoing. I became an expert at procrastination. How many times could I read the morning paper? Who could I call next on the phone? Was Helen available for a snuggle break? By the time I sang my first note, it was usually two in the afternoon and I'd be exhausted after going through four songs. I was convinced I wouldn't have the stamina to complete our proposed eighty-minute show.

Every day I called at least one of the Kritix. Did they miss me? Were they getting the songs down? It turned out that they weren't humming the songs in their sleep, but they all promised to refocus on the material during the next series of rehearsals.

Twelve days before opening night, as I was gearing up for the homestretch, disaster struck. Mark Andes, my muse, my mentor, and the coattail I was riding throughout this project, called to tell me he was moving to LA to join another band. The next day! I knew from the outset of the Kritix experience that he was on a bunch of headhunters' lists, but he was pretty sure he'd be in Boulder until mid-December. He apologized in a sincere, but "that's rock 'n' roll" kind of way.

I was crushed and demoralized. Andes had been part of this fantasy since day one. His name was on all the posters, publicity, and pre-show hype. I felt like throwing in the towel and canceling the dates, but the band reminded me that he was "only a bass player." To their collective mind, he wasn't at all crucial to pulling this off and they put out an SOS to bassist Milt Muth, who played in the Rude with Michael Reese and Judy Rudin. When I delivered the cassette of the set list, the charts, and a skinny tie to him on November 22, I was meeting him for the first time. At his first practice with the Kritix two days later, he had already mastered every song. My clouds lifted.

We practiced long and hard November 24–26 and again December 1–2. I was equal parts excited, nervous, and worried. The encouragement from family, friends, media, and band members was uniformly positive, but suddenly the pre-show backlash erupted.

"NUKE KENNY" bumper stickers were plastered on every kiosk and bulletin board at the downtown Pearl Street Mall, distributed by a group of anonymous pissed-off musicians called P.R.O.T.O.N. ("Pro Rockers Opposed To Over-selfindulgent Newscolumnists").

Reports were also flying around about a longtime Boulder musician named David Givens, who was gathering people armed with tomatoes to hurl at me as soon as I hit the stage. Givens confused me with another writer who had taken some cheap shots at his ex-wife/musical partner, Candy Givens, in a 1974 magazine article and had hated me ever since.

I could live with the bumper stickers, but the possibility of assault tomatoes freaked me out. I decided to nip this in the bud and looked up David Givens in the Boulder phone book. I located his name and called him up.

"Hello." Calm, gentle voice.

"David? This is Kenny Weissberg."

No response, no hello, nothing.

"Uh, well, first of all, I wanted to tell you that I never wrote that article about Candy. All these years, you've been pissed off at the wrong person. I've been told that you're assembling a small army to come to my show and throw tomatoes. I'm *begging* you not to. This is the first time I've ever performed onstage and I'm nervous enough as it is."

No reply.

I kicked my plea into overdrive. "David, I swear I've *never* written anything negative about Candy. I *love* Candy! I'm just asking you to put yourself in my place. Can we have a truce? I want this gig to be a positive experience."

Five more seconds of dead air and then a confused voice on the other end of the line. "You've reached the wrong David Givens. I'm a geophysics professor at CU."

I gave Dr. Givens an awkward "Oh, my God" apology and hung up. The band had a belly laugh when I reenacted that conversation at our final rehearsal and assured me that if I was pelted with produce, they'd jump off the stage and maul the perpetrators. Despite our repeated requests, we couldn't convince the Blue Note to install tomato detectors at the entrance to the club, adding to my already-heightened anxiety.

And then opening night arrived.

The day of the show, I paced the floor of my home music room and tried to be mellow. No drinks, no drugs—just miso soup. I intentionally got to the club just fifteen minutes before our 9:30 set time so reality wouldn't consume me until the last minute. I did the password knock that got me into the back door of the Blue Note and slipped unnoticed into the dressing room directly across from the restrooms.

"Hi, guys," I said, trying to muster up some moxy 'n' machismo. I was dressed in the stage clothes for my opening skit: hospital pants and a straitjacket obscuring my skintight satin pants and ripped emerald-green T-shirt bedecked with ornamental chains.

"My, don't you look niiiice," one of the boys lisped, homo in-nuendo to the bitter end.

"You look good enough to eat," another chimed in. "Bend over and I'll drive you home." It was their way of getting me to relax, but it didn't work.

A stagehand peeked in the room. "Two minutes." I didn't want to wait that long so I assembled the band and told them to lead the way. I wrapped myself in a bed sheet to hide my costume and trailed my mates closely as we passed through the sold-out crowd toward the stage.

"Go for it, Kenny!" That was a gruff masculine voice.

"We're with you all the way!" A female voice. Helen? Or did I have a groupie already?

"Woooooo!"

Awaiting me onstage was a gimmicked wheelchair with a type-writer duct-taped to one arm and a cartoonishly oversized radio microphone mounted on the other. I sat down gingerly and stared straight ahead as an audiotape describing my catatonic condition be-gan rolling. I was portraying a critic, disc jockey, record collector, and fan who fell into a stupor because he had never made his own music.

A "doctor" and "nurse," clad in hospital garb, flanked me and discussed my hopeless condition. Their discussion was interrupted by snippets of rock anthems like "Born to Run," "Anarchy in the U.K.," and "In-a-Gadda-da-Vida," which were intended to give me a needed jolt of electro-rock therapy. Just as it seemed that I was about to emerge from my doldrums, corporate-rock hooks from Journey and Styx knocked the stuffing out of me and rendered me mute once again.

There were a few more teases of my recovery and eventually the narrator's voice boomed, "Do you want good music? Then make your *own* music!"

The band launched into the opening strains of the blues-rocking "Don't Let Them Push You Around." Two stagehands lifted me out of the wheelchair and tore off my Velcro-attached sanitarium duds in one sweeping motion, unveiling the elated, cartoonish punk rocker I had become.

At the end of the first song, the audience erupted with applause so sustained that it overwhelmed me. I meekly thanked everyone for coming, strapped on my Fender Telecaster, and powered into the next song. As my mouth grazed the microphone to deliver the opening lyrics of "High School Confidential," I had the first of two white-light experiences that night. My classic Fender tube amp hadn't been properly grounded during soundcheck and the static electricity nearly killed me. When it happened a second time, I decided not to play guitar for the rest of the show (the problem was corrected by the following night) and somehow managed to regain my equilibrium.

My confidence and bravado increased with each song. The stage began to feel familiar. Even when I scanned the audience and noticed that critics were taking notes, it fueled me. Nothing could rattle me.

Four costume changes later, the show ended as it began, with an Iron City Houserockers cover. The Pittsburgh rockers were my favorite band of the moment, and even though I'd grown up in an upper-middle-class family in suburban New Jersey, I fully inhabited their urban, working-class grittiness.

As the song came to a crashing climax, I wrenched my body with a contorted leap off the drum riser and the crowd went crazy. Yes, I had a lot of friends and family sitting up close, but the Kritix got a legitimate encore. I had one final special effect in my arsenal.

The typewriter-equipped wheelchair was placed center stage, and I took a seat as the cassette player rolled. As I feigned typing to the taped sounds of pounding keys, my prerecorded voice narrated my own review of the Kritix performance. My words were sufficiently laced with self-deprecating humor, but I also heaped on fawning accolades and hinted at a sequel.

I took an unrehearsed bow to spine-tingling applause and walked through the crowd to towel off in the dressing room. On the way, I passed Stevie Wonder, who was winding down with his entourage after performing in front of ten thousand people at the CU Field-house. Had I known he was in the club, even though it was only for the final two songs of the show, I would have been rendered limp and swaggerless. Later I was told he was rhythmically bobbing his head to the music.

When I emerged from the dressing room, dry and refreshed, I was greeted by a small group of lingerers. The first person to ap-proach me was Michael Clarke. Extending his hand, he said gruffly but sincerely, "I don't hate you anymore."

I didn't see David Givens (who had thankfully refrained from throwing tomatoes), but his ex-wife, Candy Givens, a powerhouse of a singer, grabbed my arm and said, "You've got a great voice." She was bleary-eyed and sloppy drunk, but I didn't debate her assessment and gave her a bear hug of thanks.

Other random comments:

"Nice try. It doesn't matter that you can't sing. People had a great time."

"You have unbelievable balls. You must know that."

"I'm amazed. I didn't know you had talent."

"It was fantastic. It was everything you cracked it up to be. It was hot. It was pretentious. It was tongue-in-cheek. It was wonderful."

"You should have eliminated that ballad."

"You're a great singer with more charisma than any local per-former I've seen in years. You mesmerized the crowd."

Even my opera teacher, Barbara, flashed an upward thumb on her way out the door.

The entire experience had been exhilarating and then I real-ized I had a video shoot and another performance the next day. Just thinking about it gave me an anxiety attack. It renewed my appre-ciation for what performers have to go through to get up the goods night after night. I was too brain-drained to embrace the notion of a second night.

Years later, I have no recollection of the Kritix' next show. Opening night remains vivid to me, but night number two does not. You lose your virginity only once. The sole evidence I have that I showed up for a second night is the audiotape Jim Walton made. He was a local artist who passionately chronicled and archived unique musical events. As long as he could have a copy, he'd do it for free. Why not?

What I do remember are the reviews. I've received hundreds of letters to the editor over the years praising or pummeling my writing, but this time, newspaper and magazine critics were dissecting my vocal nuances and stage presence. As surreal as that was, I was reminded about the perverse power of the pen, how uplifting or disturbing a review can be.

From *Colorado Daily*'s Chris Clark:

Lester Bangs would be proud. Nobody in Boulder thought a rock critic, vermin and scum that we are, could actually front a real live rock band without lapsing into a catatonic stupor, stunned by the relevance of it all. You proved us wrong, Kenny.

Before I could let that opening paragraph go to my head, Clark leveled me a few sentences later:

Ah yes, your vocals. Let's just say Ray Davies you're not. Nor are you Bruce Springsteen, Elvis Costello, Garland Jeffreys, or even Iggy Pop. You held your own with Nick Lowe, though; you pulled off a great Jim Carroll, and the reggae number, while not exactly up to Rastafarian standards, sounded more authentic than any given single by the Police. Some likened your vocalizing to that of a wounded kazoo. I thought you sounded as proficient as any aging punk backed up by an intergalactic all-star combo.

I wasn't too eager to read the review in the *Boulder Daily Camera*. I had recently been fired for insubordination after being their weekly music columnist and rock critic for four and a half years. My editor, a former crime-beat hack, was furious when I defied his order in 1978 to write a review of the Bee Gees' *Saturday Night Fever* LP (which had already sold ten million copies) and turned in a thought piece about Graham Parker instead. He held a grudge for two years until I handed in a column called "Avoiding Music at All Costs," which detailed a week I did everything *except* go to concerts and listen to records. These activities included attending a minor league baseball game, watching David Bowie star in a traveling production of *Elephant Man*, and interviewing fans at a pro wrestling match. He fired me on the spot.

But I was gratified to see what my replacement, Mark Lewis, had written:

> *On December 3 and 4, a true drama unfolded at the Blue Note. Kenny Weissberg, long regarded as the Dean of Boulder Rock Critics, took the stage for a conceptual show featuring his custom-made band, Kenny & the Kritix. Weissberg assembled top-notch local talent to accompany his vision but it was indeed heartening to see Weissberg dominate the stage. Surely there were a number of locals who came hoping to be disappointed in Weissberg's idea of art, but his song selection was impeccable. He covered the range of styles that earned him the tag "self-indulgent" over the years, but his falsetto swoops during the soul revue section belied his tongue-in-cheek approach. Now, will they tour?*

G. Brown of the *Denver Post* and R. Alan Rice of *Audience* magazine chimed in with raves and suddenly I was confronted with a dilemma. I had poured my heart and soul into this one-shot production and gotten more out of it than I'd ever imagined. But even though we had sold out two nights and our percentage of the door receipts topped $2,000, the bottom line of my ledger was awash in red ink after I paid the band, the prop designer, the spotlight operator, and the doorman (for keeping track of the paying customers), as well as absorbing the costs for posters, postage for the direct-mail postcards, a first-class rehearsal space, and a video shoot (the latter for vanity, not necessity).

I probably lost a grand on the project and spent three months sans income to see it to fruition. No, this foray into singing, playing, and performing was never about money. Now I had to delve into another art form I had yet to master: the art of making a living.

I proudly sent my parents all the prepublicity and subsequent reviews from my debut performances. They hadn't been interested in flying from New Jersey to see their oldest son prancing around the stage straddling a mic stand. When they received the package, I got a phone call.

Mom: "When are you going to get a real job?"

Dad: "This seems like a gigantic ego trip."

If the wind had been taken out of my sails, it made me more determined not to capsize.

12.

the second incarnation

WEIGHING THE OPTIONS OF CONTINUING to make music versus finding a job to adequately support my family became a constant dilemma. Brushing pragmatism aside, I kept returning to the Kritix over the next three years. Although I still had regular freelance writing assignments and coproduced a weekly radio show called *Fear of Fridays*, I earned such minuscule income during that time that I blushed every April at the accountant's office, embarrassed by my net zero year after year. In fact, the fee from my tax preparer from '81 to '83 was greater than my tax obligation to the government.

I couldn't have pursued my Kritix vision had I not been married to a woman who understood what compelled someone to work so hard with no guarantee of compensation. Helen, a lifelong artist who has experienced numerous income droughts throughout her career, encouraged me to follow my heart and I did. If she had known that I'd succumb to all of rock 'n' roll's pratfalls, she might not have been so supportive.

Spurred on by the positive response, not to mention the orgasmic rush of performing in front of wildly enthusiastic, packed houses, I couldn't wait for the next chapter of the saga to unfold. Helen assembled a scrapbook and press packet with all the reviews of the first performances. The Kritix rode a speeding locomotive of buzz, hype, and momentum. The Blue Note called and offered us a rare three-night return engagement from August 27 to 29, 1981. The Thursday-through-Saturday slot was a rapid rise from our Tuesday-Wednesday debut.

For the next eight months, I began defining myself as a musician, as opposed to a critic or DJ. I started trolling the bars, making cameo appearances with whoever would let me share the stage. I became good friends with a power-pop band called Pearl. I had booked them into Molly's Back Room, a club I'd designed and consulted for in 1979. Whenever Pearl headlined the Blue Note, the Hotel Boulderado, or the prestigious Boulder Theater, lead singer Craig Skinner would make a gushing "special guest in the house" introduction and call me up for two songs (usually "Don't Let Them Push You Around" and "The Hard Way").

The Rave, Boulder's British Invasion tribute band, invited me to lead them through the Kinks' "You Really Got Me." Rocker Judy Blair, who doubled as a Celestial Seasonings Tea executive by day, played Tammi Terrell to my Marvin Gaye during a misguided rendition of "Ain't No Mountain High Enough" at a lesbian bar in Denver. I joined garage rocker Willy Cruz for a Springsteen/Little Steven duet (I was Bruce) on "Two Hearts," and brainy new wavers China Breaks let me play guitar and sing backup on several of their originals. A week didn't go by that I didn't bask in the glow of a local spotlight.

When it came time to reorganize the Kritix, I made a few personnel changes, retaining Sam Broussard, Brian Brown, and Jamie Kibben while adding multi-instrumentalist David Muse (Mark Andes's former bandmate in Firefall), bassist Greg Overton (who played with Broussard in a group called Spoons), and guitarist-vocalist-music director Chip McCarthy from Pearl. A spectacular but high-maintenance band member, Chip would stick with me through all future Kritix lineups.

Having recruited Muse, a dynamic sax player, I decided to incorporate more R&B into the second incarnation of the band. I added two Arthur Conley chestnuts, "Sweet Soul Music" and the more obscure "Funky Street." I was probably the first person ever to cover the Bill Medley album cut "I Don't Know Much" (which later became a huge hit for Linda Ronstadt and Aaron Neville). And who could blame me for trying to nail the Marvin Gaye/Kim Weston classic "It Takes Two," especially with the gorgeous Karen Sony guesting as my female foil?

Rehearsals were productive. Twenty-seven songs made the final cut, including Garland Jeffreys's epic "Mystery Kids," a lilting version of the Heptones' reggae gem "Book of Rules" (Bob Weir must have been in the audience—he covered that song years later), and a white-hot pub rocker from Ducks Deluxe called "Fireball."

We were further buoyed when the program director from Denver public station KBDI-TV expressed interest in videotaping our Saturday night show for a future television special. The idea of a critic fronting a band wasn't original—I had seen Lester Bangs's Birdland open for the Ramones in New York a few years earlier—but it was new turf for the Colorado music scene.

I assumed that we'd play to capacity crowds every night, so I was surprised when I snuck in the back door of the Blue Note and noticed a slew of empty tables in the rear of the four-hundred-capacity club. I was a bit perplexed, but Sam Broussard shrugged and drolly spit out, "Welcome to the real world of show business."

Club manager Patrick Coffey peeked into the dressing room to remind us of our hit time. "You did it again. Great crowd."

"How many so far?" I asked.

"Right now, 182 paid and about 25 comps, but the night is young."

"Do you think the four-dollar cover scared them away?"

"I'll lower it to three during the first set if I have your permission. But this is a big crowd for a Thursday. I'm sure Friday and Saturday will sell out."

I okayed the reduced cover charge, and by the middle of the first set, the club was filled. Did shaving a buck off the ticket price have that much to do with doubling the capacity? I'd become obsessively concerned with determining ticket prices when I became a concert promoter two years later.

My opening skit was completely revamped from the catatonic motif of the Kritix' debut performances. This time, slouched at a desk, I drank wine from a bottle and furiously typed away at a record review (a voice-over of my musings played through the Blue Note's sound system). Wincing at my own words, I repeatedly ripped the pages out of the manual typewriter, crumpled them up, and hurled them into the crowd. The "doorbell" rang and a UPS man, played demonically by Kamikazi Klones bassist A. J. Coon, dropped a pile of fifty LPs on my lap. I leafed through them, screaming and groaning about the lackluster quality of the new releases. Then I hopped off the stage and gave them away to startled audience members.

The point I was trying to make was that the record business was already in a shambles, signing mediocre acts, focusing on finding matinee idols, and eschewing adventurous content altogether. That strategy continues to plague the music industry today.

I jumped back onstage and hid behind a makeshift dressing-area screen. While the tape continued to dwell on the dismal existence of the music critic, I "changed" clothes, throwing brassieres, panty hose, and negligees on top of the partition. As the story concluded with the premise that the only way I'd ever be satisfied with music was to make my own, I exploded through the screen in a Superman shirt and spandex pants, suddenly the leader of a kick-ass rock band. Then we powered into the Springsteen anthem "Badlands."

I was a more generous bandleader this time around, which was tactical as well as altruistic because it gave me a chance to rest my

voice while turning over center stage to my comrades. Sam Broussard's soaring vocals accompanied his Hendrix-worthy guitar chops
on "Little Wing." Chip McCarthy romped through the Swingin'
Medallions' "Double Shot of My Baby's Love," and Greg Overton
delivered a soulful-for-a-white-guy take on "Mustang Sally," adapt-
ing the Young Rascals' arrangement instead of the Wilson Pickett
original. I watched my own band voyeuristically from the quick-
change booth on the side of the stage, rejoining them in new attire
four minutes later.

By Saturday night, we were oiled and ready for the glare of the
TV lights. I didn't take into account the intimidation factor that the
three-camera shoot might have on the audience, and the dance floor
remained uncharacteristically deserted during the first two songs.

"Get 'em to dance," Broussard whispered to me. Nothing is more
of a death knell to a rock band than an empty parquet.

I implored the crowd to ignore the cameras and reminded them
that they were going to be on TV. Then David Muse launched into
the opening sax riffs of "Sweet Soul Music," and the floor was filled

for the rest of the night. There's a unique bonding between performer and audience when everyone is drenched in sweat.

As Frankie Valli once falsettoed, "Oh, what a night!" The finale of the three-night gig was both exhilarating and anticlimactic. The Kritix were besieged with offers to attend after-parties, and I told a half-dozen adoring hostesses I'd be there.

But when it came time to choose, I opted to go with my brother, Roger, to a twenty-four-hour Denny's for steak 'n' eggs and a strawberry milkshake. Roger had flown in from Rochester, New York, to see the show and was flying home the next morning. Quality time with my kid brother trumped all the cocaine and tequila that awaited me elsewhere.

"What am I gonna do now?" I asked Roger, dipping my toast into the runny egg yolks. The reality was already setting in that I was about to crash after a three-night high. Whereas the other Kritix would resume their real lives with their full-time bands the next day, I was a rudderless ship at sea.

13.

back for more

I HAD NO CHOICE BUT TO DO IT AGAIN.

Well, theoretically, I had a choice, but I suffered from a severe shortage of common sense. Plus, the Blue Note brass, thrilled with our attendance figures as well as the bar sales, offered us another three-day weekend stint, with the Friday falling on my thirty-fourth birthday (April 30, 1982). I accepted the dates without hesitation.

When I studied the expense ledger from Kritix version 2.0, I noted that despite drawing 90 percent capacity crowds over the three nights, I still lost $400 on the venture. My original vision of working with hungry musicians had shifted to the "hired gun" formula when Mark Andes signed on. During the first two incarnations of Kritixdom, I paid the band members $10 for each rehearsal and $50 for each performance. When Jamie Kibben moved to San Francisco after our maiden voyage, I decided I wanted him badly enough in Kritix 2.0 that I threw in a round-trip plane ticket on top of his performance stipends. It cost me more to stage those shows than I had the potential to earn back. Later in my life as a concert producer, I learned the term "sellout money"—paying the band the guarantee

they demanded and having to sell every available ticket just to break even. I could no longer afford to abide by that formula.

So I shifted things around and reluctantly said goodbye to the high-priced spread. I could barely envision continuing without Sam Broussard, Jamie Kibben, and Brian Brown, but I had to cut expenses. I'd brought in David Muse and Greg Overton as one-time ringers, and they had performed brilliantly during their three-day careers as Kritix. I had become deeply connected to and reliant upon Chip McCarthy, who was happy to continue as my primary sidekick and musical director.

I set out to surround the two of us with a band of team players who would rehearse for free and split the gig receipts evenly.

First I approached Jeffrey Wood, Boulder's most creative record producer, who played keyboards and guitar in the quirky band China

Breaks. Several months before, after I had written a magazine profile on him, he had offered his musical expertise to me anytime I might need it. I'm sure he didn't think I would take him up on it, but when I asked him to be in Kritix 3.0, he somehow fit me into his packed schedule.

All the drummers I've dealt with over the years have been lovable whack jobs, and I had always enjoyed the playing of Peter Roos, Boulder's seminal new-wave drummer. He was an art supplies salesman by day and pounded skins for such bands as the Immortal Nightflames and Joey Vain & Scissors at night. His current band, Willy Cruz and the Dreamboats, had been my handpicked opening act for the very first Kritix performance. I don't think Roos ever said no to an invitation to play music and he didn't say no to me.

My Springsteen/Southside Johnny fanaticism was at peak levels in the early '80s and the sound in my head was filled with guitars and horns. Jeffrey knew a young multi-instrumentalist who played R&B guitar and sax and possessed an elastic vocal range, so we approached Jamie Polisher, a member of a harmony band called the Chutney Brothers. A diminutive powerhouse, sort of the Nils Lofgren of Boulder, Polisher brought some Philly funk to the new Kritix. Affable to a fault, he was shier under the spotlights than during rehearsal, and I had to constantly goad him to let loose onstage.

Not shy by any means was our new bassist Michael "Hawk" Hawkins, who worked days at Robb's Music, Boulder's hippest music store, but hated retail and dealing with the public. A muscle-bound bodybuilder usually sporting a tank top, Hawk was a solid player from day one and someone I'd depend on (along with Chip and Jeffrey) for the next two years of my Kritix experiences.

For the first time since Mark Andes had volunteered to help me formulate my vision, I felt like I was part of a band, which is considerably different from being a leader who employs backup musicians. That dynamic brought with it a closeness I hadn't encountered during the first two incarnations of the Kritix. I would never have gotten to point C without the learning curve and confidence building that points A and B provided. But this was brotherhood. We were a gang of six.

The new camaraderie exacerbated a number of bad habits. After snorting coke to get through our rigorous three-hour rehearsals, we consumed pitchers of kamikazes and closed down the bars. Then we moved on to the post-2 a.m. parties with hungry, nubile (and not-so-nubile) groupies. Although I enjoyed the fawning attention, I somehow managed to keep my zipper locked. I often stumbled home and fell into bed just as Helen was waking up to get Nicole and Paul off to school.

For a long stretch, I'd roll out of bed at 11 a.m. in time to watch *The Young and the Restless* in my pajamas before wolfing down my morning OJ and English muffin. I wasn't too far removed from total dereliction.

I finally saw the light (stars, in fact) one night as we left the Olympic Lounge, a bowling alley that doubled as a music venue. A potent combo of cocaine, Courvoisier, and half a Quaalude had turned me into a slurring lump of moist clay. As I floated toward my car, I momentarily lost consciousness and got a face full of parking lot. That woke me up, literally and figuratively. I should be toothless because of that fall, but all I had to show for it was a split lower lip. You can see it on the black-and-white band promo photo that was taken the next afternoon. I vowed to cut my drug and alcohol consumption at least in half.

Okay, so I wasn't fully awakened, but I did devise a focal point for our next performance. "Is There Rock after Death?" became the faux theme. Borrowing from Screaming Jay Hawkins, I began the show lying in a closed coffin while an audiotape rolled with John Fahey fingerpicking a gospel-tinged "Old Black Joe." After the Persuasions sang "People Get Ready," the voice of Tim Duffy, a superb Boulder musician and event designer, took on the guise of a gospel preacher and bellowed from a script I had written.

Friends of the Thirteenth Pentecostal Submission, please take your seats. We thank you for joining us on this sad, solemn, confusing evening. It didn't have to be this way. You see, we didn't come here to praise Kenny, but to bury him.

It's painfully clear why he isn't with us tonight. You see, Kenny lacked commitment. He lacked a focused vision. Perhaps, most importantly, he never knew what he wanted to be when he grew up. Poor Kenny . . . he never grew up! And being a resident of Boulder, the convenience store of disorganized religions, Kenny always sought guru after guru. He was a part-time believer in his holiness, Chogyam Springsteen Rinpoche. He was a part-time believer in Andre the Giant. He laid his body down for the Maharishi Indiana Jones and he would occasionally read aloud an Allen Ginsberg poem.

And, yes, his band the Kritix, another in a long line of part-time endeavors. Living out the fantasy. Thriving on perpetual whims. "Let's put a band together!" Rehearsals, self-promotion, songwriting, self-promotion, power chords, harmonies, vertical leaps on the stage, and more self-promotion.

As Duffy rambled on about my lack of commitment and fear of playing music and choo-chooed toward the denouement, I propped the lid of the coffin open with the neck of my Telecaster.

Yes, Kenny loved to rock and Kenny needed to rock. Yet it was the fear of rock itself that led to his untimely passing and brings us here together tonight. If rock is in your blood, then you had better bleed. Kenny refused to bleed. He refused to believe. It makes a country preacher wonder . . . does it absolutely have to happen this way? If you can't rock when you're alive, can you rock after you die? IS THERE ROCK AFTER DEATH?

Dressed in a white dinner jacket and a bright red shirt, I slowly emerged from the coffin as the band played "Taps." The audience roared its encouragement as I shimmied up the mic stand until I was fully erect. In a sudden burst of life force, I leapt atop the drum riser and began belting out the lyrics to Jim Carroll's "People Who Died." That song about losing friends to assorted mishaps, suicides, and overdoses had become one of our signature pieces and worked every time, whether as a show opener or an encore.

For this new, stripped-down version of the Kritix, I kept it uncomplicated. Other than a homage to Sam Cooke with an a cappella "Chain Gang" to kick off the second set, it was crunchy, aggressive rock 'n' roll, with especially good renderings of Bowie's "Suffragette City" and the Clash's version of "I Fought the Law." I had wondered if the lack of "big name" sidekicks might diminish our drawing power, but we sold out all three nights. Our equal split after expenses was about $175 apiece.

To contradict Frank Zappa, we obviously weren't in it for the money. Still, our minimal amount of time onstage led to maximum exposure. I amassed a stockpile of reviews and photos, and Denver-based television producer-director Mike Drumm did a "rockumentary" on me that incorporated live footage of the Kritix. He also asked me to become the on-camera host of a new hour-long show he was producing called *Waveform Rock Video*. The program predated MTV by about a year and featured the earliest rock videos from future MTV icons Peter Gabriel, Culture Club, and Pat Benatar, as well as creative clips from bands who'd have short shelf lives, like Joe "King" Carrasco & the Crowns, Altered Images, and Translator. We hosted in-studio performances by the hottest Boulder and Denver bands, including an appearance by Kenny & the Kritix.

The Kritix started gigging more often. We performed at a benefit for handicapped children in October, did a two-night stand at the Blue Note in early November, and got the coveted opening slot at the historic Boulder Theater's New Year's Eve gala (our biggest crowd: 900; our biggest payday: $1,200).

In 1983, the band urged me to book more shows, make a record, and capitalize on the growing popularity of the Kritix. I didn't take that encouragement too seriously, realizing that our next three-night Blue Note engagement would coincide with my thirty-fifth birthday. I didn't embody the demographic that record companies were lusting after. Besides, I needed to find a *real* job. Throughout my eleven years with Helen, I had barely made enough money to pay the mortgage and buy groceries.

We didn't know it would be the last chapter (unless you count the thousand bucks we got from a group of Boulder public defenders and emergency room physicians to play at their Halloween party), but our final Blue Note performances from April 30 to May 2, 1983, were joyous. The first night we celebrated my birthday ("Kenny's an old fart now," the emcee said before bringing us onstage), and Hawk turned thirty-three on the final night.

It was the most rollicking Kritix performance to date, a mixture of obscure rockers from Blotto, Felony, and the Payolas with personal favorites by Little Steven, Gary "U.S." Bonds, the English Beat, and Love.

As we partied in the dressing room, the recurring question was, "When's the next gig?" I didn't want to spoil the fun but I announced I was heading to California for a series of job interviews. If nothing materialized, we'd compare Day-Timers and I would start booking shows. New interest in the Kritix was coming from Beaver Creek, Vail, Breckenridge, Aspen, Winter Park, and other ski resort towns. But every other Colorado band coveted those slots, so I needed to act soon.

"Did any of you guys know Brent Morgan?" I asked.

Blank stares. No recognition.

"He's an old friend of mine who wants me to work for him. But he's so full of shit that I'm sure nothing will come of it. I'll be back in two weeks and we'll have a band meeting."

Kenny & the Kritix never played together again.

PART 3

Unstable Cliffs

14.

my new best friend

THE YEAR: 1971. THE PLACE: Boulder, Colorado. The location: KRNW-FM radio station, 1410 Pearl Street. The time: most weekdays, approximately 7 a.m.

When the phone rang about an hour into my morning radio show, I knew it was Brent. He was listening from his cabin in Rollinsville, a small mountain town twenty-two miles northwest of Boulder, while getting ready for his hour commute to Denver, where he was a psychologist in training.

He'd get straight to the point. "I'm stopping at Rocky Mountain Records on my way home this afternoon. What album do you think I should buy?"

I always had a quick response. "Have you heard the new Cowboy album, *5'll Getcha 10*?"

"I've heard the songs you've played on your show."

"Every song is at least good. Most of them are great."

The next morning, Brent would call again, thanking me for my recommendation and letting me know he shared my enthusiasm. He was always effusive with appreciation and eager for more suggestions.

Brent was one of a legion of faceless callers, most of whom made requests, asked me for information about upcoming concerts, or just wanted to vent to a sympathetic ear. I was always polite to my listeners, remembering times when certain disc jockeys had rudely brushed me off. Yet, unless it was a sexy-sounding female coming on to me, I usually kept my conversations brief so I could concentrate on my work.

Because there was something appealing about Brent's banter and demeanor, one day I invited him to visit the station on his way to Denver. He showed up the next morning.

Although I had no preconceptions about what Brent looked like, I was still surprised when he walked into the studio. A ruggedly handsome mountain man, he was about six foot three and a solid 215 with long, straight brown hair that fell beneath his shoulder blades and a valiant, but incomplete, attempt at a full beard. He had a big smile and twinkly eyes—charming from the get-go.

He visited for about a half hour and watched intently as I segued from one turntable to another, hopped up to grab records off the shelves, and read a few live commercials. I hinted that I had to pay attention to my show and he got the message and split, but not before we made a lunch date for that weekend.

Brent and I bonded over an assortment of common interests and our friendship evolved over the next few months. We were both sports junkies and at similar levels of proficiency in tennis and basketball, despite our Mutt and Jeff size differential (he was six inches taller and ninety pounds heavier). We spent long hours playing two-on-two half-court games at the CU Fieldhouse. I was Mr. Outside, arcing up my patented rainbow jumpers, and Brent, Mr. Inside, crashed the boards, often getting into pushing contests with larger, muscle-bound football players. Our tennis matches were best-of-three set matches that would all go down to the wire.

We were also evenly matched as guitarists and vocalists, barely adequate but good enough to make it through a bunch of songs and figure out harmonies without emptying the room. We both loved country rock and did duo arrangements of Mason Proffit ("Two Hangmen"), the Byrds, and Flying Burrito Brothers. Brent was a trite lyricist but occasionally crafted a memorable enough melody that I can still hum it in my head forty years later.

Professionally, he was seething with frustration. He had dropped out of graduate school before getting his doctorate in psychology, limiting his opportunities for meaningful advancement in his chosen field. He complained bitterly that his boss was making $25K a year (twice Brent's salary), while Brent was doing all the crucial work. When I got tired of hearing the same story for the umpteenth time, I suggested that he accept his situation and make the most of it or move on. It was simple dime-store advice, but he took it to heart and told me a few weeks later that he had given notice.

"What are you going to do next?" I asked. My father had always pounded into my head that you should never leave a job unless you had another one lined up. Even though I never followed that advice, I was concerned for Brent.

"I've got some irons in the fire." He certainly did and they had nothing to do with psychology. His only stated goal was to make more than his incompetent boss's $25K per annum.

Fluent in Spanish, with a diverse set of friends he never told me about, Brent became one of the early pioneers in international cocaine smuggling, branching out into the lucrative marijuana trade as well. He'd disappear for months at a time and the only way I'd know where he'd been was from the postmarks on his letters he sent to my PO Box. Bogota, Colombia. La Paz, Bolivia. Lima, Peru. I'd open up the envelope and inside would be a folded piece of blank notebook paper concealing scrunched up chewing gum tinfoil that contained a large rock of cocaine. I habitually stopped at the post office a few times a week to pick up promo LPs, but my trips became more frequent now that I had other parcels to look forward to.

Throughout most of the '70s Brent used Boulder as his base of operations while maintaining rental properties in Aspen and Hawaii. Although he didn't ascend to the level of having a private fleet of planes and boats doing his trafficking, he generated a substantial cash flow and achieved unqualified success in his new profession.

He never returned to grad school, but that didn't stop him from handing out business cards emblazoned with "Dr. Brent Morgan, PhD in Clinical Psychology." When those not in the know asked him about his frequent trips to South America, he responded that he was doing postdoctoral research on Mayan civilization. For years I struggled to keep a straight face while hearing him lie repeatedly and was further compromised by having to cover for him with his revolving stream of unsuspecting female companions.

After switching professions, he physically morphed into another person. First the beard went and then his long locks, replaced by a stylish close-cropped haircut with blond highlights. And for the only time since I've known him, he slimmed down to about 180 through a combination of diet, cocaine consumption, and a strict exercise regimen.

He constantly lived on the edge. In Oahu, he had been robbed and beaten up at his home by a bunch of local thugs with inside information, necessitating a move to another luxurious rental property. When I visited him on the island of Kauai in November of '78, fleeing from the coldest recorded Boulder winter in six decades, we wound up checking into a hotel because he had been tipped off that the Feds were onto him and might raid his residence.

Despite being on the lam, he insisted that I see where he had been living to impress upon me how affluent he had become. We circled the neighborhood several times in his Range Rover, and once he was convinced the coast was clear, he parked the car in the alley and we climbed the back fence to gain access to the house. He couldn't turn on the lights for me to see the ornate furnishings or the elaborate kitchen, so pocket-flashlight illumination had to suffice.

Although convinced he'd be arrested soon, he still spent scads of money on antiques, jewelry, clothes, and cars. But it wasn't complete narcissism. He was extremely generous with his friends and lovers, always picking up the tab for expensive dinners and supplying dessert in the form of Dom Perignon, Peruvian flake, and Quaaludes.

Shortly after I saw Brent in Hawaii, his time ran out. One of his hired pilots was busted, detained, and tortured during a smuggling stopover in Tahiti. He named names, including Brent, who was sentenced to three years in prison. I kept in touch with him via letters to Terminal Island off the coast of Long Beach and, later, to Lompoc State Prison. He was released after serving fifteen months and confided to me that even after paying the huge fine accompanying his incarceration, he had socked away a small fortune and could still maintain his chosen lifestyle.

On probation, Brent had to get a job and report to a parole officer once a month for the next year and a half. I visited him in West Hollywood, where he was living in a small one-bedroom apartment on Crescent Heights, and laughed silently as he poured himself into a tight-fitting tuxedo to head for his maitre d' job at Rex's Fish Market on Sunset. He was the only person I knew making six bucks an hour who drove to work in a blue Porsche 924 ragtop.

Late in 1980, Brent was formulating a legal strategy that would make him a player once again. By 1983, he had purchased an estate in Malibu with sweeping Pacific Ocean views, started a music management company out of his house, and invested in companies in San Diego and San Rafael. I began receiving cryptic messages from him on my answering machine saying that my days in Boulder were numbered. He then offered me a job with a decent salary at whichever company most appealed to me.

Before I would even consider making such a drastic move and relocating, I made Brent swear that his drug-dealing days were behind him. He assured me that everything in his life was legit. He was moving forward and needed to surround himself with people he liked and trusted. I was at the top of his recruiting list.

I was dubious yet intrigued. On one hand, Brent was such a pathological liar that it was nearly impossible to believe anything he said. On the other, I was underpaid and underappreciated by so many Boulder employers at radio stations, newspapers, and magazines that the enticement of a steady paycheck and new adventures in California was overwhelming.

"How can you trust Brent?" Helen asked when I ran this by her. Her concerns echoed mine.

"I know, I know. My gut tells me that he's turned over a new leaf and this is for real. We've always fantasized about living in the Bay Area. Let's check out San Rafael first."

I called Brent and picked some travel dates. He sent us plane tickets the next day.

"You won't regret this," he said. "We're going to have a *lot* of fun!"

15.

san rafael

ELEN AND I ARRIVED AT the San Francisco airport on a late
May evening in 1983. Rick Bornstein, my potential employer,
greeted us at baggage claim. He owned an entertainment and marketing company that cross-merchandized music and sporting events. If I
took the job, I'd be responsible for arranging concerts by mainstream
rock acts like the Beach Boys, Chicago, and the Doobie Brothers
that would take place on a rolled-out stage immediately following
Golden State Warriors games. It was a value-added promotion intended to boost basketball attendance while giving these bands a big
paycheck and a guaranteed audience of at least ten thousand people.

Bornstein and an inebriated friend loaded our bags into the trunk
of his Lincoln Town Car and we headed north on I-280. Within
minutes, Bornstein passed a large bag of coke to me in the backseat.

"Help yourself. Beer?"

"No . . . no . . . thanks," I said. "I had a few on the plane."

Helen pinched my arm severely enough to leave a black-and-blue
mark. "You're *not* taking this job," she whispered.

"Don't worry," I mumbled under my breath as Bornstein began

impersonating a deranged NASCAR driver, swerving confidently on the winding hairpin turns that led up the mountain to his mansion. We exhaled only after he pulled into his seven-car garage.

Bornstein showed us around his house, noting that if I accepted the job offer, we'd be living rent-free on the west side of the house. We would have our own kitchen and a bathroom with a Jacuzzi and steam shower, and Helen could convert a segment of the garage into an artist's studio—an ideal setup if Bornstein hadn't been insane.

It was approaching midnight and Helen announced she was going to sleep. Bornstein looked at her quizzically but didn't put up much of an argument. The two of us convened in a cavernous den, and after snorting a few wide lines of coke, my job interview began.

"The first thing I want to tell you is that you'll become a millionaire if you work for me." Not a bad intro. Pointing to his gold Rolex, he said, "Five grand." The stunning piece of African art on the wall . . . "Twenty grand." More examples of his affluence followed, with price tags attached.

His delusional monologue continued for the next two hours. By 2 a.m. we must have consumed an eight-ball of blow. My nasal passages were crusted, and despite my coke-whore proclivities, I started waving off the baggie.

"You pussying out on me?" Bornstein asked with a mock sneer. "Why am I *always* the last man standing?"

I started flashing on the old *SNL* skits where Belushi was "The Thing That Wouldn't Leave." I knew that this would be the first and last time I'd hang out with Rick Bornstein, but I was trapped. I endured the rambling accounts of his life history, feigning interest and not once interjecting, "You've already told me that."

Suddenly, he shifted back to being the interviewer. "What are your hopes and dreams?"

I told him I'd been a journalist for the past ten years. "Eventually, I hope to write a book about the rock 'n' roll industry and—"

"You think you're going to become a millionaire by writing a book? Why am I wasting my time with someone whose dream is to write a *fucking book*? I need a partner that hits the streets, cuts deals, thinks business 24/7."

He glared at me as blood started trickling from his nose. I passed him a box of Kleenex. He ignored my gesture and continued his rant, dishing out a barrage of low blows. Since I didn't care if I got the job, I think I even laughed at one point.

Finally he dropped the hammer. "Do you or do you *not* want to become a millionaire?"

"Sure I do," I said, lacking conviction, but playing along.

"Then get rid of *her*!" he screamed, pointing to the guest bedroom where Helen had been asleep for the past several hours.

"You don't even *know* her," I shot back, my manliness returning.

"I don't fucking need to know her to know that she's fucking holding you back," he said in a maniacal tone that revealed both confidence in his prognosis and a desire to curtail the job interview.

A car pulled into the driveway, startling Bornstein. Glancing at his $5,000 wristwatch, he moaned, "Shit, it's seven. The cleaning service is here. Let's get some sleep and continue this tonight." He scraped the coke detritus from the countertop into the master baggie, sponged down the residue, threw the paraphernalia into a satin pillowcase, and disappeared.

I tiptoed into the bedroom where Helen lay half-awake.

"Are you okay?" she asked with an unbalanced blend of concern and contempt.

"Yeah, I stopped doing drugs about five hours ago, so I should be able to sleep. I'll call Jamie to get you out of here." I was referring to the Kritix keyboardist who had moved to San Francisco in 1981. "Be back here by six. We'll have dinner and leave."

Coming to the rescue, Jamie got Helen off the property, and I slept until four in the afternoon. When I woke up, Bornstein was still sleeping, but his nineteen-year-old girlfriend, Jessica, was sunning herself by the pool.

I introduced myself and she started gushing about the great Chinese restaurant Bornstein was taking us to that night. "You know, Rick really likes you," she said. "I mean really, *really* likes you. Before he nodded out, he said he needs someone like you to help him run this business."

"You must be confusing me with someone else," I said, deciding to suppress a capsule summary of our seven-hour job interview.

"No, he wants you and Helen to move in with us."

Over hot-and-sour soup, Kung Pao chicken, braised green beans, and a whole Peking duck, a refreshed and clear-eyed Bornstein was as cordial as he had been demonic the night before. He regaled us with stories about how he had met Jessica at a bus stop next to her high school a few years before and they had instantly fallen in love despite a fifteen-year age difference. She moved in with him before getting her high school diploma and was being groomed for a PR position with his company. Rick asked Helen questions about her art career with genuine interest and I started daydreaming about Jekyll and Hyde. While we drank Tsingtao beer, Bornstein guzzled Diet Cokes.

We had arranged for Helen's friend Connie to pick us up at the restaurant and take us to her home in nearby Woodacre. I told Bornstein I'd get back in touch after following up on a few other job possibilities. Two days later, I wrote him a note thanking him for his time and hospitality. I passed on his job offer and have never seen or spoken to him again.

16.

america's finest city

"WELL, YOU STILL HAVE MALIBU and San Diego left to choose from," Brent said, laughing after I described the details of my nocturnal interview with Rick Bornstein.

"I'll try San Diego," I said, nixing Malibu as a possibility. "Helen doesn't want to live in LA."

What I didn't tell Brent was that Helen didn't want to live within five zip codes of him and thought I was nuts for even considering another option after the Bornstein fiasco.

"If Rick is an example of Brent's taste in business partners, why do you think San Diego's going to be any better?" was her sensible question.

"Hey, it's another free trip and we've never been there. What do we have to lose?"

"You're on your own on this one," Helen said with a shrug. "I don't believe anything that man says."

I decided to check it out alone.

Brent had purchased a failing San Diego concert company called Jerry Mack Presents. Mack had hit majestic heights in 1981 promoting a Rolling Stones stadium show and then lost his life savings by putting on a series of shows by Spanish singing-sensation Camilo Sesto. Although a superstar in Europe and Latin America, Sesto was not well known in the States. The seven shows were box office disasters and Mack had teetered on the edge of bankruptcy.

Less than a month after my ignominious twenty-four hours with Rick Bornstein, Brent flew me out to San Diego to meet Mack and his staff. We were put up at the Half Moon Inn, a family-style resort on Shelter Island.

Mack's company had produced a handful of concerts on a lawn area between the hotel and the adjacent Humphrey's Restaurant. San Diego Bay, with its impressive flotilla of yachts and motorboats, was immediately to the left of the stage, prompting the name Humphrey's Concerts by the Bay for the mini-series of shows. It was an idyllic site for live music and I instantly fell in love with it.

We spent three days in San Diego, having meetings with the staff of Southland Concerts (the reorganized company's new name). The term "dysfunctional" was yet to be in vogue, but the Southland employees could have served as the dictionary definition.

Mack, the head honcho, was a short, pudgy wheeler-dealer with shifty eyes and a voice that rose an octave and cracked whenever he was lying. Caring little about music, he was fluent in the language of numbers, although his crunching abilities were clearly in decline.

The real brains behind the operation was Marc Geiger, a twenty-one-year-old UCSD student majoring in management science. A workaholic who occasionally wore a starched white shirt and tie to the office (in the *concert* business?), Geiger was as passionate about music as Mack was disinterested. He ran the hipper-than-hip Assorted Vinyl record store on the UCSD campus and championed the new breed of alternative rockers like REM, the Smiths, the Psychedelic Furs, and Simple Minds.

Geiger was completely at odds with Mack, but needed the affiliation to further his career as much as Mack needed Geiger for his work ethic and knowledge of music. Despite our differences in age (my thirty-five to his twenty-one) and political persuasions (my liberal Democrat to his Reagan Republican), Geiger and I bonded from day one.

The office manager, a bleached-blonde, long-nailed ditz with a dangling lip named Kaylee, was Mack's on-again, off-again paramour. The friction between them was relentless. Throughout my three-day office orientation, Mack and Kaylee snapped at each other like territorial crabs. After answering the phone with a cheery "Southland Concerts," she'd put the caller on hold and, without even a nod in his direction, shout, "Steve Montague for you, *asshole.*"

Central casting couldn't have chosen a more stereotypical production team. Lance, sporting a potbelly and a perpetual four-day stubble, handled the concerts' technical aspects. Drenched in Old Spice, he'd stumble into the office every day at two, look blankly at his pile of phone messages, and start swigging Martell cognac from the bottle.

Lance's sidekick and protégé was a twenty-eight-year-old Brit named Trip. Very personable with a mumbling accent that begged for subtitles, Trip was second in command but knew he was just one fuckup away from ascending to Lance's throne. I'd later learn of Trip's laundry list of scams, although he made a solid first impression.

Southland was a full-service concert company, producing shows at medium-size clubs like the Bacchanal and the Spirit, theater shows at the Fox, Civic, and Golden Hall, and occasional mega roll-of-the-dice spectaculars at the San Diego Sports Arena. Humphrey's was an afterthought, a venue that served as a last resort if all other options had been eliminated.

I couldn't get over how beautiful Humphrey's was. Brent, Mack, and Geiger took me on a whirlwind tour of other San Diego venues, but they were all generic and smoke-filled. They could have been in any city. Humphrey's, on the other hand, presented music with a panoramic view of the water, palm trees, boats, and the downtown

San Diego skyline. Gentle ocean breezes, obviously unavailable at indoor facilities, accompanied the music. An added attraction was cocktail service provided by stunning waitresses.

"You should build the company around Humphrey's," was my unsolicited advice to Brent.

"You're not seeing the big picture," he said, with an air of condescension. "It's a cute place, but we're not in this business to book a 650-seater at a hotel. You can't put on Prince, Billy Joel, or Springsteen at Humphrey's."

From both business and grandiosity standpoints, I understood his position. The portable stage was a foot off the ground. The few lights were hanging off trees. The sound system was adequate at best. But my mind was racing like an architect's. With a half-dozen well-orchestrated improvements, Humphrey's, blessed with a one-of-a-kind location, had the potential to be extraordinary.

Unfortunately, the magical allure of Humphrey's evaporated when I stepped back into the concert office on my final morning in San Diego before heading back to Boulder. Mack and Kaylee tormented each other like eleven-year-olds. Lance and Trip exchanged racist jokes and mocked Geiger about his post-adolescent zits. It was like *Romper Room* with a mean-spirited edge.

When Brent drove me to the airport, he nudged me. "Go home, think about it for a week, talk to Helen, and make a decision. The job is yours if you want it." My job description was hazy, but ostensibly it was to learn the concert business while making sure that Brent's financial investment wasn't being abused or squandered.

"Don't get me wrong—I had a great time," I said, thanking him for his five-star courtship, which included taking me out to gourmet restaurants, fueling me with nonstop bumps of cocaine, and having a limo escort us around San Diego. "But you saw the chemistry in that office. The only one who knows what he's doing is Geiger and he'll never last with all the daily hazing they put him through. I don't want to rain on your parade, but you're crazy if you think this'll work."

When I deplaned at Denver's Stapleton Airport, it was ninety-six degrees with no ocean breeze. I was returning to an uncertain future of ongoing scuffling in Colorado. Suddenly the scenic overlook on the Denver-Boulder Turnpike didn't feel so welcoming.

The next day, after hours of soul searching with Helen and weighing pros and cons (the cons won by a landslide), I put my faith in Brent and accepted his offer of $27,000 a year plus moving expenses. Helen decided to remain in Boulder for a few months to support Paul through most of his final year in high school.

I bought a one-way plane ticket to LA for December 1, 1983.

17.

el tio

"IJUST NEED TO MAKE A QUICK STOP," Brent said as his Malibu-bound Mercedes detoured from the 405 and headed toward West Hollywood. I nodded numbly in the passenger seat, trying to wrap my brain around shifting from friend to employee.

Brent turned onto La Cienega and pulled his Benz into an underground parking garage of a nondescript condo high rise.

"Where are we?" I asked, still dazed from the plane trip and a sleepless night in Boulder doing last-minute packing.

"At an investor's," he said nonchalantly. "We'll be in and out in five minutes."

We took the elevator up to the eighth floor and Brent knocked twice on the door of 8-E, rang the doorbell, and knocked twice again.

"*Quien es?*" asked the voice behind the door.

"Brent, *amigo.*"

The door opened slowly and a handsome fifty-something Hispanic man came out into the hallway. Dressed in a stunning Armani suit, he shook Brent's hand perfunctorily but blocked our entrance into his apartment.

"He's cool," Brent assured his "investor" *en español* with a nod in my direction. "He's one of my closest friends. Kenny, this is El Tio."

El Tio and I had a guarded limp-wrist clasp and he waved us in. I still didn't fully understand what was happening, even when I noticed all the brown-paper-wrapped bundles stacked at the far end of the living room. Brent and El Tio retreated to a guest bedroom and I tried to eavesdrop on and translate their conversation through the wall. Amid the garble, I made out "seventy-three," "one point three million," and "two weeks." I figured it out. My stomach churned in queasy disbelief.

On the endless elevator ride down to the garage, I had visions of being greeted by a hail of bullets to the face or, if I was luckier, dozens of G-men screaming, "Get down on the floor!" When the automatic door slid open and neither of those visions materialized, I could finally breathe again, although I'm still convinced I aged two years during those ten minutes in the building.

"You swore you were out of the business! How could you fucking lie to me so blatantly?" I screamed as Brent sped toward Pacific Coast Highway, back to our original route. "And how could you put me in harm's way like that?" I was still more freaked out than pissed, but my anger level was on the verge of surpassing my fear.

"C'mon, man, you don't think we can make money in the concert business, do you?" Brent asked with his characteristic salesman smile. "I need money to pump into the concerts and I'm very good at making money moving drugs. And gimme a break. You were never in danger. I thought that since you were a journalist, you'd like to meet a Colombian drug lord and see what seventy-three kilos of cocaine looked like."

I spent the rest of the ride pondering my fate. Should I cancel the moving company in Colorado? Did I dare share this with Helen, my wife and soul mate, whom I never hid *anything* from? Would she insist that I catch the next plane back to Denver? Or should I go with the flow and hope that the undertow wasn't too severe?

When we arrived at Brent's sprawling digs, he showed me to the guest wing of the house and told me to freshen up because he was throwing a party in my honor and expecting a horde of loose women. There would be scantily clad waitresses pouring Cristal and a bottomless urn of blow to satiate the stream of coke whores in attendance.

I closed the bedroom door, raced for the bathroom, and threw up intermittently for the next forty-five minutes. My nerves were shot. My self-esteem flew into the toilet with the rest of the bile. How could I have been so fucking stupid? How could I have trusted Brent? My instincts told me to get a cab to LAX ASAP.

Instead, I collected myself and joined the poolside revelry, convincing myself that day one was an anomaly. Things could only get better from here.

On day two, the abyss grew deeper.

18.

doing the laundry

Avoiding small talk with the porno starlets at the party might have been antisocial, but I couldn't risk derailing my quest for clarity. I cornered Brent's girlfriend du jour and begged her for insight as to how he could have conned me into making such a drastic move with such blasé dishonesty.

"Nothing Brent does surprises me," she said.

So it shouldn't have surprised me either that my new employer was cracking the whip at nine the next morning, peppering me with assignments. Even though I had been hired, theoretically, in an executive capacity, my first dictate was to travel around Malibu and Santa Monica laundering money.

"We all have to do some grunt work to get this business started," he said, before handing me a large briefcase with $90,000 in $100 bills.

Since I was being paid a decent starting salary, I followed my marching orders. I divided the money into ten packets of $9,000 each and drove one of Brent's five cars up and down Pacific Coast Highway. At each bank, I handed a rubber-banded wad to a teller with printed instructions to purchase a cashier's check payable to Brent's accountant. As long as each check request was under $10K, we wouldn't be raising any governmental red flags.

It took me a full business day to complete all the transactions, and even though I had nothing left in my system to regurgitate, I felt more nauseated than I had the day before. I stopped questioning Brent about his modus operandi. I had allowed myself to get sucked into his game plan and there would be no turning back.

"Okay, I did my gofer thing for you today. Let's head for San Diego," I said. "I want to get to work."

"We'll get there soon enough. First I want to make the rounds and introduce you to some of the major agents you'll be dealing with."

I agreed that that would be prudent, so I donned my black jeans, black shirt, and black sneakers (standard music industry attire) and headed for Beverly Hills and Century City to visit mega-agencies like William Morris, ICM, Regency Artists, APA, and CAA.

At each stop, a similar scenario unfolded. A receptionist seated us on an Italian leather couch in the lobby, asked us if we wanted anything to drink, and announced our arrival to the respective agents, who, even if their phones were quiet and calendars empty, kept us waiting for fifteen minutes before sending an assistant out to lead us through the office maze.

Brent had gotten his entrée into the concert business via his roommate in Malibu, Ken Rosene, a former music critic for the *Honolulu Advertiser* and one of three major concert promoters in Hawaii. Happy-go-lucky and gregarious, Rosene sponged money and cheap rent from Brent in exchange for imparting much-needed tutorials about the biz and introductions to all the right people. I learned a lot from my brief interactions with Rosene, mostly about working the phones, which agents to focus on and which to avoid, and the importance of following up every meeting with constant volleys of communication.

Rosene had set up appointments for Brent and me with heavyweight agents like Tom Ross, Mike Piranian, Hal Lazareff, Marty Beck, Peter Sheils, and David Snyder. Most of these characters would play a significant role in my early years as a concert promoter, but they virtually ignored me at first.

"Nice meeting you," they'd say, looking through me to see if Brent's leather man-purse had a coke-vial shaped protrusion. "Brent, let me show you our new conference room."

Brent and each agent would disappear for a few minutes, leaving me to stare blankly at the gold and platinum records that dotted the office walls. Upon their return, the conversations were decidedly more animated and borderline manic. I felt left out.

The power schmoozing continued for three days. Each night, I became the designated third wheel as Brent and Rosene traipsed from trendy restaurants to hipster hangouts, looking for malleable women. I tagged along like an unwanted kid brother, standing around stoop-shouldered with both hands in my pockets.

At this point, my self-esteem was nonexistent. I pondered my plight during all my waking hours, wishing I were back in Boulder with my wife, kids, friends, and bandmates, collecting unemployment and struggling to make ends meet.

When it was finally deemed appropriate to head for San Diego, Brent surprised me by flipping me the keys to one of his lesser Mercedes. "This is for you to drive until you go back to Colorado to pick up your Maxima," he said, knowing that I'd get hooked on the fancy ride. "And I'll bring some goodies for the condo."

The condo in question was located in a four-story building about twenty feet from one of San Diego's most spectacular beaches. Brent had assumed monthly payments on the place before the bank repossessed it from its delinquent owner, Jerry Mack.

I gladly moved into the plush, two-bedroom oceanfront apartment with a private underground parking spot for "my" Mercedes. Most nights I watched the sunset while sitting on the sand, or if I was too lazy or preoccupied to take the elevator down and make a quick barefoot trek into the surf, I could see the sun dip below the horizon from the chaise lounge on my balcony.

If Brent's plan was to seduce me with materialistic temptation, he was succeeding. But he hadn't finished attaching the feedbag to my snout. Shortly after I moved in, he left behind a bulky Ziploc bag. "This is for just the two of us to do," he said.

An ounce of coke lay before me, twenty-seven grams more than I was used to having in my possession at any given time. My eyes got buggy just looking at that much blow, but after doing a line, I cringed. It was shitty stuff. I'd have no trouble playing by the rules and saving the stash for Brent's occasional visits.

Yeah, right.

19.

1984

WHILE BIG BROTHER WAS MICROMANAGING the lives of an entire population of fictitious characters in 1984, I was having some real-life catastrophes of my own.

Amid the nonstop in-house sniping at Southland Concerts, I struggled to learn the rudiments of the business. Marc Geiger, my twenty-one-year-old mentor, left the company in June to become an agent at Regency Artists in LA. He was the only person in the company I could relate to, so his departure was traumatizing, In retrospect, it was the best thing that could have happened because it forced me to take charge of my own destiny, for better *and* worse.

In the first few months of the year, I flew back and forth between Colorado and California six times to help Helen pack and coordinate our move. When we were separated geographically, we spoke constantly. I felt giddy to be basking in balmy eighty-degree temps in San Diego while it was twenty below in Boulder.

But I felt awful about leaving behind my stepchildren, Nicole and Paul, and taking their mother with me. Nicole was living in an apartment with some girlfriends and finishing her freshman year at the University of Colorado, while Paul was wrapping up his senior year at Boulder High.

My history with Nicole was complicated. She was devastated when her parents got divorced and very confused when I moved into her family home. When Nicole was seven and I was the twenty-four-year-old neighbor doling out candy, we got along famously. When she was eight and I was suddenly the twenty-five-year-old roommate sharing her mother's bed, her smiling face pretty much vanished.

It took at least two years before Nicole began to trust me again. One time she was so upset with us that she packed her clothes and favorite stuffed animal into a giant pillowcase and ran away from home. She made it only half a block before returning in tears.

I made a point of not stepping into a paternal role. The kids' father still lived in the neighborhood and saw them regularly. Nevertheless, I wanted to offer Nicole plenty of support. I cheered her on during her elementary school track meets, went to her dance performances, and invited her on my radio show as a guest character (The Pepper Queen). When she hit puberty, our relationship became both closer and more strained. Helen and I had to reprimand her many times for sneaking her boyfriend into her bedroom, well aware that our own thinly veiled sexuality around the kids was not setting the best example. Even so, Nicole and I became more compatible during her teenage years, and she danced joyously at our wedding in 1977. Her friends viewed me as the "cool stepfather."

Paul and I, on the other hand, hit it off from day one. When I was still the neighbor, I had witnessed his father reprimanding him in his backyard and cuffing him across the back of his head. I wondered if that was a usual occurrence or merely an anomaly. After Helen's divorce was finalized and I moved in with her, Paul and I became pals. Before he turned ten, I took him to see musical acts as diverse as Kiss, the Kinks, and Frank Zappa. He and I developed a mutual admiration for each other—I enjoyed watching his progress as a young artist, and he listened to me on the radio every morning, read my newspaper columns, and skipped classes to attend my University of Colorado Trivia Bowl contests, sitting in the front row and cheering for all my correct answers.

Alas, adolescence set in and the conflicts began. Paul quickly became one of the most flamboyant teenagers in Boulder. He dyed the bottom half of his jet-black hair platinum blonde and shaved off his eyebrows. He began dressing like Fred Astaire, wearing retro suits and skinny ties to school, making him an easy mark for taunting.

When he was in the tenth grade, his high school drama teacher called Helen to let her know about the rampant rumors that Paul was gay. I took him to Tom's Tavern for a cheeseburger as an excuse to bring up that distressing conversation.

"Mrs. Higgs called your mom the other day," I said. "She thinks you're great in the play, but she's concerned that some of your antics are rubbing your classmates the wrong way. Some of them even think you're gay."

"I am," Paul said without hesitation. Instead of cowering, he seemed thoroughly relieved to tell the truth.

I shouldn't have been startled by this revelation, especially given the giant poster in his room of Prince clad in nothing but a thong, but I was still caught off guard. "We're obviously going to have to tell your mom," I said.

"I know." There was no trepidation in his voice.

Helen was overwhelmed and concerned, not that Paul *was* gay, but that *being* gay would make his life more difficult. It certainly made our family dynamic more challenging. Like the time I knocked on Paul's bedroom door to check on him and found a teenage boy under the covers waiting for Paul to get home from school. Or the day that Paul left his journal on his bed. I got what I deserved when I flipped the pages to his most recent entry, a salacious recounting of his sexual encounter in the men's room stall at Fred's Steak House a few hours before one of his busboy shifts.

By the time Brent offered me the job in San Diego, I had been an integral part of my stepchildren's lives for eleven years. Communication and camaraderie had improved among the four of us, and even though the kids didn't call me Dad, we were obviously a family unit.

In deciding whether or not to relocate, Helen and I rationalized that Nicole and Paul were both already fiercely independent and rebellious, so it wouldn't make much difference if we stayed in Colorado or headed to California.

Wishful thinking . . .

As I was spending the bulk of 1984 dealing with movers, finding a rental property to take the place of our beachfront condo, learning a new profession, adjusting daily to a dysfunctional cast of colleagues, taking trips to LA and NYC to meet the power players of the concert industry, writing two thousand trivia questions for a rock 'n' roll board game, working every day, going out every night, and doing way too much coke, both kids dropped bombshells on us.

First Nicole. When she and Paul came out to visit us in April, we sensed her melancholia as soon as she got off the plane.

"I have to talk to you, Mom," she said, avoiding eye contact with her mother and ignoring me altogether.

Helen didn't hesitate. "You're pregnant," she said.

At nineteen, Nicole had her whole life in front of her. She'd been sexually precocious since age fourteen, so her pregnancy didn't shock us. But it was disturbing that the father was an ultra-Orthodox Jewish massage therapist from Israel in the U.S. on a student visa. He had no intention of staying here, marrying Nicole, and raising a child.

I found myself in the illogical position of trying to be the voice of reason. Helen and I sat with her on the beach, gazing at the endless expanse of ocean and feeling comforted by the breeze.

"Nikki, . . . you're pursuing a college degree, you have many years ahead of you to have babies, you'll be caring for this child alone, there will likely be no support from the father, we're a thousand miles away so we won't be able to help—do you understand how much it will cost to have a child?"

I was sleep deprived myself and mildly incoherent, but I tried to maintain a gentle, reassuring demeanor. Helen displayed a calm exterior but her insides were being roto-rootered. Without forcing the issue, we discussed the pragmatics of her having an abortion. "Under the circumstances, don't you think it's the prudent thing to do?"

"I'm having the baby," Nicole said, refocusing her attention on embroidering what would become her child's first blanket.

We didn't try to talk her out of that extremely personal decision. We became supportive allies of Team Nicole, helping her navigate the next eight months via sporadic trips to Colorado. Helen spent the month of November in Boulder and I mistimed my one week away from work, returning to San Diego two days before Nicole gave birth to Shira Isabelle Rose on November 28.

I flew back to Colorado on November 30 to hold and bond with my two-day-old granddaughter for a day before returning once again to San Diego and my confusing new career. As I wheeled my suitcase into our Spanish adobe rental, I wondered aloud, "Are there any other thirty-six-year-old grandfathers in the music business?"

Then Paul. We planned for Helen to stay with him until the spring of 1984, and then we'd hire a house sitter to see him through to the end of the school year. The day in April that Helen joined me in San Diego, he was shooting up a variety of drugs in our Boulder bedroom.

Always one of the brightest bulbs in the lamp, Paul breezed through his senior year. Rather than going to college in the fall, he headed for San Francisco, where his charm quickly landed him a job scooping cones and blending lattes at a Double Rainbow ice cream shop.

But the city was primarily a way station for Paul's unbridled experimentation with sex and drugs. He was spiraling downward in a dangerous way and Helen and I had no clue how to help him.

When he came to visit us again in October, he had dyed his hair a garish shade of orange. I muffled my groan but found myself discussing his misguided choice of color with him a few days later, also suggesting that he have his ragamuffin mop trimmed and shaped. It reminded me of having dinner with my parents in the summer of '69 before I headed back to Madison for my senior year. I had miscalculated coming down from an afternoon acid trip and was still seeing the melting walls behind my mother (whose face had morphed into a boxer-bulldog mix) as she harangued me about having my hair styled. Fifteen years later, I'm dishing out the same advice to my tousled stepson.

Late one evening, Paul started talking with me about drugs. He was afraid that his usage was getting out of control. Now shooting speed, he had attempted to recreate Lou Reed's epic five-day binge chronicled on his *Berlin* album. He added too matter-of-factly that he was sharing used needles with his friends, an open invitation to contracting AIDS or hepatitis.

We talked for hours and I offered my total moral support. I admitted that I wasn't the most qualified drug counselor, considering all the blow I was still doing myself. When we drove him to the airport for his return flight to San Fran, I made him promise he'd call me every time he was about to shoot up. I would ask what we could do to help and try to convince him not to do it.

He never called. Helen and I were worried sick that he would tempt fate one too many times.

Paul didn't quit doing drugs right away, but he quickly eliminated intravenous from his vocabulary. By the time he was twenty-two, his drug days had ended. He then had a revelation that he and San Francisco weren't a good mix and abruptly headed back to Boulder.

He's lived there ever since.

20.

we gotta get humphrey's

"**A**RE YOU READY TO RUN THE BUSINESS?" Brent asked me as 1984 drew to a close.

He and Jerry Mack were having daily fights about bookings as well as the overall grim financial picture. Mack claimed that it was essential to wrest away shows from the competition, overpaying the act if necessary, regardless of the outcome. The agents rewarded that kind of fiscal stupidity by selling you more shows. That mentality is still woefully prevalent in the concert industry today, but it made no sense to Brent, so he and Mack decided to go their separate ways.

"Absolutely," I lied.

We both realized that the odds were stacked against us. Mack would take his experienced support staff with him and I had never booked a show in my life.

During the final tumultuous weeks that led to the dissolution of their partnership, Mack and Brent had intense disagreements over how to split the mythical assets of Southland Concerts. They each attempted to pawn off the rights to Humphrey's to the other, neither of them giving a shit about it. In exchange, the promoter who inherited the outdoor venue would agree to cease going after theater and arena shows.

I refused to let Brent get rid of it. "Humphrey's is the only reason I moved to San Diego," I reminded him in one of hundreds of heated debates we'd have during the final two years of our working relationship. "You're a fool if you don't recognize what we have here."

"You can't see the forest for the trees," was his constant rejoinder. "Humphrey's is our backup venue, nothing more. If we can't find a bigger place to put on a show, it will always be there as our last resort."

Being a music lover who enjoyed sitting as close to the stage as possible, I was most interested in developing an intimate venue and Humphrey's provided that opportunity. I wasn't willing to let Brent's unrealistic and delusional ideas impede my vision.

I explained to him that Humphrey's would appeal to big-name performers as much as it did to me. For sheer convenience, the venue was only five minutes from Lindbergh Field. Airport proximity is a major plus for touring artists. On the property, the dressing rooms were luxurious hotel suites located directly behind the stage—headliners could literally do a soundcheck at 4 p.m., take a nap, have room service deliver dinner at 5:30, hop into the shower, and begin performing an hour later. They could roll out of bed and be onstage.

On the downside, Humphrey's limited 650-seat capacity, though intimate, made it tough to attract big names even if they were willing to do two performances a night. It was a daunting task to compete with 2,500-seat indoor theaters or 5,000-seat outdoor amphitheaters. The main thrust of my job would be to sell the uniqueness of the experience for both the artist and the audience at a venue that few had heard of.

Before I could test my powers of persuasion, though, we needed to land the Humphrey's exclusive, which wasn't a given. I was an unknown entity in the concert business and had limited relationships with agents and managers. No one cared about my artistic background in Colorado or my musical knowledge and integrity.

All that mattered was whether I would offer more money than my competitor. Also working against me was the fact that Jerry Mack had ten years of promoting experience, including presenting stadium shows, and knew every important mover and shaker.

As 1984 segued into 1985, I took control of the situation. On New Year's Day, I called Brent. "Get your ass down to San Diego immediately," I said. "I've made an appointment tomorrow with Richard Bartell, the new owner of Humphrey's Half Moon Inn, and it's important that you be here. Mack is in Puerto Vallarta on vacation. We need to act fast."

Rarely did Brent heed my advice but he drove down to San Diego that evening. Over a swordfish dinner at Anthony's Star of the Sea, we plotted our mini-strategy. A novice at business, I still managed to formulate a detailed plan on my trusty IBM Selectric. Southland Concerts would book the entertainment and absorb the talent and production costs, including rental fees to the Port of San Diego. In return, we'd receive 100 percent of the gate proceeds and whatever sponsorship monies we could procure. Bartell Hotels would generate its profits from sale of food and beverage and assume no financial risk.

In my entire career as a concert producer, I wore a tie to work only once: January 2, 1985. Brent and I had a cordial, get-acquainted meeting with Richard Bartell in his converted hotel room office adjacent to the putting green and a stone's throw from the enticing Olympic-size swimming pool.

After exchanging pleasantries, I ran down our proposal. When the Bartell family purchased the Half Moon Inn just a few weeks before, Richard hadn't even been aware that a summer concert series took place on the property. He rattled off a litany of logistical concerns before asking us the obvious question.

"Is Jerry Mack still involved with your company?" Jerry Mack— the guy with all the clout and concert biz expertise. We had adequate funding through Brent's large cash reserve but were short on industry connections. We didn't stand a chance.

"No, we had a falling out and he's no longer with the company," Brent said diplomatically, trying not to drag Mack through the mud.

"I hope that isn't a problem," I said, preparing to launch a camouflaged character assassination. My future in San Diego depended on us getting Humphrey's. "We believe that we can—"

"Where do I sign?"

I pulled out my roughly sketched letter of agreement that delineated each party's responsibilities. Bartell, who'd been a public defender and trial lawyer before joining the family business (which had recently sold its group of radio stations and bought a cluster of hotel properties), carefully perused and initialed each point, signed the letter, and shook our hands.

We later found out that Mack had stiffed Bartell Broadcasting on a series of contracted media buys, even though many of the advertised shows had sold out. Without elaborating, Bartell implied that if Mack had still been involved with us, he would have looked for another partner or discontinued the concerts altogether.

Brent and I looked at each other and barely contained our mirth. Brent might not have wanted an exclusive booking arrangement with Humphrey's, but he had one nonetheless.

As we headed to Humphrey's Restaurant for a bowl of corn chowder and a dozen raw oysters, how was I to know that this was the first day of my twenty-two-year association with Richard Bartell?

21.

miles in the rain

A T THE ONSET OF 1985, I sat in the catbird seat, with the money and authority to book a forty-five-show summer concert series. There were a couple of problems, though. One, I didn't know what I was doing. Two, Jerry Mack, the ousted promoter of record at Humphrey's, was coming after us with a vengeance. He immediately went down the street to the far end of Shelter Island and started a competing series at the Kona Kai Hotel.

I was unquestionably the underdog, but the cliché that all the pressure was on the favorite was a crock. It was a struggle to get agents to take or return my phone calls. I was running a uniquely quaint venue but I was just shy of invisible in the eyes of the power brokers.

As future concert seasons came and went, I would start booking the following year's lineup in October and have at least a dozen confirmations by December. But 1985 was a bitch because Southland Concerts didn't land the Humphrey's account until early January and I didn't secure a firm date until a month later.

My first confirmation after becoming "captain of the ship" was Chuck Mangione, an artist whose music I equated with cotton candy, primarily fluff with no substance. One booking and I had already compromised my artistic values. I dished out offers to any agent who would pay attention to me. That was a short list. Peter Sheils of the William Morris Agency had been plied frequently with coke by Brent so he politely picked up my calls. But Peter had a long-standing allegiance to Mack—in fact, Peter had sold him the Camilo Sesto tour that had propelled him toward bankruptcy.

Since I had no choice but to be patient my initial year at the helm, I was exhilarated when Sheils called in early February to confirm David Sanborn, one of the biggest names in contemporary jazz. This might quell the onslaught of naysayers who didn't think I was up to the task of competing against Mack, Avalon Attractions, and other more established promoters in the market.

My mild euphoria was short-lived. A few days later, Sheils called. "I have bad news," he said. "Mack came up to the office with $15,000 in cash yesterday and I have to give him Sanborn."

It was my first indication that one's word meant nothing in the mercurial concert business.

"What the fuck?" I'm generally a mild-mannered person, not prone to temper tantrums, but reneging on a promise is a quick way to elevate my blood pressure. "You confirmed the date last week. I have already written a press release and was just getting my ad campaign in order." I was stretching the truth—our ads weren't scheduled to break for a month. "How can you fuck us over like that?"

"I'm really sorry, Kenny. You should have seen Mack. He was groveling. His voice was cracking. It was pathetic."

"And I'm supposed to feel sorry for him? C'mon, Peter. He dug his own grave a million times. Plus, you confirmed the date to *me*. When is a confirmation *not* a confirmation? Jesus motherfucking Christ!" I surprised myself with my own fury.

That situation ultimately turned out well and became a timely lesson for a naïve rookie promoter. A show is never really yours until it goes on sale, and even then, it can go away. Ray Charles, who played twenty-nine shows during my career at Humphrey's, was already sold out weeks in advance in 1987 when I got a call from his notorious manager, Joe Adams, informing me that he was canceling the date because a rival area promoter had come to the table with an extra $5,000 for a show on the same day. No amount of arguing about how Ray was screwing his fans or how blatantly unethical this was could get Adams to change his mind. He yanked the show, we refunded 1,800 tickets, and I moved on with my life. The following year, Ray Charles returned to Humphrey's and subsequently played for us every year until his death in 2004. Joe Adams showed up most of the time and was a congenial backslapper.

You have to roll with the punches.

I pressed Sheils for days, trying to convince him to bring Sanborn back to Humphrey's. "I can't, but stay by your phone. I'm going to make this up to you."

Famous last words that I would hear hundreds of times during my tenure as a concert producer. But Sheils came through the next morning.

"Are you sitting down?" he asked with an air of mystery in his voice that suggested that the original Mott the Hoople might be reuniting to tour.

"Go ahead," I replied blankly, expecting an overpriced Stanley Turrentine confirmation at best.

"Okay. June 2 and 3, two nights of Earl Klugh. Confirmed. July 5, John Klemmer. Confirmed. July 20, Larry Carlton. Confirmed. And on April 21, your opening night will be . . . Miles Davis. Confirmed."

I felt like a Major League Baseball GM who had just pulled off a spectacular four-for-one trade. All these artists added instant credibility to our series, but Miles Davis was the one I did backflips over.

Davis's career was showing signs of revitalization in the early '80s after he had disappeared into a cocaine haze from 1975 to 1980. *The Man with the Horn*, his 1981 comeback LP, had garnered positive reviews and reasonably good sales numbers, although his performances were erratic: brilliant one night, unfocused and plodding the next.

I didn't know which Miles Davis would show up, but I did know that April was the tail end of the rainy season in San Diego and the forecast for April 21, which turned out to be accurate, was for sporadic rain accompanied by monsoonal winds.

I was neurotic enough about presenting my first concert without having the added distraction of intermittent rain throughout the evening. What if we had to cancel the show? Did we still have to pay the band? Of course we did, but maybe an understanding artist would give us some money back and share the loss with us. My naïveté was still in full flower.

During my first two years as a promoter, Brent hired a consultant named John Harrington, a respected talent buyer for the Hollywood Palace, to teach me the ropes and advise on the booking. Harrington came down for the Miles Davis concerts and watched me with amusement as I paced back and forth in our dressing-room office, tensing up every time it began to drizzle. Harrington had seen it all during his career, but he'd never produced an outdoor event.

"Relax, Kenny, it's a no-brainer," he said. "The show goes on, the band plays, the show ends, everyone goes home, and you wake up tomorrow and do it again." With that pearl of wisdom, he whipped out a joint, lit it up, and insisted I partake.

"I don't know, John. I still have to settle the show," I said before taking the first of a half-dozen hits. When the tour manager came by to get paid before the seven o'clock show, I was feeling no pain. I handed him the balance of the guarantee (Miles got paid $17,500 that night—supposedly a bargain) and went to the side of the stage to watch the performance. In later years, I'd sit in my designated ninth-row center aisle seat, but on this night I didn't want to be confronted by any audience members who might blame me for the weather.

The early show started on time in a steady rain. By the second song, a little-known piece of funk-fusion called "Maze," the sky responded with some up-tempo activity of its own, drenching the performers and the audience. Amazingly, the musicians played through it with smiles on their faces, including the trumpet-wielding front man.

Davis, dressed in black from head to toe, including a Gaucho hat, sunglasses, and gloves, never faced the crowd and didn't say a word the entire night. But the performances were riveting enough to keep the fans (1,339 paid for two shows) mesmerized throughout their own mud-encrusted Woodstock by the Bay.

Even though Davis's repertoire consisted of all recent material (no *Birth of the Cool*, *Kind of Blue*, or *Bitches Brew* that night), the audience was clearly excited by his playing as well as by his cherry-picked band of young lions that featured guitarist John Scofield, saxophonist Bob Berg, and future Rolling Stones bassist Darryl Jones. In George Varga's glowing concert review in the *San Diego Union* the next morning, he wrote, "If last night's weather might have been better suited for a Jacques Cousteau television show about coastal storms, no one bothered to tell Davis. The mercurial trumpeter turned in a fiery performance that burned strongly from start to finish."

When the second show came to a close, shortly before the 10:30 curfew, I wrestled with whether I should knock on Miles's door to thank him for getting me through my "debut performance." Even though he had a racially mixed sextet, he was notorious for his distrust of the white music biz establishment, especially concert promoters. As I played head games with myself, his dressing-room door opened and I stood face-to-face with Miles Davis, who was heading to the green room for some post-gig food and beverage.

More than slightly tongue-tied, I extended my hand and thanked him, identifying myself as the promoter. I'll never forget his handshake: a backhand, contorted twist of the wrist latching onto the tips of my thumb and first two fingers.

"How did you do?" he asked with his characteristic rasp.

"It really doesn't matter," I said, startled that a performer of his magnitude would be curious about the promoter's financial outcome.

"This was the first concert of my career, and no matter what happens from here on in, I'll always be able to say that I presented Miles Davis in concert. You have no idea what that means to me."

"Yeah, yeah. But how did you *do*?"

"We, uh, lost some money," I said, "but I don't care. Miles Davis just played at Humphrey's and—"

He grabbed my wrist and looked me straight in the eye. "Next time," he said, "you gotsta *charge* more."

It reminded me of the simplicity of David Carradine in *Kung Fu*. If I had charged more, the bottom line would have been higher and we might have broken even. He nodded and proceeded down the path to dinner enlightenment.

In 1986, we presented Miles Davis again. Adhering to Miles's strategy, I raised the ticket price from $16.50 to $18.50. Attendance dropped by two hundred and we lost $2,500.

22.

transition

RICHARD BARTELL HAD PROVIDED SOUTHLAND Concerts with not only a place to stage our concerts, but a buffer zone to grow our company as well. He oversaw some creative renovations on his property that expanded our capacity to nearly 1,400. Yet Brent never seized the opportunity to make the Humphrey's series the centerpiece of our operation, opting to let it dangle on the periphery.

Brent tried to hang with the big boys, furiously bidding on arena shows. As the line erroneously attributed to P. T. Barnum goes, "There's a sucker born every minute." Brent could lay claim to a few of those minutes.

"You're not going to believe this," he said during one of our ten-a-day phone calls. "I just bought three nights of Prince, March 10 to 12, at the Long Beach Arena. I paid stupid money, but we got the shows. They go on sale next week."

With all the veteran, deep-pocketed concert promotion companies in Southern California, I wondered why a superstar like Prince would cast his lot with unknown Southland Concerts. It turned out that Brent had partnered the shows with a down-and-out music industry shyster he called Filch who was trying to recapture his glory days by offering Prince twice his market value. "I'm putting up all the money and Filch is pulling in some past-due favors," Brent said.

Only in the concert business could a promoter sell out three nights and lose hundreds of thousands of dollars. When the smoke cleared from all the pyro, Brent lost $200K after selling all 36,000 Prince tickets. He had nothing to show for his investment but a tour laminate with his name on it.

It was hopeless trying to explain how much easier it was to make money while presenting a relaxed evening of music at Humphrey's. Brent needed the big bang and ego gratification that arena spectacles afforded. Plus, he could take his harem of porno starlets backstage.

Yes, Brent had a penchant for porno and the adult-film community long before the Internet was invented. He hung out on movie sets in LA, went to award shows in Vegas, and invited several "actresses" and directors to visit "his cute new venue" in San Diego. He had recently turned forty, and most of his dates were in the eighteen-to twenty-two-year-old range, including the four-foot-eleven ball o' dynamite Quikki Vikki.

Brent's involvement with porn ultimately hastened his departure from the concert business. In 1986, he provided his Malibu estate as a location for a series of XXX films, some of which included performers under the legal age of eighteen. Brent pleaded ignorance when the Feds stormed his property—he was an innocent bystander, after all—but he was still booked and charged with pandering. I heard about it on the KNX three o'clock news while driving back from the gym to my office.

The charges were eventually dropped but not before Brent had accumulated $200,000 in legal fees. The mental anguish combined with a significant financial drain took its toll on Brent, and his concentration on business affairs in San Diego disappeared. I ran Southland Concerts the best I could, but I didn't have instant access to funds and had to constantly ride Brent's LA-based accountants to wire artist deposits, replenish the checking account, and keep the creditors at bay.

My limits were being severely tested. I was losing patience *and* hope, a staggering one-two punch. And then Brent pulled a stunt that initially sent me tumbling a few rungs lower but ultimately served as the catalyst to extricate myself from his web.

Helen and I had been seeing a marriage counselor named Letitia to examine the stresses that had been steadily eroding our harmonious fourteen-year relationship. The combination of relocating, starting a new career, and leaving behind our two kids and Helen's deep ties to the Boulder arts community had wreaked havoc on our sex life. Not only was I away from home most of the time, but when I'd stagger in late at night from a concert, making love was not high on my list of priorities.

"What's left in this relationship for me?" Helen asked during our first session. Exasperated by my association with Brent and the way the job was affecting me, she had contemplated returning to Boulder . . . alone.

A respected writer with an acclaimed book on divorce, Letitia had been highly recommended to us by several friends in the throes of marriage dissolution. But I didn't want to be coached through a breakup. I desperately wanted to save our marriage, and Letitia quickly assured me that she did more than facilitate and mediate estrangements.

Shortly after we started counseling, I made a tactical error by inviting Letitia to a concert at Humphrey's on a night Brent was in San Diego. The four of us sat together at the show, and Brent immediately became flirtatious with Letitia, who had been successful on the beauty pageant circuit in her twenties, winning several tiaras and sashes before morphing into a career as a therapist and author.

Again, Helen and I had to listen silently as Brent fed yet another unsuspecting mark all his bullshit about having a PhD in psychology and abandoning the field to study ancient Mayan civilization, before becoming an entertainment industry mogul. He left out the parts about producing porno flicks and serving time for drug dealing.

A few days later, Letitia initiated a conference call with Helen and me to tell us that Brent had asked her out to dinner. She wanted to discuss it openly with us to see if we had any qualms about it. She admitted she was attracted to him, adding that she had been lonely since her own divorce and was ready to give dating a try.

Without exposing Brent as a fraud, Helen and I warned Letitia about his checkered history with women. We also reminded her that he was my boss and in our minds indirectly responsible for the dysfunction that had permeated our marriage. But Letitia assured us there would be no mention of us on any level during their date and asked for our blessings. We advised against going out with him but said we wouldn't stand in her way.

"I'm a big girl," she said. "I can handle this without it affecting our counseling."

The morning after their date, Brent called me at my office. "Hold all your calls for the next twenty minutes," he ordered. "Do I have a story for *you*!"

He proceeded to describe every sexual position he and Letitia had tried the night before in their complimentary hotel suite at Humphrey's. "She had five orgasms, at least two of them G-spots," he said, adding details about the size of her breasts, the taste of her vagina, and other apertures he had explored.

"*Why* are you telling me this?"

"You're a writer. I figured you'd like to hear a good story." It was reminiscent of the day he took me on the West Hollywood drug deal less than an hour after I'd relocated to Southern California, when he had also played the journalist card.

I took a long lunch break, drove the 1.7 miles home from my office, and related the Brent-Letitia tale to Helen. We decided to call Letitia and tell her what we knew. She was mortified and apologized profusely.

We continued seeing her professionally because we were pleased with the progress we'd made under her guidance. But how could I continue to work for Brent? Wasn't this, in fact, the very last straw?

Yes, it was. On a business trip to New York City a few weeks later, after a festive night consuming blinis, caviar, and Cristal at the Russian Tea Room, I verbally blindsided him in his hotel room at the Parker Meridian. Fists clenched, I screamed how unconscionable it had been for him to seduce Letitia, knowing I was seeing her to work on marital problems that included sexual dysfunction, and then gleefully rub my face in the athleticism of his exploits. I called him on his lifetime of lies, bullshit, and manipulation, directed not just at me but at his entire universe. I paced the marble floor and my manic, emotive monologue reached epic proportions. Suddenly Brent didn't seem six inches taller.

He tried to appease me by laying out a huge line of blow. For the first time in our fifteen-year friendship, I told him no.

Then I took a deep breath and continued. "Look, the Humphrey's season is ending in three weeks. I can't work for you anymore. So either I leave and you find a replacement for me or you quit the business and I find someone else to back the concerts."

Brent pushed the coke mirror back in my direction. "C'mon man, let's do some lines."

I declined again, left his room, and, taking my first giant step toward sobriety, ventured out into the Manhattan night.

The next morning, over a conciliatory breakfast, Brent told me he had decided to fold Southland Concerts and exit the concert business.

I'll always remember October 11, 1986, as the date of my last cocaine binge. Brent came down to San Diego and threw himself a farewell party. We stayed up all night, and on this occasion, I didn't ignore his powdered party favors.

At 7 a.m. I raced to catch an early flight to San Francisco. A good friend had an extra ticket to see the first Bridge School Benefit at the Shoreline Amphitheatre near Palo Alto and invited me to accompany him. The lineup was Crosby, Stills, Nash & Young, Bruce Springsteen in acoustic-trio format (with Danny Federici and Nils Lofgren), Tom Petty, Don Henley, and Robin Williams. We had tickets in the tenth row, and from what I was told, it was a fantastic four-hour show. We flew home the next morning, I slept for twenty-four hours, and when I woke up, I couldn't remember anything about the concert.

Without warning, a light bulb blazed brightly in my cranium. I swore to myself I would . . .

1. Give up drugs

2. Save my marriage

3. Begin a serious workout regimen

4. Reinvent my situation at Humphrey's

It was an ambitious checklist but I nailed every item. After nineteen years of drug use, I stopped on a dime. Helen and I continued seeing Letitia for another year and reaffirmed our commitment to each other. We've been free of marriage counselors ever since. I went from a paunchy schlubbo (my idea of exercise was reaching for the remote) to a toned muscleman, maintaining a five-day-a-week gym routine.

Finally, on October 15, 1986, three days after Brent folded his tent, I went to Richard Bartell, told him Southland Concerts was history, and hammered out a profit-sharing arrangement with him that lasted the next twenty years (a handshake deal—we never had a contract).

And Brent? His ongoing saga was sketchy, as it's never been easy to delineate fact from fiction regarding his adventures. After the porno pandering charges were dropped, he got involved in the drug trade again, this time as an investor, not a trafficker. Soon the heat was on and he quietly fled the country. No strange parcels showed up at my PO Box with South American postmarks. I didn't hear from him for three years.

Occasionally I would call his ex-girlfriends, and according to one rumor, he was playing professional polo in Europe, living under a pseudonym. That sounded a lot to me like his claims to be researching Mayan civilization in South America, but you never knew with Brent.

On September 29, 1991, my home phone rang, awakening me at six in the morning. I assumed it was a wrong number and didn't pick up. A few hours later, I played back the message and heard in a familiar raspy voice, "Next time you gotsta *charge* more." Miles Davis had died a day earlier, and for years after Miles had given me that advice, Brent and I did our best impressions of him, and here was Brent leaving that cryptic message for me without another word. When I reconnected with him a year later, before he started serving a six-year sentence (reduced to three for good behavior) in a downtown Phoenix correctional center, he told me he had left that message from a pay phone in Paris.

Halfway through his second incarceration, Brent was transferred to a prison outside Santa Fe, and when he was released, he settled there. As a Santa Fe resident, Brent reinvented himself as a designer and builder of luxury homes. Helen and I visited him on the way to Boulder in 2002 and he took us on a tour of his spec properties. Trying to impress upon me that he was still a boss, Brent barked orders *en español* at a crew of Mexican workers. He then regaled us with detailed descriptions of his life as a general contractor while tracing the origin of the granite countertops in the kitchen and bemoaning the travails of steam-shower installation.

Unfortunately for Brent and his investors, the three houses sat high on a mountain top, accessible only by a steep dirt road, meaning any prospective owner would need a four-wheel-drive vehicle and a high tolerance for bumps and potholes to scale the rugged terrain. The impressive properties sat empty for over a year, garnering only one or two lowball offers. Brent's partners, who had put up all the money, grew impatient and drew up litigation papers.

Brent disappeared again for another three years. This time there weren't even humorous voicemails. I contacted his exes in Santa Fe, LA, and Colorado—nothing. Even his longtime Beverly Hills accountant, who oversaw all his finances while Brent was a legitimate businessman and during both jail terms, claimed to be out of the loop. Attempted emails all bounced back.

"Brent must be dead," I said to Helen more than a few times.

He wasn't. In 2006 he called me out of the blue and acted as if he had spoken to me a week before.

"Where have you been for the past three years?" I asked, not fully understanding the care and concern I still had for him after all the swerves he had pulled on me.

"Come on, it hasn't been *that* long." He ran through a fifteen-minute recap of his escapades, including a harrowing tale during which he almost became a victim of California's three-strikes law. He had finally holed up incognito in a friend's trailer in Desert Hot Springs, with occasional hot water and one small black-and-white TV that picked up only grainy images from three local stations. Quite a comedown for a guy accustomed to twelve-foot ceilings and satellite TV in every bathroom.

Yet leave it to Brent to right the sinking ship. He soon started dating a fast-food magnate and moved into her gated community mansion in Rancho Mirage. The last time I saw him, he was driving a $150,000 Mercedes Benz CL600. He disappeared from my life again until just recently, when he called to invite us up to see the $4 million home he and his sweetheart had built in Pacific Palisades.

PART 4

Backstage at the Bay

23.

gonna be huge

I WAS FORTUNATE TO MEET WHITNEY HOUSTON long before alcohol, drugs, questionable companions, and the pratfalls of fame ruined her life and led to her untimely passing. In fact, her gig at Humphrey's on August 28, 1985, (nineteen days after her twenty-second birthday) was the first headlining concert of her career.

To be honest, I succumbed to pressure from Triad Artists agents Marc Geiger and David Snyder to book Whitney Houston and pay her asking price of $11,500 for two shows. Her first single, "You Give Good Love," hadn't even been released nor had her debut album, *Whitney Houston*. Geiger, already adept at agentspeak at age twenty-two, kept saying, "Trust me on this one. She's gonna be huge." At that point in my career, I did what the agents told me to do. If I had played hardball or haggled about the price, they might have stopped calling me. I didn't develop my negotiating skills until a few years later.

By the time I put Whitney's shows on sale, she was all over the radio and *Whitney Houston* was well on its way to selling thirteen million records. By the night of her concert, "Saving All My Love for You" was number one on the pop and R&B charts, and I looked like a genius. In fact, I had merely been following marching orders by booking an artist I had barely heard of. The shows sold out months in advance.

When I arrived at the venue to watch Whitney's soundcheck, I sought out her manager, Gene Harvey. A gregarious, middle-aged, white Jewish guy, Harvey shook my hand for an interminably long time while thanking me for taking a chance on his artist. "We'll always remember you for being the first person to pull the trigger on a Whitney Houston date," he said, beaming. "You'll *always* be our promoter in San Diego. C'mon, let me introduce you to her."

WHITNEY HOUSTON
ARISTA

Waiting patiently in her dressing room while her band did a line check onstage, Whitney was dressed in tight jeans and a satin baseball jacket. Gene introduced me as her promoter and I smiled and looked directly into her eyes because we were both the same height. She shook my hand meekly, said nothing, and stared down at the floor.

I searched for something relevant to say. "I'm from South Orange," I said, knowing Whitney had grown up in neighboring East Orange, New Jersey.

"Really?" She suddenly seemed genuinely pleased to be talking to a geographical homie. Although I was fifteen years older than Whitney, we had both been born in Newark and moved to the suburbs at an early age. Whitney mentioned that she moved when she was four years old, after the Newark riots (July 12–17, 1967) devastated her neighborhood. I followed up by telling her that I'd written my college thesis on the Newark riots, having spent the summer of '67 working as an orderly at Newark Beth Israel Hospital.

"I was *born* at Beth Israel!" she said.

"Me too," I said, although neither one of us could identify our respective delivery doctors, which would have further heightened our stream of connectivity had it been the same guy.

What really sealed what I hoped would become a lifelong friendship was when I asked if she had ever had Gruning's ice cream. I may be exaggerating for effect here, but I seem to recall her levitating.

"Strawberry milk shakes! Oh my God!" She ran outside and called over her brother Michael who was acting as her head of security. Before they showed up at Humphrey's, I had researched the Houston family and discovered that Michael had been a decent high school basketball player. I started talking trash with him, challenged him to some playground one-on-one, and told him I'd have no problem posting him up and shooting fadeaway jumpers over his outstretched arms. He didn't know what to make of me. I'm pretty sure he knew I was kidding.

My interaction with the Houston entourage continued throughout Whitney's two revelatory performances. Gene Harvey grabbed me by the elbow and took me aside as I walked down the aisle during the late show.

"I just wanted to tell you that you couldn't have done better promoting these shows," he said, drenching me with a thick New York accent that always felt strangely comforting when I dealt with East

Coast managers. "Both audiences were entirely mixed ethnically with blacks, whites, Asians, and Hispanics. We're very concerned about reaching more than just an urban audience, and your marketing brought in everyone." He reiterated that they would never work with another promoter in San Diego.

The fact of the matter was that I had reluctantly booked a young, unknown artist, thought I had been squeezed for too much money by her agency, closed my eyes, and put the show on sale. Whitney Houston's subsequent crossover hits were what drew everyone. I had nothing to do with the show's success.

Nevertheless, I basked in the glow of Gene Harvey's accolades, fist-bumped (before it was cool!) with Michael Houston, and said goodnight to an effusively grateful Whitney Houston.

You can guess the ending. I never saw any of them again.

I played the game as good promoters do. I sent flowers to Whitney that hopefully arrived at her next destination. I took my agents out to a lavish dinner at Peppone Ristorante in Brentwood. I sent Humphrey's swag to Gene Harvey to distribute among his crew. I got a Christmas card and an autographed photo from Whitney.

By the time Whitney played her debut concert at Humphrey's, she was *already* too big for our venue. For her return engagement in San Diego less than a year later, she was headed for the 13,000-seat Sports Arena. I called Triad Artists and Gene Harvey and reminded them that I was their San Diego promoter. Triad told me to submit an offer of $75,000, quite a healthy pay hike from the $11,500 I had paid her the first time around. That's showbiz, and I used my newfangled fax machine to transmit the offer.

I was still naïve enough to feel that the date was ours. After all, Whitney's manager had proclaimed that we were their exclusive San Diego promoters and we agreed to her asking price. Done deal, right?

Not when the big guns with national companies start swooping in. Avalon Attractions and Nederlander, who were vying for the LA and Orange County dates with Whitney, tried to wrest San Diego away from us by upping the offer to $90,000. Rock impresario Bill Graham offered multiple dates in six markets including San Diego. My agents, now frothing at the mouth from the seismic activity, called me and said that if we came to the table with $95K plus a back end, they'd stop the bidding and award us the date. They pointed out that I had a history with the act (albeit a brief one) and a vote of confidence from management.

Long story less long: We dropped out of the bidding at $125,000. The show was awarded to Avalon for $135,000. They ultimately came a thousand tickets short of selling out the arena and lost $30,000. This was my first major taste of the industry's bidding-war mentality where the bottom line is superfluous to getting the act at all costs. I was never offered another Whitney Houston date.

I may not have made a lasting love connection with Whitney, but I'll always be able to say that I was her first.

24.

it's a bird, mr. charles

I HAVEN'T KEPT ACCURATE COUNT OF the number of events I produced but it was in the vicinity of two thousand. Twenty-nine of those were Ray Charles concerts, which were attended by about thirty-four thousand people.

The Genius of Soul was a dependable, if erratic, performer. Most nights he was fire, but occasionally he would be more perfunctory. When contracted to do two shows, Ray limited his performances to fifty-five minutes apiece. Not fifty-four or fifty-six—exactly fifty-five. He achieved this timing perfection by putting a talking wristwatch up to his ear several times during the show. When the watch said "fifty minutes," he immediately launched into "What'd I Say," jumped up from his keyboard bench at the fifty-four minute mark, hugged himself, bathed in applause for a minute, and then was led off the stage.

I never got tired of watching Ray Charles perform. He always changed his set lists, the staples being "Georgia on My Mind" (usually his third song), "I Can't Stop Loving You," and a finale of "What'd I Say." "Busted" and "Hit the Road Jack" were given preferential treatment but weren't there every night. My favorite moments were often when he'd dig up B-sides or obscurities like "I Gotta Woman," "Mississippi Mud," or "Come Back Baby." He always got a rise out of the crowd when he covered the Beatles or Hank Williams as well.

Eager to nurture our ongoing professional camaraderie, I made an effort to greet Ray personally whenever he appeared at Humphrey's. The first time I met him was between shows in 1984. "The sound here is wonderful," he said to me. "You know, sound is all I have." Honing my nascent skills as a promoter, I made sure to tell him that I hoped he'd make Humphrey's an annual stop on his in-demand itinerary. He gave me that signature Ray Charles smile and promised he would.

During the first of his two-night/four-show engagement on August 31 and September 1, 1985, an avian phenomenon took place on opening night that could have derailed our budding rapport. Humphrey's had a row of tall, skinny palm trees behind the stage.

An overly protective egret and her growing family nested in one of them. When feeling threatened or simply in a conversational mood, this particular egret—we called her Eleanor—squawked in a volume comparable to a dozen angry crows. It was particularly annoying during solo acoustic guitar concerts by Michael Hedges or Leo Kottke, but the performers adapted to Eleanor with grace and good humor, often working her into the show by making snide remarks at her expense.

Toward the end of a solemn rendering of Ray's 1962 smash hit "You Don't Know Me," Eleanor started "singing along," drowning out the flummoxed star of the show.

Ray signaled for the band to stop the song, turned sideways, and faced the capacity crowd. "You know, I'm getting paid a lot of money to be here and I don't have to put up with this," he said to the audience. "If you didn't come to hear me sing, then you might as well go home."

There was a hush and an audible gasp in the crowd as Ray sat stoically beside his organ, waiting for the rude patrons to shut up or be eighty-sixed. His production director frantically ran onstage and whispered in his ear, "It's a *bird*, Mr. Charles. It's a *bird*."

No longer miffed and visibly amused, Ray Charles grabbed his vocal mic and said, "I think it's time that the Raelettes come out and help this old man finish the show." A rapid-fire medley of "Unchain My Heart," "Let's Go Get Stoned," and "What'd I Say" turned an uncomfortable confrontation into a harmonious denouement.

My relationship with Ray Charles continued to be mutually beneficial for two decades. Declining health forced him to cancel a sold-out show in 2003 when he was deemed too sick to travel. He passed away the following year.

I talked with him for the last time just before he took the stage in 2002. As usual, I asked his tour manager if I could peek into Ray's dressing room to say a quick hello and thank him for returning to Humphrey's. At each introduction, after reminding Ray who I was, he'd add, "This is the place with the bird." Upon hearing that, Ray Charles would throw back his head in laughter. He never forgot Eleanor, the loquacious egret.

Since Humphrey's Concerts was originally an offshoot of a well-respected restaurant of the same name, our event catering elicited minimal complaints over the years. Most musicians and their crews, who ate buffet-style in the green room, were thoroughly satisfied with the cuisine.

For the headliners, who ate in the privacy of their own dressing rooms, we provided more individualized meals. Most of the stars I dealt with had specific dietary requirements. Some were concerned about their health ("boiled, skinless chicken with NO SALT"), many eschewed cow products, and others refused to eat with plastic utensils and put the kibosh on Styrofoam plates. Over the years, the number of vegans increased. Ray Charles was one of the least demanding artists I've ever worked with. In fact, his autocratic manager, Joe Adams, insisted that we not pamper the members of the band and crew by feeding them at all. That saved us hundreds of dollars in catering fees every year.

When Ray performed twice a night (1984–1994), he liked to have his meal waiting for him as soon as he finished his early show. Normally, his own staff took care of his food, but at his final Humphrey's appearance in 2002, he asked us to do it.

I went into his dressing room before the early show, joined by the chef who'd be preparing the meal. I read him the entire Humphrey's menu from soup to desserts. Recommendations included seafood corn chowder, oysters Rockefeller, jumbo shrimp cocktail, mixed green salad with crumbled bleu cheese, steak Diane, macadamia-crusted halibut, trout amandine, Dover sole, strawberry cheesecake, mort au chocolate—a mouthwatering selection.

Ray focused intently on every item and description. He made his decision. "Is there a Denny's nearby?"

"Yes, about a mile away."

"Can someone run down there and get me a chicken fried steak?"

We were glad to oblige. As I exited Ray's room, the tour manager took me aside to apologize for troubling us and needlessly insisted on explaining. "It took us six hours to get here from Phoenix," he said. Normal flight time is slightly more than an hour. "We had a two o'clock flight, but when Ray went through security, they told him to take off his shoes. Ray looked at the guy and said 'I'm Ray Charles.' The guard couldn't have cared less. Ray is a proud man and he wouldn't take off his shoes. The dude wouldn't let us board the plane.

"So we walked to the other end of the airport and bought tickets on another airline. The same thing happened at that checkpoint. They wouldn't let Ray through unless he took off his shoes. He refused. Then Ray told me to charter a private plane. We just got here a half hour ago, so that's why we didn't have time to fix his meal."

It was less than a year since 9/11 and airports were still on high alert, but this was *Ray Charles*! It cost the seventy-one-year old legend $5,000 to keep his shoes on that day but we picked up the tab on the chicken fried steak. When we delivered it to his room, he beamed appreciatively without a trace of the day's agitation on his face.

25.

the domestic goddess

DOING FAVORS FOR AGENTS IS an essential part of a concert promoter's lot in life. If an agent needs to fill in a Monday on one of his artist's tours and that Monday falls in your market, the promoter has no choice but to help the agent out, fully realizing that people don't usually go to concerts on Monday nights unless they *really* want to see the act. Other times you have to book acts that you know won't sell tickets because the same agent sold you two home runs ("I just sold you Crosby, Stills & Nash and Ringo Starr—you *have* to do John Tesh!").

It's also common to be force-fed opening acts that mean nothing in terms of ticket sales, but you still have to put them on the show and pay them $500 because the agent dictates the terms. "We'll come back and play for you when we're big" is the throwaway one-liner that accompanies the gouge. Some of the acts I added to shows that never made it big included Shurman, I'Kona, Anthony Szpak, Girlyman, and Aslyn.

In 1985, I was riding the late-August hot streak that included the three sold-out evenings with Whitney Houston and Ray Charles.

Because Triad Artists booked those shows, when my territorial agent Nanci Stevens called to tell me I'd be paying $1,000 ($333 a night) for an unknown comedian named Roseanne Barr to do fifteen minutes of comedy to warm up the crowd, I accepted it in stride.

"Is she any good?" I asked. When inappropriate or downright awful comics are slapped on shows without much forethought, they often victimize concert audiences. One that I'll never forget involved a "comic" whose entire act was giving a primer on oral sex techniques. Not too serious an offense, except that he was opening for a gospel show by the Reverend Al Green and the crowd consisted of middle-aged churchgoers in their Sunday finest.

"I know nothing about her," Nanci admitted, "other than she'll be on *The Tonight Show* with Johnny Carson next week and we need to surround that with some Southern California shows."

Five days after the historic *Tonight Show* appearance that introduced America to the "domestic goddess," I knocked on the door of her Humphrey's dressing room. I always introduced myself to the opening acts, mostly to make them feel welcome but also to glean some information about them because I was the emcee who brought them onstage.

Before I could open my mouth to tell Roseanne who I was, the five-foot-four housewife and mom greeted me with a shrill, yet friendly, "I know who you are. I used to watch you on TV from my trailer in Denver." My television "career" had lasted all of twelve weeks when I hosted the low-profile rock video/live music show on Denver's public TV station. Roseanne, a huge music fan, had seen every episode. We started talking about Colorado and determined that we had several mutual friends. It was an unexpected and enjoyable getting-to-know-you encounter.

As soon as we dispensed with the pleasantries, Roseanne got down to business. "My manager claims that the reason you're paying me so low is that these shows were already sold out. Is he telling me the truth?"

"Yes," I said. "I didn't budget any money for a support act, and your $333 a night is coming out of our profit." I didn't tell her that I'd never pay more than that for an unknown comic or that other promoters sometimes have opening acts pay them just to get exposure in front of a capacity crowd. I'm glad I bit my tongue.

"So if the shows hadn't been sold out, you would have paid me much more, right?"

What could I say? "No question about it."

"And you promise you'll pay me more the next time?" She was smiling and sort of flirty, but she was dead serious. "I'm developing a TV show and by the time I come back here, I'll be famous."

I'd heard it all before and I would continue to hear it forever. Rarely did such a self-aggrandizing prediction come true.

"I'll definitely pay you more the next time," I said, and it turned out that I wasn't lying.

During her three nights and six shows that week, she absolutely killed in front of both Whitney Houston's and Ray Charles's disparate audiences. Roseanne's working-class brand of humor that elevated the esteem of all housewives (while skewering their husbands) connected with women on a deep, hysterical level. She told her jokes with a winning smile and an infectious cackle that softened the sting of her biting barbs. A huge following was being molded one show at a time.

Despite my enthusiasm for her act, I almost had to fire her. During her opening slot for Ray Charles, she closed her show with an off-color joke that referenced Ronald Reagan farting in bed and pulling the covers over Nancy's head. The audience convulsed with laughter, with one exception. Ray's manager, Joe Adams, came into my dressing room between shows with a wrinkled brow and gave me a stern reprimand.

"Did you hear what the comedian said about our president?" he asked. Without letting him know that it had cracked me up, I admitted that I had. "This is a family show. There are old people who love President Reagan and they were offended. There are children who come to see Mr. Charles who shouldn't be subjected to this kind of humor."

The last thing I needed was to piss off the headliner's manager, so I didn't stick up for Roseanne. "I understand where you're coming from, Joe," I said, scrunching my shoulders. "Look, if you want me to, I can pay her and tell her not to play the second show. I don't want you to be upset because you don't like the opening act."

Adams considered my offer but quickly said that wasn't what he was looking for. "Don't get me wrong. I'll be repeating her entire act with the boys on the bus and I'll be telling all her jokes in the office tomorrow. But we can't have her belittling the president."

Assuring Adams that I'd take care of it, I took Roseanne aside as she noshed in the green room and gave her the feedback from the Ray Charles camp. It was the only time I ever attempted to censor an artist's performance. Years later, Roseanne Barr became notorious for her temper tantrums and on-set tirades, but at this early point in her career, she calmly said, "I'll take that joke out of the show."

Today, whenever there's a *Roseanne* rerun on Nickelodeon or she shows up as a panelist on *Real Time with Bill Maher*, I remind myself that she used to watch *me* on television and that I once had to advise her to tone down her act.

●

Roseanne did return to Humphrey's. She co-headlined (with Louie Anderson) in 1987 and headlined on her Honeymoon Tour in 1991 with her then husband, Tom Arnold, as her opening act. I followed through on the "promise" I made in 1985 and paid her significantly more than $333 a night. Her '91 paycheck was $35,000, a pretty hefty payday at the time.

Although she was a huge TV star, she had alienated San Diegans at a Padres game in August 1990 with her intentionally shrill rendering of the "Star Spangled Banner," which she punctuated by grabbing her crotch and spitting on the grass. Bad press abounded. Paid admission was only 1,707 for her two shows, considerably less than her 1987 gigs. No one heckled her, but her fan base in flag-waving San Diego was evaporating despite her soaring national profile.

Dealing with Roseanne was always a pleasure. The only minor friction occurred when the catering crew delivered a mediocre bottle of champagne to her dressing room when her contract had called for Dom Pérignon. She called me into her room, showed me the cheap champagne, and asked with a slight edge in her voice, "What's this?" Realizing it was one of my boss's ill-conceived cost-cutting strategies, I ran to the restaurant and got her the Dom.

I never saw Roseanne in the flesh again. Her groundbreaking TV show lasted nine seasons and she pretty much put her stand-up career on the back burner. I booked her in 2002 for a concert that was going to be half comedy, half Roseanne with a rock band. Advance sales were abysmal and she eventually canceled her entire tour, which was probably fewer than ten dates.

26.

the fat man's baggage

T HE PHONES HAD BEEN QUIET ALL DAY. It was a Monday evening in late August and we had only eight shows left in the '86 concert season. The year had been stressful, but productive. My main objective had been to keep the company viable financially while veering away from the smooth-jazz emphasis I had inherited when I took over the booking in 1985.

The diversified lineup included appearances by country-rock innovator Emmylou Harris, Canadian political activist Bruce Cockburn, cowpunk rockers Lone Justice, the quirky Leon Redbone, rock 'n' roll originals the Everly Brothers, reggae superstar Jimmy Cliff, psychedelic folkie Donovan sharing a bill with Jesse Colin Young, and an ill-conceived (by me) double bill of the Roches and Roger McGuinn (which would have sold out a theater in Boulder but only generated 536 paid admissions for their two shows at Humphrey's).

I jumped when the phone rang at six.

"Kenny, Jack Green from Willard Alexander. Glad I caught you."

I didn't do much business with Jack, who specialized in selling big bands to ballrooms, cruises, and casinos, but I had aggressively pursued his one rock 'n' roll package that teamed Fats Domino and Jerry Lee Lewis. I was skeptical charging twenty dollars a ticket, a record high at the time, but the two shows sold out weeks in advance.

I was happy to hear his voice. "Three days and counting, Jack," I said, referring to our imminent agent-buyer collaboration. "What can I do for you?"

"Well, don't get worried, but Fats has a sore throat and he's flying in early so he can rest for a few days before the show. In fact, his plane lands in an hour. Can you get a limo to the airport for him and find a first-class hotel?"

Troubleshooting hadn't become my middle name yet. "Oy yoy yoy, Jack," I said. "An hour? My production director is out of town, and I have no clue what limo company we use, and it's August in San Diego—every hotel is sold out."

"C'mon, kiddo, you're a pro. Get him a taxi. Find him a room. Actually he's traveling with his tour manager, so they'll need two rooms. And hire a van to haul his luggage. He doesn't travel light."

"I'll figure something out," I said, glad that Jack couldn't hear my pounding heartbeat.

I quickly called the Seapoint Hotel, one of Richard Bartell's properties, conveniently located about a mile from the airport. That was one of the blessings about working with a hotel company. We had access to seven San Diego locations to accommodate our artists. The Seapoint had a few rooms set aside for emergencies (did they call them emergency rooms?), and I told the GM to hold them for Antoine Domino and his tour manager-valet Rip Rogers. I also arranged for the Seapoint to send a driver with their fifteen-passenger bus to provide transport for two humans and lots of luggage. I called Helen to let her know that we'd be picking up Fats Domino at Lindbergh Field in forty-five minutes.

Fats Domino was one of my childhood heroes. Among the first 45s I bought was "Blueberry Hill" in 1956, and I'm certain that the first LP in my eventually humongous collection was called *Ricky*

Sings Fats, twelve Fats Domino songs performed by Ricky Nelson (although I no longer have the LP and there is absolutely no evidence on any website or reference book that it ever existed).

I owned an arsenal of Fats's 45s, including all the "walking" songs: "I'm Walkin'," "I Want to Walk You Home," and "Walking to New Orleans." Anticipating his upcoming concert, I was hoping he'd resurrect secondary hits like "I'm Gonna Be a Wheel Some Day" and "My Girl Josephine." Helen had her fingers crossed that the Fat Man would pull out "Shu Rah" from his bag of tricks because his pronunciation of the title character sounded like "Shira," the name of our granddaughter.

We parked our Maxima station wagon in the short-term parking lot and went inside the terminal to meet Domino's plane. The airport was surprisingly empty and only a handful of passengers descended the escalator from the inbound flight from New Orleans.

It wasn't hard to recognize Fats Domino. A diminutive five foot four, he must have tipped the scales at 275. Dressed in a green leisure suit and an open-collared matching shirt, it seemed like he was rolling toward baggage claim. Accompanying him was Rip Rogers, who resembled a blonde grizzly bear with long straggly hair and an unkempt beard.

I introduced myself to both the legend and his handler, trying unsuccessfully not to fawn all over Fats. I kept my adulation to 20 percent below the maximum allowable gush level and asked if he needed help with his luggage.

"Lotta baggage," he said in a distinctive N'awlins patois that was both charming and indecipherable. I hailed a porter and asked him to bring a cart to pile Fats's suitcases. One cart wasn't nearly enough.

"Tha one, tha one, tha one," Fats pointed as the matching ensemble revolved around the carousel. In all, he had twenty-one pieces of luggage and, as far as I knew, just two dates on his brief West Coast tour.

Fats handed the porter a crisp hundred-dollar bill and we wheeled the carts to curbside where the Seapoint bus and driver were waiting for the "Domino party." I explained to Fats and Rip that the hotel was about a mile away and the driver would take good care of them. I gave Rip a business card that included my home and office phone numbers and told him to call me anytime during the next few days if Fats needed anything from groceries to medical attention.

"Wheh de cah?" Fats asked. That question and Fats's inflection have been ingrained in my head ever since.

"Excuse me?"

"Wheh de cah?" he asked again, still calm but on the verge of agitation.

"Where's the limo?" Rip Rogers translated.

For the first time, I started stammering, trying to explain my dilemma that their agent had called me less than an hour ago, that my production director was covering a state fair in Idaho, and that it had been too late for me to arrange for proper limousine service.

Rogers took me aside. "Fats Domino doesn't ride in no bus! Do something."

"I'll be back in a minute," I said, leaving Helen in the charming company of Messrs. Domino and Rogers while I raced to the parking lot to get the station wagon. The Maxima was no limo but it was less than five years old, comfortable, and suitably plush except for random fast-food wrappers littering the floor.

I pulled up to the curb and, doing my best chauffeur imitation, jumped out of the car and opened the back doors for Fats and Rip.

"Wheh de cah?" Domino said yet again.

"Would you rather I pay for a taxi?" I asked, realizing that I was in a quagmire without an escape hatch.

"Fuck it. Let's get in," Fats said, his blood clearly beginning to sizzle.

During the four-minute ride to the hotel, Helen told Fats how excited we were to welcome him to San Diego, how we had been listening to his LPs for months leading up to the concert, and how her absolute favorite song was "Shu Rah" because it made her think of our granddaughter.

Helen's ebullience was an effective thaw in this ice block of discomfort, but the Maxima interrupted her monologue. "Fuel level is low," announced a female voice. Ding, ding, ding. "Fuel level is low."

"What's *that*?" asked a startled Rip Rogers.

"Oh, this is a talking car," I said, nerves fraying. "It tells me if my passenger door is ajar."

As if on cue, it talked to us again. "Fuel level is low." Ding, ding, ding. "Fuel level is low."

"Damn, we gwine run outa gas." I didn't need to look in the rearview mirror to see who was talking.

Fortunately we made it to the Seapoint with a half gallon of gas to spare. The fifteen-passenger bus loaded only with Fats's luggage pulled up behind us. I ran inside, got a team of bellmen to assist the Domino party, and filled my tank at the adjacent Chevron station.

On the way home, I made the mistake of exhaling, assuming that my work on this particular project was done. Karen Carpenter's ghost might as well have been perched on my shoulder cooing, "We've only just begun."

When I got to the office Tuesday morning, I had three messages from Jack Green. I learned early on in my tenure as a promoter to face the music and return calls promptly.

"What's up, Jack?" I asked cheerfully.

"It's not good. Fats had a sore throat to begin with and the hotel you put him up in had central air conditioning. He checked out this morning and moved to the Bay Club. Rip will bring the hotel bill to settlement, but I don't even know if there will be a show. If he doesn't feel well, he won't play."

I tried to digest all of this without losing my composure. The Bay Club was three times as expensive as the discounted rate I had negotiated at the Seapoint. Plus, Fats and Rip Rogers were staying there for three nights. There went a good chunk of our profit.

When my mind stopped calculating future balance sheets, I obsessed on the main issue of whether or not Fats would play. It was out of my control, so I decided to focus on details of other upcoming shows to avoid thinking about Fats Domino. I also insisted that Helen stop playing his music repeatedly at home. I wanted this hero of mine to hit the stage on Thursday, play the gig, and go home.

On the afternoon of the show, I went to the soundcheck. Usually those are relaxing, sometimes boring affairs where the band adjusts the volume, gets a proper drum sound, and makes sure that the instruments don't drown out the vocals. On this day, chaos reigned.

It started humorously enough when I literally bumped into Jerry Lee Lewis as I entered the backstage area. I introduced myself as being the promoter of the show.

"Hi there. I'm Jimmy Swaggart," he said with a devilish grin.

"Funny, you don't look anything like your cousin," I shot back, letting him know I was aware of his genealogy. We exchanged pleasantries and he pointed out his seven-year-old son who was chasing ducks down the aisle of the venue, then headed for his hotel room.

As I climbed the stairs to my day-of-show office in room 408, I heard a booming voice with a Southern accent calling my name (and mangling the pronunciation). It was Rip Rogers.

"Listen, we gotta talk," he said. "Fats still feels like shit and he's talking about canceling the show. He hates doing two shows in one night on any night, but he doesn't think he can make it. So this is what I'm telling you to do—do *not* pay us the balance of the guarantee until after he does the two shows. If you pay him now, he may pocket the money and blow off the show."

This was confused logic at its zenith. The protocol for promoter-artist relations, especially a new relationship like this one, is that you pay the artist's agency a 50 percent deposit a month in advance to secure the date and then pay the artist or his tour manager the 50 percent balance before he takes the stage. If the artist cancels for any reason other than a weather-related act of God, the promoter gets his deposit back. So there was no reason at all to withhold Fats's payment. If he was too sick to perform, Rip would return the balance to me, and the agency would refund the deposit via bank wire.

"Okay, you're the boss," I said. "The money's right here. Just come and get me when you want to get paid." I then sat down with Jerry Lee's manager and settled their end of the deal.

I exhaled again, which was another misstep. In fact, I even allowed myself the luxury of sitting in the audience to watch Jerry Lee Lewis open the show. His unique "hunt 'n' peck" piano style, index fingers ablaze, electrified the audience, who rose to their collective feet by the time "Breathless," "Whole Lot of Shakin' Going On," and "Great Balls of Fire" feverishly closed the show.

At the intermission, Helen leaned over and asked, "Do you think Fats will do 'Shu Rah'?"

"I doubt it, but I can go ask him." I went back to the dressing room area and was intercepted once again by Rip Rogers.

"Get me Fats's money. Now!" He was screaming in a manic tone that belied his previously rugged Southern-hospitality demeanor.

"Okay, okay, but I thought you told me not to pay him until the end of the night."

"Now—or he won't play!"

I led Rip back to the dressing room to count out the $6,250 balance due.

"Just out of curiosity, why the sudden change of plan?" A stupid question.

"He knows you already paid Jerry Lee," he said, stuffing the money in his boot before rushing out of the room.

I made my way to the side of the stage where Fats and his thirteen-piece band were waiting to go on. Tapping him on the shoulder, I smiled and asked him, "Can you play 'Shu Rah' for my wife?"

Returning to my seat in time for the opening song, I looked at Helen in disbelief when the first words out of Fats's mouth were "Here comes my baby Shu Rah, how you doin' Shu Rah . . ."

"He's doing it. First song!" Helen beamed.

The only problem was that the band was playing "When the Saints Go Marching In" in another tempo and another key. Fats had called an audible but his players hadn't picked up on it. The result was a distorted cacophony that left both the audience and the band members disoriented. Fortunately, everyone was back on the same page by the second song and the set gained momentum. Fats's voice opened up after some early hoarseness and the show reached its customary crescendo during which he pushed the white grand piano across the stage . . . with his stomach.

We set up the evening's schedule so Fats would close the early show and open the late one. His voice improved dramatically as the night wore on and the second performance outfunked the first. He left the audience screaming for more—the ultimate goal of most rock 'n' rollers.

My personal melodrama with Fats Domino was finally over. He had overcome the lack of airport limo, central air at the Seapoint, a persistent sore throat, and the fuckup during "Shu Rah" to deliver back-to-back knockouts.

At last I could exhale, relax, and have a drink.

Not quite.

Helen, who had left to go home after Fats's second show, came running backstage to get me. "Fats Domino is standing in the parking lot with his garment bag. I think he's waiting for a limo!"

"Holy shit!"

When my production director abandoned me to take a more lucrative gig in Idaho for the week, he didn't leave behind any instructions or game plan for his stagehands. I grabbed Helen's hand for moral support, and we raced to the parking lot, jumped in the Maxima, and pulled up to the box office kiosk where Fats and Rip were standing. I jumped out of the car and reprised my role as chauffeur once again.

"Wheh de cah?" asked Domino as he had at the airport three

interminably long days ago. If I hadn't believed in déjà vu before, I was its strongest proponent now.

What was the sense of even trying to explain? "My production director screwed up," I said. "I'm firing him on Monday."

I opened the back door for Fats. He looked at Rip, his trusty valet, and said "Fuck it, let's walk." The entrance to the Bay Club was no more than fifty yards from where they had been waiting for the great lost limo.

"C'mon, Fats, we ain't walking," Rogers said, ushering his boss into the car.

We drove the endless fifty yards in silence, and as I pulled up to the lobby entrance, I turned around to shake hands with one of my heroes. "Thank you for everything you did tonight. I know that you were under the weather, but you still did two great shows, the crowd loved you, and I appreciate everything you put into this effort. Did you have a good time?"

Fats let my hand dangle. "Everything was okay, but I had problems with the promoter. He's racist." Domino was momentarily unaware of who he was talking to. "Wait a minute . . . aren't you the promoter?"

"Yes. Why do you think I'm racist?" I was sweating bullets now, a fine line arising between fear and anger.

"You paid Jerry Lee and you wouldn't pay me."

"I beg your pardon, but I paid you the minute you asked for your money." I refused to take the fall. I looked at Rip Rogers and then back at Fats. "Your own tour manager told me not to pay you until the shows were over. It was his idea. I always pay acts whenever they want their money."

"That's bullshit," Rogers mumbled, no doubt trying to save his job. In fact, I've often wondered if Fats didn't fire Rip on the spot.

Then, suddenly, Fats zeroed in on Helen. "And you—asking me to do 'Shu Rah.' The band didn't know it and it ruined my music for the rest of the night."

At this point, I just wanted Domino and Rogers to get out of my car *and* my life. "I apologize for the misunderstanding, Mr. Domino. I grew up loving your music, I paid you good money to perform it tonight, and I'm sorry you feel like this. Have a safe trip back to New Orleans."

Fats stepped out of the car, looked menacingly at Helen, and said, "And good night to *you*, Miss Shu Rah."

I left the car in neutral with the gas running for at least five minutes. I was too weak to put my foot on the accelerator and switch the gear into drive. I looked at Helen, who was equally stunned. "What just happened?" I asked, wanting an answer that didn't exist.

Equilibrium slowly returned and we headed home. I squeezed Helen's hand. "If you hadn't been with me, who knows how this would have all played out. No one will ever believe this story."

Because the show had been financially successful and artistically satisfying, I put the past behind me and made an offer for Fats and Jerry Lee to return to Humphrey's in tandem the following year. They accepted my offer and the show went on sale in early April and quickly sold out again.

Ten days before the scheduled appearance, Fats Domino canceled his entire West Coast tour because he didn't want to leave home. Representatives for Jerry Lee Lewis said that their artist would play the date if we gave him all the money earmarked for Fats Domino, essentially doubling his fee. We canceled the show.

27.

pretty woman
running scared in dreams

I GREW UP SAFE AND SEQUESTERED in South Orange, New Jersey. Adventure was taking the #7 bus to Newark to buy a pair of skin-tight casino pants at Cromwell's. If my friends and I really craved rebellion, we'd jump on the #52 to Irvington, transfer to the #107, and get off at Port Authority in New York City, a few blocks from the arcades that lined Times Square. After an hour of Skee-Ball and pinball-machine hopping, we'd walk to the Horn & Hardart Automat and deposit coins for a machine-delivered ham and Swiss on a hard roll.

It was 1961, pre-Beatles and post-Elvis army enlistment. The soundtrack in my head was dominated by Roy Orbison. He was such an enigma with the oversized sunglasses that made everyone wonder if he was blind, a puffy pale face more common among ad execs than rock 'n' roll stars, and a voice more like Ezio Pinza's than Eddie Cochran's.

Listening to Peter Tripp count down the Top 40 on Wednesday nights on WMGM was my weekly ritual and I always hoped that Roy Orbison would scale the charts to number one (which he accomplished twice with "Running Scared" in '61 and "Oh, Pretty Woman" in '64).

Even though the Beatles revered Orbison and opened shows for him in England in 1963, it was the hysteria of the British Invasion that ironically nudged Orbison into relative obscurity in '64. "Oh, Pretty Woman" would be the last hit of his career and he pretty much disappeared from the pop music landscape.

Roy Orbison's music has made a lifelong impression on me. After becoming a concert producer and realizing Orbison was still on the road singing his canon of hits to small audiences in clubs, I made several queries to see if I could get him to come to Humphrey's in 1987.

Nanci Stevens, Roy's agent at Triad Artists, wasn't sure she could secure a West Coast tour. There simply wasn't much interest.

"I might be able to get you a date, hon, but you'll have to pay one-off money," she said. If a tour is "routed," with multiple dates in neighboring markets, the artist's fee is usually more reasonable than a "one-off," which means there are no surrounding dates and the artist has to fly in for a single performance.

I bit the bullet and made an offer of $15,000 for two shows, even though Roy's draw didn't merit that high a guarantee at the time. This was one example of me "booking with my heart, not my head," a criticism often leveled at me by my deep-pocketed boss. In this instance, the stars started to align when Orbison was inducted into the Rock and Roll Hall of Fame in January '87. When my September concert went on sale in April, enough of a Roy Orbison reawakening had occurred in the U.S. that tickets sold briskly from the outset.

When concert day arrived and it was time to send the limo to pick Roy up at his hotel, I had the driver pick me up first so I could tag along for the ride. That was the only time I did that in my career, but this was an icon I wanted to greet. As Roy and his wife, Barbara, approached the limo, I leaped out of the car to open the back door for them. I went to shake Roy's hand and my overzealousness must have alarmed Barbara as she wedged between us and sneered at me.

I explained that I was the promoter of the show and a devoted fan, stopping short of saying that I had been listening to Roy's music ever since discovering him on my transistor radio in 1960. Barbara relaxed a bit, but she remained protective of her shy husband's privacy.

Walking with Roy and Barbara to their dressing room, I told him that both shows were nearly sold out. He nodded and softly said, "Nice little place you got here." Then he disappeared. Helen and I sat in our ninth-row seats and waited for the show to begin.

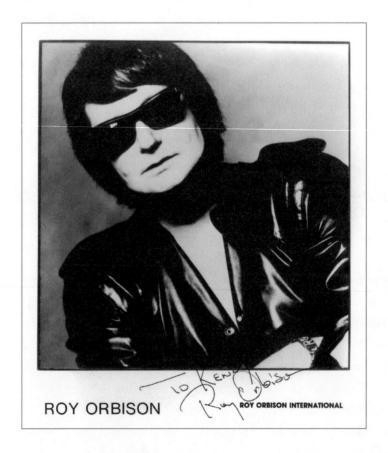

ROY ORBISON   ROY ORBISON INTERNATIONAL

Sans emcee introduction, Roy and his band walked onstage to a spirited ovation and immediately launched into "Dum-dum-dum-dumdy-doo-wah," the opening strains of "Only the Lonely." The live version sounded exactly like the record and I wouldn't have been surprised if it clocked in at the same two minutes and twenty-four seconds. I didn't see how the show could improve on such a chill-inducing beginning, but it did.

By the time he hit the high note in "In Dreams," tears were trickling down my face. I really lost it during "Crying." The growls during "Oh, Pretty Woman" were simultaneously comical and spine tingling. And when Orbison hit that majestic peak at the end of "Running Scared" not once, but twice, he brought the crowd to its feet for the tenth time. That song surely contains one of the greatest cliffhangers in the history of pop music.

At the conclusion of the first performance, I ran backstage to my office and paced the floor, screaming, "Roy Orbison! I just saw Roy Orbison! I brought Roy Orbison to San Diego!" No one was in the room to hear the sounds of my thirty-nine-year-old heart pounding with pride.

When I left Humphrey's after the 2006 season and went through a litany of press interviews, I was always asked, "Out of the 2,000 shows you produced, which one was your favorite?"

Without hesitating, I would answer, "Roy Orbison, September 12, 1987."

I had very few confrontations with customers during my career as a concert producer. I sat anonymously in the audience during the shows I wanted to see and hung out backstage schmoozing with tour managers and crew personnel during the others.

After regaining my composure in the dressing room after Orbison's first show, I ventured out to the box office to see if the second one had "gone clean," promoter jargon for sold out. About a dozen people stood in line and one angry first-show customer was trying to dissuade them from buying tickets.

"What a rip-off," she snarled. "Seventeen fifty a ticket and all he did was forty-five minutes. Don't go—it was a total rip-off."

Normally, I would have kept walking, but not this time. Without identifying myself as the promoter, I approached the potential patrons. "First of all, the show lasted exactly sixty-two minutes. He did seventeen songs and every minute was spectacular. This is a rare opportunity to experience greatness. Roy's voice is as good as it ever was. This may have been the best concert *ever* at Humphrey's, and I've seen a lot of them."

The complainer looked at me with disbelief and stomped away. I went to the cash register, grabbed $17.50, and followed the woman to her car. It was the only time in my career that I gave anyone a refund *after* a transcendent concert and the only time I ever looked at a paying customer, forced a phony smile, and said, "Please don't come back."

28.

extortion
chuck berry style

MUSIC AGENTS TRY TO SELL a promoter anything, whether or not they believe the act can sell tickets. A day didn't go by without sales pitches for Tony Orlando, Ben Vereen, Juice Newton, or David Cassidy. They might be viable headliners for "soft ticket" shows at state fairs, casinos, or corporate events, but even if all four of them appeared on the same bill, they wouldn't sell out an evening at Humphrey's.

During my first three years on the job, my William Morris agent Peter Sheils never tried to sell me Chuck Berry. Whenever I brought up his name and aggressively tried to buy a date, Peter said, "I want us to remain friends. Trust me—you do *not* want to present Chuck Berry." We'd drop the subject and move on to other bookings.

In early '88, the William Morris agents shifted territorial responsibilities, and my account was passed on to Kevin Murray, a former lawyer who later became a California state senator. Very gregarious and eager to please, Murray would try to deliver anything I wanted.

I had a ritual about booking the Humphrey's lineup. The shows took place from April through October. When one concert season ended, I'd take a few weeks off to decompress and then begin a serious round of agency hopping in November, wish lists in one hand, calendar in the other. Sitting across a desk from each agent, one-on-one, we'd peruse their talent rosters, searching for appropriate acts for the following summer.

"How about Chuck Berry?" Murray asked when he got to the *B* page.

"I've wanted to present Chuck Berry," I said, "but Peter Sheils always talked me out of it. He says it's a clusterfuck and not worth the pain and suffering."

"That might have been true in the past but Chuck is behaving himself these days. He's no problem."

That's all I needed to hear. I made a $27,500 offer for Berry to play two shows. The date was confirmed so fast I knew I had done something wrong. It's inbred in a concert promoter to become paranoid when confirmations happen too quickly.

The contract turned out to be a one-pager, not the novella length I had come to expect from superstars. Unlike most artists who try to wangle airfare, hotel rooms, limousine service, Dom Perignon, and sterling silver guitar picks, Chuck Berry had only one major demand: The promoter had to hire a "backup band familiar with Chuck Berry songs." He traveled alone, picked up his own rental car at the airport, and found his way to every gig.

The only snafu in the contract was the line that said that Berry would perform two forty-minute shows. When I struck the deal with Kevin Murray, I made it clear that we needed two sixty-minute shows. After all, it was our highest priced ticket of the year at twenty-two dollars, and the audience would scream bloody murder if Chuck hightailed it out of there after only forty minutes.

"Let me put you in touch with Dick Alen," Murray said, gracefully passing the buck to Berry's longtime responsible agent, a power player in the business who represented everyone from Little Richard and Rod Stewart to Tom Jones and Aretha Franklin.

"No problem," Dick told me. "Just cross out '40' and put in '60.' I'll make sure Chuck's aware of it. He loves to play. You'll have a hard time getting him to stop."

Having gotten his reassurance, I didn't think about the set length again. I hired San Diego's funkiest blues band, the Mighty Penguins, to handle backup chores and an LA-based comedian named Martha Jane to provide fifteen minutes of introductory filler.

Friday, July 29, arrived, both shows were sold out, and I had projected a profit in excess of $13,000 on ticket sales alone. Food and beverage sales were gravy. This was a big winner for a small venue like Humphrey's.

Martha Jane began the 7 p.m. show on the dot, and when she came offstage at 7:15, I still hadn't seen any sign of Chuck Berry. I called Dick Alen at home and got his answering machine. "Dick . . . I know you're probably in Tahoe or Carmel for the weekend, but our show starts in fifteen minutes and Chuck Berry isn't here." I didn't hide my anxiety very well.

Five minutes later, the front desk manager at the Half Moon Inn called me and said, "Mr. Berry is in the hotel lobby and would like to see you."

Relieved beyond measure, I trotted from my backstage office to the lobby, where the tall and lanky Chuck Berry was standing, dressed in an elegant suit, guitar case in hand. I enthusiastically welcomed him, shook hands, and told him that his band was eagerly awaiting his instructions in the dressing room.

"You and I have a *big* problem," he said, still smiling and still pumping my hand.

"What's the problem?" I asked, my heartbeat accelerating.

Berry slowly reached into the inside pocket of his jacket and pulled out our contract. "What does it say at the very bottom of the contract?" he asked, smiling even more broadly.

Reading the very small print aloud, I said, "'Any alterations to this contract shall render it null and void.'"

Without waiting for my reaction, he pointed to the crossed-out "40" I had replaced with "60." "This contract is invalid," he said matter-of-factly, almost like a nonchalant "checkmate."

We walked toward the backstage dressing room and I tried to reason with him. "Dick Alen assured me that you would do two sixty-minute sets. It was Dick Alen, *your* agent, who told me to change the contract."

"Dick Alen never ran this by me. I *never* would have agreed to do two sixty-minute shows. I'm an old man!" Berry, a spry sixty-one at the time, clearly enjoyed messing with my head.

We reached the dressing room and I asked how much extra I'd have to pay him to do two sixties.

"Fifteen," he replied, without hesitation.

"Fifteen hundred?" I asked, ready to bite the bullet.

"Fifteen thousand," he said with a straight face.

"What? I can't do that," I said, throwing my hands up in the air. "Okay, do two forties. Your fans will be disappointed but I'll take the heat. Sorry for the misunderstanding."

Berry's portion of the show was scheduled to start in five minutes, so I quickly introduced him to the band. Affably, he pointed to each musician and correctly identified his respective instrument. "You must be the drummer . . . I'll bet you're the bass player . . . and you're on keyboards." After decades of playing his hits with strangers accompanying him, Berry had developed an uncanny sixth sense.

"What songs are we playing?" asked drummer Paul Kimbarow.

"Chuck Berry songs!"

"Are they in the same keys as on the record?"

"Look, all you have to know is when I lift my foot up, you start, and when I put my foot down, you stop. It's easy."

No rehearsal, no set list, no direction whatsoever.

I interrupted the repartee. "Showtime's in two minutes."

"Let's hit," said the suddenly enthusiastic Berry. He removed his suit coat. Underneath was a multicolored paisley polyester shirt, as loud and lively as his performance was about to be. He led the band to the stage.

Throughout the first show, Berry sang out of tune, played out of tune, and stopped in the middle of a few songs, forgetting his own lyrics. "I'm an old man," he kept reminding the audience. But he could do no wrong. The crowd ate up every minute of his performance—all *sixty-seven* minutes!

Even though I was too stressed out to enjoy the show, my spirits soared when it reached the one-hour mark. Berry's crass efforts at extortion had failed and his threats of doing abbreviated performances had been idle.

Relaxing in my office between shows, I answered a timid knock at the door. A woman in her late thirties with a skyscraper of teased blonde hair introduced herself as Carolyn and said that Chuck wanted to see me in his dressing room, right next to mine. The door was ajar and she led me in.

"Great show!" I said, exaggerating. "And thanks so much for doing an hour."

Berry, clad in his dress pants and a sweat-drenched undershirt, stared at the floor. "I did my part. Now you do yours," he said, avoiding eye contact.

"I told you that you could do forty minutes," I said, once again spiraling down our interpersonal chasm. "You made the right decision and gave your fans the show they came to see."

"Do you *want* a second show?" he said, still gazing at his shoe tops.

"Are you saying there won't *be* a second show?"

"Don't push me."

"Jeez, Chuck, how much do you want?" I asked, my voice rising an octave.

He held up four fingers.

"The show starts in twenty minutes. I'll never be able to come up with four thousand dollars."

"You figure it out," he said, more sullen and ornery than he had been all night.

I knew that Richard Bartell and his wife were having dinner at Humphrey's Restaurant and planned to attend the second performance. I walked briskly to the restaurant and barged in on them between bites of salmon. I gave Richard an abbreviated version of the situation and pointed out the de-escalation of Berry's financial demands.

Unaccustomed to this kind of behavior in his world of business, Bartell was furious. "What a lowlife! I don't want him on my property. Tell him to go home and let's cancel the second show."

Even though I agreed with him in principle, I appealed to Bartell's bottom-line mentality, hoping it would overrule his sense of morality. "Look, Richard, we're making $13,000 at the door, maybe another ten grand in food and beverage profits. If we cancel the show, there will be twelve hundred dissatisfied customers and our profit will be cut in half. Remember, we've paid Chuck in full. He's ready and willing to do the show and it'll be over in an hour."

"What do you think we should do?"

I suggested meeting Berry halfway. There was cash in the safe earmarked for the Ronnie Laws/Kirk Whalum concert on Sunday. We could borrow from that and replace it with cash from weekend restaurant receipts.

Reluctantly, Bartell went along with my plan. He counted out $2,000 in $100 bills, and I jogged back to Berry's dressing room.

The door was locked and no one responded to my frantic pounding. I peeked in the window and saw Berry still in his T-shirt, still staring at the floor.

Carolyn finally answered the door. The audience for the second performance had already sat through Martha Jane's comedic musings and was eager to hear "Maybellene," "Sweet Little Sixteen," and "Johnny B. Goode." They couldn't wait to sing along with "My Ding-a-Ling." The band was in position onstage, waiting for its leader.

"Chuck, this is all I could come up with," I said, handing him the stack of cash.

He counted the loot deliberately, smiling broadly upon reaching the final $100 bill.

"When do we hit?" he asked victoriously.

"Five minutes."

"I'll be there," he said, tossing his undershirt across the room and donning a solid black long-sleeved shirt.

The late show clocked in at a satisfactory sixty-five minutes and Berry was much more proficient and electric. Maybe his $2,000 "bonus" had spurred him on. Maybe the backup band's increased comfort level and confidence added to the improved execution. I certainly enjoyed it more than the early show.

Customarily in the concert business, when one night ends, you immediately forget about it and start preparing for the next. I was organizing my paperwork and getting ready to lock up and go home when Carolyn appeared in the doorway.

"Chuck would like to see you," she said demurely.

Wait a second, I thought to myself. The shows are over. He can't be thinking of hitting me up for more money. What could he want?

I almost didn't follow Carolyn next door to Berry's dressing room. I never wanted to see him again. But my curiosity outweighed my lingering sense of outrage, so I followed her down the hall.

Berry was still in his stage clothes when I entered the room. Wearing the same smile he flashed after counting his extra cash, he asked, "So how did you like it?"

"I would have enjoyed it much more if we hadn't gone through so much hell to get here," I said, trying to be diplomatic for no apparent reason. I had felt like telling him to eat shit and die.

"Listen, we just had bad communication. Next time, make the deal with me directly," he said, handing me a piece of hotel stationery with his home phone number initialed with a capital *C*. "Don't go through the agency."

I wondered if Berry did this dance with every promoter. Here he was, after successfully extorting $2,000, trying to forge a personal relationship with me that would bypass his longtime agent, Dick Alen, and the 10 percent fee he needed to pay William Morris for brokering his deals.

I pocketed the number that I never called, thanked him for two spirited concerts, and turned toward the door.

"Hey, don't go. We just called out for some Chinese food and I ordered enough for three. Why don't you join us for dinner?"

Not that I was craving wonton soup, but I wish I had dined with him to add even more colorful details to this story. Instead, I politely declined his invitation and went home.

The following Monday, I called my friend and fellow promoter Bruce Labadie, who had presented Berry at the Paul Masson Winery in Saratoga two days before my show, to compare notes. His story dwarfed mine. Berry had refused to take the stage unless he was paid an additional $9K. Labadie didn't have a safe with extra cash on the property and he was too freaked out to negotiate. He sent every stagehand and volunteer on his staff out with their ATM cards to get the loot and ended up giving Berry the total sum in twenties. His story had a different ending than mine, however: He went to the press, got front-page publicity, and was reimbursed in full by William Morris. I merely attributed an additional $2K in my concert expense report to "bogus miscellany."

I swore I would never book Chuck Berry again, but we concert promoters tend to have short memories. For the next seven years, I said no thanks whenever my revolving cast of William Morris agents would pitch a Chuck date. One day I bumped into Dick Alen in the William Morris elevator on my way to a meeting to discuss potential 1995 bookings.

"Why don't you make an offer for Chuck?" Alen asked, my 1988 nightmare long since obliterated from his memory banks. "He's doing great business and not pulling any of his crap anymore."

I've always liked Dick Alen, so I caved in and made a $22,500 offer for one show on Monday, June 5. Again, the date was confirmed immediately. Chuck Berry might have still been a decent draw, but he had burned so many bridges that his calendar was somewhat barren.

When I arrived at my office on June 5, I had a frantic message on my voicemail from the general manager of the Half Moon Inn. Apparently, Chuck Berry had shown up at 3:30 a.m. and demanded a free room (which is never part of his deals, because he always handles his own accommodations). Since the overnight front-desk clerk had no prior instructions to give a free room to Chuck Berry, he turned him away. Berry was furious and told the hapless employee that he was canceling his show and going home to St. Louis.

"Here we go again," I thought. I called Dick Alen and, of course, couldn't reach him. I called my territorial agent, Guy Richard, one of the most thorough agents in the history of the concert business, and he assured me he'd find Chuck and work this out. Agents are paid the big bucks to double as fire fighters.

Suddenly it was 7 p.m., ninety minutes away from showtime, and no one had heard from Mr. Berry. The concertgoers filed into the venue and I was upstairs composing a short speech that I would reluctantly deliver at 8:30. "We regret to inform you . . ."

I went to the parking lot to alert the valet crew that we might have a problem and noticed a couple of excited ticket holders milling around a new Cadillac parked in the handicapped zone a few yards from the venue entrance. Chuck Berry was slouched in the driver's seat with a dazed look on his face. Who knows how long he had been there?

He rolled down his window and signed some autographs before security guards realized what was happening, surrounded the car, and shooed the fans away.

"Can we escort you to the dressing room, Mr. Berry?" the head of security asked.

"Leave me alone. I'm in a bad mood," he said.

One of the other security guards approached me to apprise me of the situation, and in a rare case of runaway avoidance, I said, "I want nothing to do with this. It will work itself out."

It did. Chuck motioned to the security chief as the opening band pounded out its final song. The concert came and went without incident, the 1,100 fans gave Berry a standing ovation, and the night was over.

I didn't say a word to Chuck Berry that night. I didn't have Chinese food with him at the end of the show. And I've never seen him again.

29.

static
from the godfather

I WAS WARNED THAT I MIGHT experience mental anguish and heartburn if I booked a James Brown show. Jeff Allen, Brown's agent, used to regale me with stories about how working with his client was both the highlight of his career and a recurring nightmare. Allen said that he had a collection of bizarre faxes from Brown (mostly sent in the middle of the night), some firing him with vitriol and others rehiring him with gushing affection. Allen used to read them over his morning coffee. I'll be first in line at Barnes & Noble if Allen publishes these communiqués. His working title is *Just the Fax*.

Despite Allen's friendly admonitions, I booked the Godfather of Soul for two nights on July 11 and 12, 1994. I had grown up admiring not just his music but his social conscience as well. I remember watching televised reports about how James Brown had performed in Boston and Washington, D.C., on consecutive nights after Martin Luther King was assassinated and how his combination of charisma and finesse had quelled potential riots in both cities. I used to scream along with "Say It Loud—I'm Black and I'm Proud" when it was released in the fall of '68, even though I was a pasty white kid.

Dealing with James Brown's entourage was a logistical and financial challenge. We had to spend $4,000 a night for rental gear, feed
forty people, and provide twenty-two hotel rooms, including a luxury
suite for Mr. Brown. Since Humphrey's operated under the Bartell
Hotels umbrella, setting aside the rooms wasn't the issue. But when
James Brown arrived at the Half Moon Inn and insisted on moving
to the Sheraton, the businessman in me had to get involved. If we
acquiesced to his demand, it would cost us an additional $5,000 a
night assuming he took his band with him (plus limo service back
and forth to the Sheraton). On top of that, the Half Moon Inn
would be left eating twenty-two empty rooms. The rest of the hotel
had been sold out for months.

The tour manager met me at the entrance to the hotel and led me
to Mr. Brown's car. Sitting in the backseat of a Lincoln with James

Brown was pretty surreal. After a cursory exchange of pleasantries, I expressed our concern that the accommodations we offered apparently were unsatisfactory and asked what the problem was.

"Static electricity."

"Excuse me?"

"Static electricity."

I was dumbfounded. I had heard stories of James Brown rambling incoherently to reporters or at arrest scenes, but this was just a two-word answer and I *still* didn't know what the hell he was talking about.

I relied on his tour manager for a translation. He leaned over and whispered, "His hair."

I was still confused but pretended to understand. Then Mr. Brown strung together a few more words. "Static electricity messes with my hair," he said. "Your rooms have carpets."

Suddenly it all made sense. The most immaculately coiffed man in show business had grooming dilemmas caused by uncooperative carpets. He was used to staying at Sheratons because their suites had marble floors. How could I argue with that logic?

Fortunately the rest of the traveling party remained at the Half Moon Inn. We gave the limo driver directions to the Sheraton and a smiling James Brown bade me farewell.

Although James Brown's performance was joyous, it fell far short of impressive. He played solid, full-length renditions of his hits—"Papa's Got a Brand New Bag," "I Got You (I Feel Good)," "Cold Sweat," "Living In America"—but spent an inordinate amount of time with his back to the audience, conducting his mini-orchestra through aimless jazz-funk instrumentals. Too many passages had been included specifically so his troupe of garishly costumed go-go dancers could do their thing. And the then sixty-one-year-old entertainer, no longer quite the hardest-working man in show biz, wasn't spry enough to excite the crowd with his signature splits. His dance moves, which have inspired everyone from Michael Jackson to Prince, were sporadic and limited to brief, economical interludes.

Still, it was a memorable night for me, especially because our son, Paul, was there to see one of his heroes. Twenty-eight at the time, he spent the entire concert dancing wildly on the bayside boardwalk and asked if it would be possible to meet James after the show. I made arrangements, reminding Paul to call him "Mr. Brown."

We were kept waiting for an hour because a pushy and persistent Ike Turner had aggressively worked his way backstage to have a private reunion with his one-time touring pal.

Finally, we were ushered into Brown's dressing room and I re-introduced myself, adding, "This is my son, Paul, who flew in from Colorado just to see your show."

Paul was suitably starstruck and started reciting a tribute he must have been rehearsing for the past hour. "It's such an honor to meet you, Mr. Brown. I can't thank you enough for everything you've done for me, for music, for the world . . ." Suddenly, he abandoned his script. "Oh, the hell with it, James, give me a hug!"

He grabbed James Brown in a bear hug and lifted him slightly off the ground. I was momentarily mortified, but my concerns disappeared when the Godfather looked at me, while reciprocating Paul's embrace, and said in a sincere staccato, "Your son's got soul. Your son's got a *lot* of soul."

I smiled broadly and noticed that the carpeted floors had absolutely no adverse effect on Mr. Brown's perfect hair.

30.

a higher voice

WHEN I DETOURED TO BOULDER, COLORADO, in July 1971, I had no way of knowing that it would become my home for the next twelve and a half years, that I would meet my future bride less than a year after planting myself in town, or that I would forge an enduring friendship with Richie Furay, the lead singer of Buffalo Springfield and Poco.

I was such a fan of Furay's that I would often block out an hour on my radio show to play nothing but songs by his two bands. "Nowadays Clancy Can't Even Sing" would segue into "Kind Woman," and when I ratcheted up the tempo, the country-rock whimsy of "Consequently So Long" would blend right into "C'mon," the live rave-up from Poco's *Deliverin'* LP. Although I never had the opportunity to see Buffalo Springfield perform during their brief two-year career (which was influential enough to garner them a spot in the Rock and Roll Hall of Fame in 1997), I rarely missed a Poco concert if they played anywhere within driving distance of my zip code.

I interviewed Richie on my KRNW morning show in early '74 after he had left Poco to form the Souther Hillman Furay Band, the

David Geffen–fueled project that was supposed to catapult him toward that elusive superstar status. I interspersed Furay songs throughout the interview, featuring his brooding nine-minute orchestral homage to Gram Parsons called "Crazy Eyes" and my Poco fave at the time, "Just for Me and You."

In mid-June, I drove three hours to Aspen to catch SHF's debut performance at a 200-seat club called the Gallery. The place was packed with an A-list of record company execs and agents from the West Coast. I also spotted Glenn Frey from the Eagles.

I was reviewing the show for *Cake Eaters*, Boulder's vibrant arts-and-entertainment monthly. I expected to write a rave review, reintroduce myself to Richie, and conduct a follow-up interview back in Boulder. Instead, I witnessed a band that lacked onstage chemistry and seemed more like three singer-songwriters showcasing their own material backed by indifferent sidemen. It was an anticlimactic performance that failed to live up to the hype.

Feeling uncomfortable about giving SHF's concert a mediocre review, I shied away from calling Richie. Then about four months later, our lives intertwined in one of those serendipitous non-accidents.

I was sitting in the *Cake Eaters* office, editing copy, when my friend John Lee called from Stapleton Airport in Denver. "Can you pick me and a buddy up at the airport?" he asked. "Neither one of us remembered to arrange a ride."

"C'mon, John," I said. "It's snowing, it's freezing, my tires are worn out, and I'm under intense deadline pressure."

"I forgot to mention that my 'buddy' is Richie Furay."

"Be right down," I said, grabbing the keys to my Datsun 510 wagon.

The snow started falling harder on the Boulder/Denver Turnpike and I questioned why I was doing this when it would have been so much easier for them to hail a cab. But the journalist in me viewed it as an opportunity to be in an intimate space with Richie Furay for an hour, even if I was his designated chauffeur.

After stashing the luggage and guitars into the back of the car, we headed for I-36 to Boulder. John said that he had recognized Richie in line at LAX and started singing "Pickin' Up the Pieces" while Richie tried in vain to ignore him. Eventually they struck up a conversation and John offered my services as the driver who would deliver Richie to his doorstep in Sunshine Canyon.

Almost immediately, I started pumping Richie with questions: How were the SHF recording sessions going? What had they chosen for their first single? How was he getting along with Souther and Hillman?

Although forthcoming with his responses, he admitted his mind wasn't on music, but on his marriage. His wife, Nancy, wanted a divorce.

I halted my Q&A from the driver's seat, and Richie explained that his relentless quest for rock 'n' roll stardom and all that went with it had driven a wedge between him and Nancy. The night before he flew back to Colorado, Richie had accepted Jesus Christ as his lord and savior, primarily due to the encouragement of his bandmate Al Perkins. Since Nancy had recently been "born again," Richie hoped that his new commitment might provide the ultimate commonality and heal their marriage.

Despite the snow and dangerously icy road conditions, I began driving faster, trying to get Richie home. I switched the subject, delving into his musical history, but there was no further response. I looked into the rearview mirror and saw him deep in meditation, eyes closed, whispering to himself, praying for a miracle.

John and I dropped him at the bottom of his driveway and unloaded his luggage and gear. He politely refused our offer to help him lug it up to his spacious log cabin. He barely thanked me for the ride, though I could see the gratitude in his eyes.

For many years after the airport pickup, when Richie introduced me to his friends, he would say, "This is the guy who saved my marriage."

My friendship with Richie deepened as the years went by.

After I became the first journalist to chronicle his conversion to Christianity in a 1975 *Creem* magazine profile, we kept in touch professionally and personally throughout my remaining years in Boulder. Whenever Richie released a new solo album, he made sure the record company sent me an advance cassette, and there were occasional lunch dates and visits to his welcoming mountain home.

By the time I moved to San Diego in 1983, Richie had dropped out of the secular music business to become the pastor at Calvary Chapel in Boulder. Pastor Richie and I talked now and then, but it never dawned on me to ask him to play at Humphrey's until 1995 when I booked the Stephen Stills Band and they requested an opening act.

Always a musical alchemist eager to concoct the perfect brew, I called Richie at his office and left a long-winded message on his answering machine inviting him to open the show. Furay hadn't played with Stills since their days together in Buffalo Springfield. When a week passed with no return call, I assumed he wasn't interested. I needed to fill the slot, so I tried for another inspired combination by asking Chris Hillman (Stills's former bandmate in Manassas) to open the show. He quickly accepted my offer and the date was set.

Two days later, Richie called me back. "Listen, I'm sorry I didn't get back to you. I've been going back and forth on this for days and I've decided I'd like to do the date."

I gulped and stumbled over my words. "When I didn't hear from you, I figured you didn't want to do it and gave the gig to Chris Hillman. I can't take it away from him, so I have to call Stills's manager and see if I can make this a three-act bill. Would you open for Stephen and Chris?"

"I'd love to. Can you try to make it happen?"

I immediately called Stephen's manager, Gerry Tolman. I expected him to shoot down my request because adding a third act might cut into his client's set length. But it turned out that Tolman was both a fan and an acquaintance of Richie's so he gave me his enthusiastic okay.

It was a dream come true: I had arranged for three Boulder residents from the early '70s to share the same stage in San Diego in 1995. Furay and Stills had played together in Buffalo Springfield. Stills and Hillman cofounded Manassas. And Furay and Hillman had teamed up in the Souther Hillman Furay Band. The *San Diego Union* did a big feature on the "reunion" and praised my creative approach to concert producing.

The concert came and went way too fast. Chris joined Richie during his half-hour opening set for a spirited version of the Everly Brothers' "Bye Bye Love," comically forgetting a few of the simplistic lyrics. Stephen did a cameo during Chris's set, dueting on a Manassas song called "It Doesn't Matter." Stills called Hillman up during his portion of the show to contribute mandolin and vocals to a few songs, but inexplicably did not invite Furay to join him on the rousing finale of "For What It's Worth."

When he said goodbye to me at the end of the night, Richie masked whatever disappointment he may have felt about being ignored by Stephen. "I had way too much fun," he said, giving me a characteristic bear hug. "I hope you're not getting me into trouble!"

Sure enough, this little taste of playing his music in front of 1,300 people churned up the positive memories of his past life as a traveling musician. In ensuing years, I put together five more Humphrey's shows featuring Richie as a "special guest." He supported Emmylou Harris and America and twice opened for the modern-day version of Poco (with longtime members Rusty Young, Paul Cotton, and George Grantham). After opening the Poco shows, he joined them onstage as a full-fledged band member. I also spliced together another reunion by creating a triple bill of Jim Messina, Richie Furay, and

Chris Hillman, during which Richie joined Jim for acoustic duets of Buffalo Springfield classics.

When Richie let me know he was serious about pursuing more secular concerts to go along with his church performances, I worked with colleagues of mine in Orange County, Santa Barbara, and Saratoga to land him the supporting slot on a series of Linda Ronstadt dates.

In the summer of 2007, Richie Furay embarked on his first national tour in nearly thirty years. The band included his youngest daughter, Jessie, and his assistant pastor, Scott Sellen. Richie's re-emergence and willingness to hit the road led to the long-anticipated Buffalo Springfield reunion with Neil Young and Stephen Stills in 2011. That tour, rumored to be touching down in thirty cities, was limited to two nights each in Oakland, Santa Barbara, and Los Angeles, as well as a prestigious festival date at Bonnaroo in rural Tennessee. Reviews were sensational. Richie and Stephen were gearing up for more when Neil did a 180, dropped the idea, and hit the road with Crazy Horse instead.

Richie's consolation prize was returning to Boulder to conduct his Sunday morning services at Calvary Chapel in Broomfield, much to the delight of his congregation. Recently celebrating their forty-sixth wedding anniversary, he and Nancy revel in the joy of eleven grandchildren. Sometimes I sense he'd rather go trout fishing than deal with the rigors of touring, but when he reaches those plaintive high notes in "Kind Woman," you know that he was born to sing.

31.

lady soul
at the hotel del

"Yes, of course we have the cash," Mitzi said, "but there's no way Kenny's going to drive a half hour to settle this show at one in the afternoon on a concert day. He'll pay Ms. Franklin tonight before she goes onstage."

Mitzi Stone was my assistant at Humphrey's Concerts for nineteen years, and part of her unwritten job description was to protect me from vultures and other dubious intruders who gobbled up my time. She screened a hundred calls a day for me and knew exactly who to put through. I never would have lasted as long as I did in this business without her.

Still, I'm glad I overheard her trying to lighten my workload on September 14, 2005. I walked into Mitzi's portion of our two-room office and whispered to her to put the caller on hold.

"Who's that and what's up?" I asked.

"It's Tanya," she said, referring to Dick Alen's assistant. Alen was Aretha Franklin's agent. "She expects you to go down to the Hotel del Coronado and pay Aretha this afternoon. I told her that that wasn't going to happen."

"Are you kidding? How many chances do you get in life to go into Aretha Franklin's hotel room and watch her count $50,000 in $100 bills? Not only am I doing it, but I'm taking you with me." I picked up the phone and got the details from Tanya.

It was arguably the major coup of my career as a concert producer to land an Aretha Franklin date at Humphrey's. She was on my wish list every season, but so much was working against us logistically that the odds of my bringing that fantasy to fruition was the equivalent of a sixty-to-one long shot with a burr in its hoof winning the Preakness.

For one thing, there was Humphrey's limited capacity. I had seen Aretha perform for 10,000 people in Chicago the day after my nephew Ted's bar mitzvah the previous summer. But the major obstacle in getting Aretha Franklin *anywhere* on the West Coast was her aversion to flying. She had canceled several engagements at LA's Greek Theatre in recent years because she refused to fly. She hadn't appeared in San Diego for more than thirty years—and that was a brief set in an R&B revue at a 50,000-seat stadium.

Nevertheless, all concert promoters shoot for the moon regardless of the unlikelihood of getting a confirmation. An agent's job is to take offers. While I've wasted a fair amount of time—my own and various agents'—by making futile offers for Springsteen, Dylan, Joni Mitchell, and Van Morrison, you never know when an artist might opt for a change of scenery and play a small outdoor theater in San Diego.

So when Guy Richard, my supportive William Morris agent, called and asked if I wanted to make an offer for Aretha, I tried to wrap up the deal immediately. "Just tell me how much she needs and I'll tell you what the ticket price will be," I said. Usually, promoter/ agent negotiations are extended back-and-forths with lots of cat-and-mouse maneuvers, wiggle room, and gamesmanship. Not this time.

"I think 150K would get it done."

Up until that point, the most we had paid an artist was $110,000 for a Tony Bennett date in 2003. Not wanting to cross the three-figure threshold, we had priced those tickets at $98. If I agreed to Guy's asking price, a ticket to see Aretha at Humphrey's would cost $140 (plus Ticketmaster fees).

I faxed the offer a few minutes later and the date was confirmed the following week. Our anxieties regarding the enormous guarantee and bloated ticket price proved to be unfounded—the show sold out within thirty-six hours (not a record-breaking pace, but quickly enough).

Mitzi and I drove to the Hotel del Coronado, the jewel of San Diego hotel properties, located across the bay on Coronado Island. When "the Del" opened in 1888, it was the largest resort hotel in the world and the first to use electric lighting. Over the years, regular guests have included Rudolph Valentino, Charlie Chaplin, Babe Ruth, FDR, JFK, and Bill Clinton. It was prominently featured in Billy Wilder's classic *Some Like It Hot* in 1959.

Following Tanya's instructions, we were to meet Scotty, Aretha's head of security, in the lobby and he would escort us to Ms. Franklin. Mitzi called him on his cell as we pulled into self-parking.

Inside the hotel, we spotted only one six-foot-five, three-hundred-pound man, so we quickly gravitated toward him. Clad in a loose-fitting jogging suit and white socks (no shoes), Scotty greeted us warmly and we rode the elevator to the third floor. He told us why Aretha never stays above the third floor in any hotel, but my anticipation of meeting the Queen of Soul was so overwhelming that I couldn't concentrate on his explanation.

Exiting the elevator, we were greeted by Big Mike, who might have been Scotty's cousin. Similar size, identical outfit, also sporting white socks. Another friendly hello before he knocked on room 308. A third bodyguard, Tony, opened his door and joined us in the hallway. The guys had apparently split a three-pack of white socks. Suddenly, Mitzi and I were surrounded by nineteen feet and nine hundred pounds of jocular brute force, an amiable Detroit power trio.

Tony knocked gently on the door directly across from his. It opened ever so slightly. "The promoter's here," he said. Aretha Franklin invited us in.

Dressed casually in stretch pants, a cotton shirt (shockingly braless), and a short brunette wig, Ms. Franklin avoided eye contact while graciously ushering us in. She had been staying at the Hotel Del for the past few days and her room looked like it had been tousled by a small cyclone. Room service trays and empty cereal boxes were scattered randomly all over the floor and on every countertop. Three days' worth of assorted newspapers obscured the carpeting. Fake eyelashes dotted her unmade bed. Despite the warm mid-September temperature outside, the air conditioner was off and the windows were closed.

I claimed the only chair in the room, while Aretha held court from her king-size bed, at the edge of which Mitzi was granted permission to sit (Mitzi spent the next month telling anyone who'd listen that she "was in bed with Aretha Franklin!"). I made some small talk about her gutsy performance as a last-minute substitute for an ailing Pavarotti at the 1998 Grammys. It didn't register at all with Aretha, who was singularly focused on getting paid.

As I handed her the thick manila envelope containing $50,000, I thanked her for making a rare trip to San Diego and choosing our venue. I reminded her that a $75,000 deposit had already been sent to the William Morris Agency and another cashier's check for $25K would be overnighted to the agency in the morning. She nodded knowingly.

Without saying a word, Aretha deliberately counted her lucre. Eschewing a recount, she acknowledged that it was all there and thanked us. A satisfied expression replaced her previous veneer of trepidation and indifference. I took advantage of her softening and asked if I could glance at the set list that I noticed on her bed.

"Sure," she said, not looking entirely comfortable with my nosiness, but I was the guy who had just handed her $50,000.

The set list was amazing: "Respect," "Natural Woman," "Chain of Fools," "Baby I Love You," "I Never Loved a Man," "Think," "Since You've Been Gone," "Rock Steady," "Bridge over Troubled Water," "Spanish Harlem," "Freeway of Love"—nearly her entire arsenal of hit singles.

"I was excited before, but after seeing this set list, I'm bouncing off the wall," I said. "I think you'll really love our place."

For the first time in our half hour together, Aretha engaged me in spirited conversation. "I love your gift shop. The cheesecake is out of this world—absolutely to die for. And the ice cream is excellent too." She thought that the Hotel del Coronado was "our place." I didn't correct her.

Aretha walked us to the door and peeked out tentatively. She motioned to one of her white-socked teddy bears, still stationed in the hallway, and said, "It's okay," meaning that we were free to leave. Business had been transacted to Lady Soul's satisfaction.

Aretha Franklin's performance that night deviated completely from the set list I had seen that afternoon. While she could have filled her hundred-minute performance with hit after hit, she oddly changed directions after starting like a house on fire with "Respect" and "Natural Woman." She mixed in gospel, show tunes, scat singing, a touch of opera, an overwrought rendition of "The Greatest Love of All" (who needed that?), and a great-on-paper, but woefully unrehearsed duet with San Diego–based saxophonist James Moody on the old standard "Moody's Mood for Love." I've never been one to insist on a hits-only performance from any artist, but Aretha's ill-conceived choice of material that night left the audience feeling deflated, especially after the combustible opening ten minutes of the show.

Backstage, Aretha politely posed for photos with me, Mitzi, and Mitzi's teenage son. I can count on one hand the number of times I've asserted myself to get a photo op with a star, but I wasn't going to let Aretha escape without subjecting her to a few quick snapshots. Disappointingly, she had changed from her gorgeous sequined gown into a casual sweat suit (her new wig was also less spectacular), but whenever I'm plagued with self-loathing about having spent so long as a concert producer, I pull out the picture of me with my arm around Aretha Franklin.

32.

diva demands

I LOVE STRONG, INDEPENDENT WOMEN. I've been married more than forty years to one of the pioneers of the feminist art movement. Helen has devoted her life to inspiring women of all ages to pursue creative endeavors. If you placed Frieda Kahlo, Germaine Greer, and Isadora Duncan into a blender and hit "puree," you'd concoct a Helen Redman smoothie.

Musically speaking, I'm similarly drawn to edgy, provocative women. I'll take Joni Mitchell over Celine Dion, Etta James over Whitney Houston, and Fiona Apple over Enya. My radio playlists were always pretty evenly split between men and women. I tended to showcase thoughtful singer-songwriters who hadn't broken through to the mainstream, like Sandy Denny, Catie Curtis, Eliza Gilkyson, Regina Spektor, and Nanci Griffith, mixing them up with soulful vocalists like Bettye LaVette, Eva Cassidy, Lila Downs, and Nina Simone.

As a concert producer, I was flummoxed and disturbed that I had some of my most difficult encounters with the very women whose music and mentality I've long supported. While my experiences didn't alter my feminist leanings, they were discouraging reminders that divas would always roam the earth.

NATALIE COLE

I booked a Natalie Cole concert in 1986 after she had bounced back from her first career descent. Five years of inactivity caused by drug addiction scared promoters away and her calendar was nearly empty. I was skeptical as well but accepted a sweetheart deal from an agent I respected.

We did mediocre business, selling a scant 985 tickets for her two-show appearance, but her strong vocals, clear eyes, and outgoing personality impressed me. I had briefly introduced myself to her before her afternoon soundcheck and was pleased when she addressed me by name after the show and asked if I enjoyed her performance. It was heartening to see her making significant strides toward a full-fledged comeback.

I invited Natalie back in 1988 and attendance increased by 50 percent. Again, she was charming and in great spirits, buoyed by her huge hit with Bruce Springsteen's "Pink Cadillac." I told her I hoped she'd make Humphrey's an annual stop on her itinerary and she assured me she would.

So I was mildly surprised when the statuesque diva brusquely walked by me on the way to her dressing room on September 7, 1989, without stopping to say hello. I asked her longtime manager, Dan Cleary, if anything was wrong, and he shrugged and said, "We all have good days and bad days." I went about my business.

The first show was excruciatingly loud, so bass heavy that the customers in the first five rows sought refuge in the rear of the venue. Dozens of people approached me and asked if there was anything I could do about lowering the sound level. The last person a sound-man wants to talk to is the concert promoter, but I tried anyway. I was told that Natalie *needed* to play at this volume.

Between shows, I cornered Cleary in the catering room. Managers are skittish about jeopardizing their 15 percent by upsetting their meal ticket for any reason, but he said he'd talk to Natalie before the second show. I explained that not only had we received numerous complaints from concertgoers, but we had also far exceeded legal noise-abatement restrictions.

I returned to my office, adjacent to Natalie's dressing room. The rooms at the Half Moon Inn are soundproof, but I heard high-pitched screaming through the walls. Then I heard something crash and found out later that room 407 needed a new lamp.

The second show came and went. The volume issues were not rectified. Dan Cleary offered a sincere yet cursory apology, and I thanked him for trying.

The irony is that two years later, Natalie underwent a profound image change that took her career to new heights. She did that gimmicky hologram "duet" of "Unforgettable" with her late father Nat King Cole. Their images and vocals were spliced onto a CD and video that made it appear that they were singing onstage together. She won Grammys for Record and Song of the Year.

In one fell swoop, Natalie Cole went from rock chick in tight leather pants to sophisticated torch singer in sequined gowns. Her backbeat changed from an electric Fender bass with the amp turned up to ten to an acoustic stand-up bass muted ever so delicately. Distorted, ear-shredding sound would never be an issue at Humphrey's for Natalie Cole again.

But there never was an "again" for Natalie Cole at Humphrey's. I made her offers on an annual basis for the next ten years. She declined every time. I finally stopped trying, her agent admitting to me that she had an elephant's memory and never forgave us for asking her to turn it down.

PATTI LABELLE

When the curtain was about to fall on my on-the-job training season on October 24, 1984, I glanced at the calendar of Post-it notes on the wall behind my desk and stared at the name I had looked forward to all year: Patti LaBelle. Ever since seeing LaBelle collaborate with Laura Nyro in 1974, a concert that brought me to tears, I had hoped to cross paths with her again. I never guessed I'd be presenting her in concert.

By the end of that first season, I was so mentally and physically drained and my social skills so eroded that I decided to lay low the night of Patti's performance. I made no effort to welcome her to the venue and isolated myself in my office until showtime. The performance was spectacular on every level and hit its peak during the final encore when Patti belted out her signature version of "Somewhere Over the Rainbow."

She left the stage with the band still playing and continued singing into a wireless mic up the flight of stairs that led to her dressing room. The band finished vamping and left the stage, the houselights went on, and Patti was *still* singing a cappella behind closed doors as the deliriously happy crowd headed toward the parking lot.

Those ten minutes of joy reminded me that what I was doing was meaningful and that I should produce concerts again the following year. It was a microcosm of my lifelong passion for music. I promised myself to thank Patti LaBelle in the flesh if I was ever lucky enough to be her presenter again.

Six years later, I had that opportunity when Patti LaBelle returned to Humphrey's in July 1990. My sister, brother-in-law, and nephew were visiting from New York City; my stepdaughter and five-year-old granddaughter were also in tow. Prince's ex-drummer Sheila E. was in the audience and Patti called her up onstage to do a five-minute drum solo. It was one of those rare goose-bump evenings.

After watching the first riveting performance, my family and I headed to my backstage office to stretch out and have some wine, cheese, and spicy chicken wings. When we got to the steps leading up to the second-story suite, Patti's tour manager blocked our path. "You can't go up there," he said. His thick British accent was the red flag. It's unfair to pigeonhole anyone by race, religion, or country of origin, but British tour managers (with a few wonderful exceptions) were *always* the most anally compulsive, overprotective, paranoid, nitpicking, ballbusting jerkoffs a U.S. promoter had to contend with. Most of them were named Ian, Graham, Simon, or Clive. I think Patti's guy was a Nigel.

"Excuse me?" I asked politely. "That's my office. I'm the promoter and this is my family."

"I don't care who you are. You would have to walk past Patti's dressing room on the way and she'll throw a fit," he said in a whiny voice.

"Hey, we'll tiptoe. We're hanging out between shows and I have to prepare your settlement paperwork."

"If Patti sees you or *anyone* go by her window, she'll throw a fit and she may not play the second show. You've got to believe me."

"Her door is closed, the blinds are drawn, the walls are sound-proof, and I need to go to my office." My voice was getting testier and if I wasn't ruby red, I was at least pink in the face.

Nigel didn't stand down and continued to forcibly block my path. My family observed all this with bemused disbelief. Five-year-old Shira, who had grown accustomed to being the center of atten-tion with every artist who played Humphrey's, tugged at my sleeve, wondering when she was going to meet Patti.

"Trust me, you *don't* want to do this. I've been with Patti for six years. I know her every mood, and you better not go up there."

This was a first. A tour manager forbidding me from going to my own room and threatening cancellation of the show if I didn't abide by his rules. Of course, I had no way of knowing if he was ac-tually speaking for Patti or fabricating the whole thing to justify his lot in life. It was one more lesson I learned about swimming with the tides in this business.

I led my family into the green room as the crew prepared the stage for the second show. Patti was absolutely transcendent again and I marveled at her ability to do back-to-back ninety-minute shows with such fervor and dexterous vocal acrobatics.

I never did get the opportunity to tell Patti LaBelle that her ten-minute encore in 1984 cemented my career as a concert producer.

DIONNE WARWICK

"Anyone Who Had a Heart" would just "Walk on By" as opposed to treating people the way Dionne Warwick abused my crew during her two-night stand at Humphrey's in September 1991.

I sensed it was going to be a rough couple of days when I received her contract rider. I laughed aloud when I saw the demand that we provide a full-size Ms. PAC-MAN video game in her dressing room. I stopped laughing when her agent told me, "Sorry, this is a deal breaker. If Ms. PAC-MAN isn't waiting for her, it's a breach of contract and she'll cancel the show." We had to search arcades all over town for the outdated game, but we eventually found one to rent for $150 a night plus cartage and delivery.

When Ms. Warwick arrived at the venue, I went to greet her in her hotel room. We shared a geographical history—both of us lived in South Orange, New Jersey, during the '60s—and my mother was very close with Val Sommer, one of Dionne's best friends in our lily-white suburb. I had gone to summer camp with Val's two sons, of whom Dionne had been very fond. The name-dropping and South Orange references were icebreakers as the chain-smoking Warwick coolly acknowledged our six degrees of separation. Unfortunately, that didn't protect my crew from her wrath during her two-night engagement.

Minutes into her soundcheck, she dressed down my stage manager because of the specks of dust on the grand piano. That night, when the spotlight operator flubbed a cue, she stopped the song and berated him on mic for his lack of professionalism. When he blinked the spotlight on and off in playful admission of his faux pas, she said, "That's not funny!" She also had a few tiffs with our monitor mixer, who never seemed to satisfy her needs. And she expressed occasional dissatisfaction with the fourteen-piece string section we had hired for her.

What Dionne Warwick didn't realize or care about was that her verbal diatribes disrupted the pacing of her show and made her audience visibly uncomfortable. It didn't matter that her angelic voice nailed such timeless classics as "Do You Know the Way to San Jose," "You'll Never Get to Heaven," and "Don't Make Me Over." Her rants ruined her performance, and despite the fact that we made a healthy profit, I never invited her back.

We checked the usage meter of Ms. PAC-MAN before returning it to the vendor. Dionne Warwick never even turned on the machine.

ANITA BAKER

Anita Baker falls squarely into the "be careful what you wish for" category.

I'd been trying to book her ever since "Sweet Love" soothed my world in 1986. It was a career-defining track for Ms. Baker and immediately vaulted her into too-big-for-Humphrey's status. By the time "Giving You the Best That I've Got" became a number three pop hit in 1988, I didn't even bother making the annual call to her agent.

The laws of gravity apply to music careers as well, and Anita eventually stopped churning out hits and filling arenas. Rather than play "little places" like Humphrey's, she retreated from the spotlight and devoted most of her time to raising a family. I was as surprised as anyone when she announced she had a new record deal with Blue Note and was looking for some off-the-radar gigs to try out the fresh material. I threw my hat in the ring and got her for the bargain basement price of $180,000 for two nights (August 4 and 5, 2003). The $85 ticket price was a record high at the time for a Humphrey's show.

Mitzi and I celebrated this major coup over crab sandwiches and Arnold Palmers at Point Loma Seafood. Anita's prolonged absence from the concert stage was a concern, as was the relatively lofty ticket price (this was a few years before Rolling Stones tickets maxed out at $450, and three-figure tickets became the norm). Our giddiness lasted until Anita's thirty-two-page concert rider arrived via FedEx the next morning.

Artists accustomed to playing arenas and large amphitheaters usually ask for the moon in addition to their exorbitant paychecks. Requirements from most of the Humphrey's acts were more modest and only occasionally elicited groans. Anita Baker sent us her arena rider, the one that screamed, "Don't you know who I am?"

The most egregious demand was for a barrage of stage lighting that could have caused rolling blackouts in three states. I pondered such ephemeral questions as why would a balladeer insist on dozens of moving lights when she stood still on the same mark throughout her concert? Overkill, but wait, we were just getting started.

Anita insisted on white Marley-covered flooring, usually used by dance troupes in proscenium theaters. We had a black-carpeted stage that met the approval of 99 percent of the acts we booked. Anita Baker was the 1 percent. It didn't matter that our seating wasn't pitched and that *no one* in the audience could see the floor of the stage—it was white Marley flooring or the show wouldn't happen. Oh, don't forget the white cyc backdrop and the front curtains, neither of which was part of our informal outdoor-stage setup.

When I calculated the additional costs of obscure sound equipment we'd have to import from LA or Vegas, limo service multiple times a day (separate trips for her and her husband) to and from Anita's hotel in La Jolla, a seamstress, a hairdresser, and two dozen dethorned roses a day, the total came to about $20,000.

After filling six pages of a yellow legal pad with hand-scrawled notes, I called Anita's agent, an old-school Jerseyite named Paul La-Monica. He had one of those thick East Coast accents and tough-as-nails demeanors that originally made me envision him as being obese, balding, cigar chomping, and weapon toting. Upon meeting him, I was shocked to see a slight, handsome blond man at least twenty years younger than I'd imagined. We had become allies in our brutal business of choice, so I didn't expect resistance when I tried to modify Anita's laundry list.

"Kenny, there's nothing I can help you with on this," LaMonica said. "The girl's a superstar and she expects this kind of treatment."

"Don't get me wrong. I'm thrilled that you confirmed these dates and I owe you one—but she's basically asking us to build a theater for her two nights here. You've seen Humphrey's. We're cute—we're not Radio City. Hundreds of major stars have been more than satisfied with our sound, lights, and production values. *No* one has asked for this much in my entire career."

We went back and forth for fifteen minutes, and I got zero concessions. Then I called Richard Bartell and let him know we would have to sell 2,500 tickets to break even. Our profit at sellout would be about $6,000, absurdly low for a high-risk $200,000 investment.

But Richard loved rolling the big dice, especially if it meant landing a one-time arena headliner for our series. "Give her everything she wants," he said.

Laying out all the pros and cons (in this case, the cons won handily in my opinion) and still getting a "do it" from the money-man made my life easier. But it didn't make things easier for my crew. As the show drew nearer, the phone calls to Mitzi and Tim, our production director, increased exponentially each day. It was as if we didn't have another seventy-five shows on our schedule. It was all Anita, all the time.

I started calling other promoters to ask about their experiences, hoping that her bad reputation was fabrication and hyperbole. But, as was the case with my Chuck Berry investigation, I got an earful of horror stories. Her employees, ranging from runners to agents, lived in fear of her wrath. She was known to fire soundmen during performances. At one point in her career, it was rumored that she had a stipulation in her contract rider forbidding any venue employee from making eye contact with her.

I kept reminding my staff of the concert biz credo: book a show, present a show, go to sleep, wake up, repeat. Anita Baker would be in the rearview mirror soon enough.

So it was miraculous (as well as another life lesson) that when Anita arrived for her afternoon soundcheck, she introduced herself to every stagehand, usher, and caterer with a warm smile and a handshake. "Hi, I'm Anita!" She made a point of thanking the chef for her specially prepared dinner. She didn't rail at me for the horrible folding chairs that had become the bane of my existence and source of way too much negative commentary. In fact, she asked me, "Is there anything I can do to make the next two days easier?"

While I ended up enjoying Anita's shows, I had to laugh at the piss-poor quality of the sound we had spent $7,500 to enhance. It was far inferior to the usual pristine quality that emanated from our front-of-house speakers. The audience was "Caught Up in the Rapture" throughout the evening and went wild when Anita singled out some of the crowd who had driven long distances to see her comeback performances. "I'm sooo nervous tonight because I have some friends who came down here to see what I could do," she said. "Please welcome . . . Miss Dionne Warwick. Please stand up, Dionne." Deafening roar. "Oh . . . and look who's sitting next to her . . . please take a bow . . . Miss Gladys Knight!" It was somewhat anticlimactic when she introduced Shawn Stockman from Boyz II Men, who had bought front-row seats from a scalper for both nights. "I've never met Shawn before, but I'm hoping that we become very good friends."

Anita performed two encores at the end of both concerts and continued to endear herself to our staff with her innocence and friendliness. As she descended the stairs after her first encore, with the crowd in a frenzy, she spotted Mitzi sipping wine.

"Mitzi! Mitzi! Is it okay if I do one more?"

It was always such a relief when a concert ended, the crowd filed out, and no one had died. On my short drive home, I had six minutes of silent reflection about the path from pursuit to performance, knowing that I had been largely responsible for making an event happen. It was especially satisfying that we emerged unscathed after dreading our two nights with Anita Baker. We had sold 2,524 tickets and made a few thousand dollars in spite of the never-ending cost escalations. I slept soundly after night two.

When I got to the office the next morning to prepare for that evening's easy-as-pie show with Herman's Hermits (starring the effusive Peter Noone) and Lou Christie ("Lightnin' Strikes"), I played back several frantic voicemails from the general manager of the Half Moon Inn.

Anita Baker had arranged a celebration, at her expense, for her crew and entourage because the Humphrey's shows were the final nights of her mini-tour. The backstage staff had set up the "green room" with hot trays of food, silver service, kegs of beer, magnums of wine and champagne—the works. When Anita heard about the party's location, she protested that it was the same room the crew had eaten dinner in. She wanted to entertain in an executive hotel suite. Reluctantly, our staff gathered everything onto rolling carts and moved the festivities, momentarily forgetting that the hotel was nearly sold out and the party was being moved from a backstage area where noise wasn't as much of an issue into a populated part of the property amid hundreds of sleeping patrons.

The celebrating went on until 4 a.m. Security had to knock on the door several times to remind the revelers that they were disturbing the other guests. The requests for silence were ignored. Dozens of people checked out of the hotel in a foul mood, venting angrily at the front desk clerks. After all their rooms were comped, the meager profit we'd made on our Anita Baker experience evaporated.

GALLAGHER

Not all divas are women.

The prize for the biggest asshole I've ever dealt with goes to Gallagher, the prop comic who made a career out of pounding produce with a sledgehammer. Regrettably, Gallagher pounded on people as well.

I realized early on in my dealings with Gallagher that he was a classic diva. As soon as he walked into the venue, he launched into a tirade about our chintzy plastic chairs, asking me, "How can you charge so much money for a ticket and make people sit in such uncomfortable seats?" I extended my hand and said, "Nice meeting you too." Since he knew I was the promoter who was paying him, I got off easy.

To call Gallagher's audience a cult following would be underestimating his appeal. We sold all four thousand tickets for his two-night engagement October 6 and 7, 1988. For a good long run, he was huge on the comedy circuit, brandishing a blue-collar appeal that would be inherited in ensuing years by Jeff Foxworthy and Larry the Cable Guy. Since his audience knew they would be assaulted with watermelon seeds, mustard, and chocolate milk, they came prepared. Most people in the first ten rows wore raincoats and the few who didn't were provided with plastic sheeting.

The show began with Gallagher rolling himself onto the stage as a human spoke in an enormous wheel. He was primarily an observational comic, an equal opportunity insulter who put down consumers, pop culture, and politicians with nonpartisan aplomb. But he saved his signature routine for the final fifteen minutes when he unleashed the "Sledge-O-Matic." His fans roared and cowered in approval as he smashed huge containers of cottage cheese, piles of Big Macs, and giant vats of ketchup. Pummeling watermelons was his denouement.

Since we had two shows a night and needed to turn the house, the cleanup in between had to be rapid and meticulous. Gallagher barked out orders from backstage, not just at our stagehands but also at his elderly parents, who traveled with him and were assigned to the janitorial brigade. I wouldn't believe that anyone could treat his parents with such disdain if I hadn't witnessed it. Gallagher's mom and dad literally swept and vacuumed the stage, getting down on their knees to scrape caked-in refuse off the carpet. They seemed utterly intimidated by their son, afraid that they might lose their jobs if they didn't toe the line.

I watched this same spectacle take place after all four shows and felt relieved that I would never have to deal with Gallagher again. I settled the show with his amiable manager, former surfing phenom Gary Propper, and tried finding out more about this raging comedian. Propper, who would go on to produce the *Teenage Mutant Ninja Turtles* movies (which enabled him to get out of the Gallagher business), was as laid back as Gallagher was hostile. He avoided my questions, winked at me, and pocketed his check.

Walking through the venue at the end of the endless night, I saw Gallagher riding an oversized unicycle back and forth across the concert area. It was past midnight, hotel guests were sleeping, and Gallagher was working up a sweat while digging up huge chunks of sod in the process. He later claimed he'd been rehearsing for a commercial shoot at Mission Beach the following afternoon.

The Humphrey's bar manager, an attractive woman named Paula (who happened to be eight months pregnant), gingerly approached Gallagher and impeded his cycling progress. She politely reminded him that he was waking up the hotel's affluent clientele and pointed at the turf he had uncarthed. Instead of acquiescing to Paula's requests that he stop pedaling and call it a night, Gallagher dismounted from his bike and stood nose-to-nose with her while unleashing expletive-laced insults that made his comedy routine seem tame by comparison. Sadly, I didn't have a tape recorder running, but the gist of Gallagher's rant recounted how much money Humphrey's had just made presenting him in concert and that he could do whatever he wanted, whenever he wanted. If he wanted to destroy the lawn, Humphrey's had made more than enough profit during the past two days to resod it several times over. And invest in comfortable chairs for patrons to sit on!

The commotion lasted so long that Paula's coworkers spilled out of the restaurant to come to her assistance. They called the Harbor police who showed up and put Gallagher in handcuffs. Our production director, Tim Mercer, ran to get Gary Propper, and their intervention was the only thing that kept Gallagher from being thrown in the back of the paddy wagon.

When I started booking the 1989 season, Gallagher was not part of my master plan. He not only tore up the lawn during his wee-hours unicycle romp, verbally abused a helpless pregnant employee, and created a commotion severe enough to warrant his forcible arrest, but also awakened several hotel guests who demanded refunds the next day.

Selective memory comes into play when the bottom line is bulging. Humphrey's netted more than $40,000 for presenting a jerk with no redeeming qualities, and I thought we should count our blessings, take the money, and run. Richard Bartell disagreed. He insisted we pursue whatever means necessary to get him back. When he weighed Gallagher's transgressions against the amount Humphrey's had banked, he reminded me what I should do in my role as talent buyer.

I went through the motions, hoping that Gary Propper would reject our offer. Seemingly, Gallagher had a worse time with us than we'd had with him. Instead, all Gary remembered was how successful the booking had been for all of us. Because of that, he asked for a raise for Gallagher's return engagement. There was the out I needed, I thought, but when I ran it by Richard, he said, "Give it to him."

I was momentarily demoralized but consummated the deal. It was far from the only time in my career that I had whored myself out. But Bartell's business instincts proved correct. Gallagher sold another four thousand tickets the following August and Humphrey's made another $40,000.

Gallagher was equally as miserable to deal with the second time around, although no handcuffs were necessary. The following year, when Gary Propper abandoned management to produce animated movies, I had the excuse I needed to discontinue my relationship with Gallagher. We never had to Power-Vac watermelon seeds off the lawn at Humphrey's again.

33.

angels

I DON'T MEAN TO IMPLY THAT every interaction I had with an artist sent me lunging for Advil. On the contrary, 95 percent of the shows I produced went off without incident and most of the acts appreciated the paycheck, the venue's glorious setting abutting San Diego Bay, and the proximity to the airport if they were touring by plane.

I usually kept my distance, affording the artists their privacy, but along the way, I developed memorable relationships with some wonderful human beings.

B. B. KING

When I transitioned from Colorado media guy to California concert producer, I wasn't confident that my new career would last twenty-three weeks, let alone twenty-three years. I quickly made a conscious effort to book my heroes, people who had made an indelible mark on my life. The masses didn't always agree with my taste, so this wasn't the most effective business strategy.

In terms of consistently delivering a trifecta of performance, personality, and promoter profit, B. B. King is the first artist who comes to mind. Gracious, appreciative, articulate, and gifted, B. B. embodies sheer wonder. When he first appeared at Humphrey's in 1984, he was fifty-nine years old and we paid him $13,500 to do two ninety-minute shows. Twenty-one years and twenty-seven B. B. King concerts later, we paid him $100,000 for one eighty-minute performance just a few weeks after his eightieth birthday.

Most headliners would stay on their tour buses until showtime, take the stage, and head directly back to the bus as soon as the show was over. Not B. B. King. He always had his tour manager and former valet, Willis "Be-Bop" Edwards, come fetch me so we could share a private conversation in his Humphrey's dressing room. I don't know if he ever remembered my name, but he recognized my face and always introduced me to his band members and crew as "the boss."

At the end of the night, he held court with his fans, having them wait in line at his door and file in four or five at a time. He'd give each of them a monogrammed guitar pin or autographed pick. He listened attentively to all their stories and adulation. It gave me the chills to hear older black people from the South tell B. B. that they had listened to him spin records at WDIA in Memphis or had seen him perform on the "chitlin' circuit" at places like the Hippodrome, the Royal Peacock, or the Cotton Club.

In 1989, I was courting my son-in-law Kevin to move from Oregon to San Diego to work for me so Helen and I could be closer to our daughter, Nicole, and grandchildren, Shira and Issac. They stayed at our house for a couple of weeks of concerts, including two shows with B. B. King. This time when Be-Bop took me into B. B.'s dressing room, I brought Helen, Shira (age four), and Issac (age two) with me. When we walked into the room, B. B.'s eyes lit up, and the massive three-hundred-pound man in a tuxedo slid out of his chair to the floor and crawled toward the kids.

Neither Shira nor Issac was startled. They were transfixed by B. B., and when asked to "come over here and give B. B. a hug,"

both of them obliged without hesitation. It was an unforgettable moment.

Of course, from a business angle, it enhanced my relationship with B. B. that we sold out nearly every show he played and consistently broke bar records (predominantly Courvoisier drinkers, according to the bartenders). It was so satisfying for me to be able to give B. B. a "raise" year after year, culminating in his six-figure payday.

I had to be careful, though, not to go to the well too often. In 1987, we had sold out two nights and four shows in June, and B. B.'s agent called in July to ask if I wanted to get in on a West Coast leg they were adding in September. When presented a scenario like that, I would normally advise the agent to skip the market until the following year, but agents have their weekly quotas to fill and the easiest path was to call on their friends to help them out. And *how* could I say no to B. B. King?

When the date played, we had sold only 60 percent of the tickets, so there were a lot of empty seats. I can count on one hand the number of artists who expressed concern that I might be losing my shirt by presenting them. But B. B. made a point of taking me aside between shows and addressing the issue.

"We didn't do very well tonight, did we?" he asked, his face contorted with genuine worry.

"I brought you back too soon," I said. "Don't worry about it. We've put on twelve B. B. King shows and this is the first time we've lost money."

"But I want you to make money *every* time!"

I went on to produce another fifteen B. B. King concerts after that one—and we did make money on every one of them.

BONNIE RAITT

I fell in love with Bonnie Raitt in 1972 when I saw her play at Tulagi in Boulder. Her bluesy vocals, slide guitar playing, and onstage interaction with her bassist Freebo was a rapturous combination. I hung out after the performance to try to convince her to come on my radio show at KRNW the following morning.

"What time's your show?"

"Six to ten."

She cackled, just short of derisively. "I probably won't go to bed before 6 a.m!" So I hooked her up with my friend Michael Muirhead, who did afternoons. At 2 p.m. the next day, I headed back to the station and sat on the floor during the interview. My hormones were raging. I was twenty-four and Bonnie twenty-three—it should have been perfect! Except for the fact that there were ten other guys in the room, all with the same desires. None of us went home with Bonnie that day.

Fast-forward thirteen years and I'm a concert promoter in San Diego, throwing out offers to all my favorite artists. Bonnie's career was in a lull, but I still couldn't convince her manager, esteemed musicologist Dick Waterman, to put his artist onto a makeshift lawn area at a resort hotel with an unknown promoter. Fortunately, John Harrington, my part-time mentor, had an extensive history with Waterman and Bonnie and convinced them that we were on the level.

We booked Bonnie for two shows on May 26, 1985, with an unwritten promise that we could bring her back on October 5. When Bonnie showed up at Humphrey's, the only thing I recognized about her were her freckles. Her body was pudgy, her face uncharacteristically bloated, and her eyes devoid of fire. But she was a delight to work with and we had a host of mutual friends to trade stories about, especially Chuck Morris who had booked Bonnie into Colorado clubs and theaters for fifteen years.

Bonnie was accompanied by her boyfriend, a renowned record producer I'll call Freddie. The whole entourage had a party-animal essence, yet when it came to business, Bonnie hit the stage on time, the band was loose and sloppy in a good way, and the shows included fan favorites like "Angel from Montgomery," "Stayed Too Long at the Fair," and the Sippie Wallace staple "Women Be Wise." I waited for her as she descended the stage staircase and thanked her for taking a chance on Humphrey's.

"See you in October?" I asked.

"I'd play here *every* night if I could," she said, smiling. I never got tired of hearing that over the course of my tenure at Humphrey's. I called Dick Waterman the next morning, who confirmed the return engagement and verified that Bonnie had loved the vibe of the place.

When Bonnie showed up on October 5, I greeted her warmly but made an innocent mistake by asking her if Freddie was with her. She regaled me with stories of how he had cheated on her with other women, run up bills in her name while she was on the road, and played off her celebrity status to garner favors from other music business honchos. When Bonnie came home from tour to those revelations, she took Freddie's wardrobe of Armani suits and alligator shoes and threw them into her swimming pool. As I listened with extreme discomfort, I noticed that Bonnie was smiling the entire time. She had already moved on to the next cartoon panel in her life's graphic novel.

After her typically spirited performance, I followed her to the green room where she'd be doing some after-show imbibing. "Wonderful, Bonnie. Thanks again. I hope to see you next year." I always said that to artists I wanted to become fixtures on my annual calendar.

"Where do you think you're going?" she said, playfully grabbing me by the elbow. "Aren't you going to be my date tonight?"

Fantasies raced through my head. I was married and very loyal to my wife. But could I pass up a chance to fool around with Bonnie Raitt?

I didn't have to stew too long in my own anticipatory juices, because she quickly hit me with her request. "I need someone to carry my guitars to the car," she said.

That someone was me, one in each hand. I got a goodnight hug as my reward.

I didn't see Bonnie again until 1987, when she returned with a tight little four-piece band that included New Orleans prodigy Ivan Neville (son of Aaron). The most memorable part of that night was the opening act I booked as a favor to my friend Chuck Morris. He had just signed a singer-songwriter from Klein, Texas, named Lyle Lovett and asked if I could find a show to put him on. Since Bonnie and Lyle were both represented by Monterey Peninsula Artists, it seemed like a possible fit. Not only did the two artists mesh during their evening at Humphrey's, but they became great friends and toured larger venues as a double bill for several years. While I was happy for both of them, the Raitt-Lovett package was too big for Humphrey's, so I was left out in the cold.

Bonnie didn't ask me to lug her guitars that night, but I noticed a real sparkle in her eyes when I introduced her to the audience. After years of alcohol and substance abuse, Bonnie was sober. You could tell in the way she carried herself, not to mention that she had shed a significant amount of weight. When she left, she apologized to me for the sparsely attended shows. "I'm not much of a draw anymore," she said. "But I hope you'll have me back."

I promised I would, but it never happened. And it wasn't because I didn't try.

Bonnie's career exploded in 1989 when all the stars aligned and her *Nick of Time* CD won three Grammys (including Album of the Year) and sold six million copies. Two years later, *Luck of the Draw* did even better, garnering three more Grammys while surpassing eight million in sales. Bonnie had graduated from Humphrey's and was doing her postdoc work in large amphitheaters around the country.

I mourned the loss of no longer being Bonnie Raitt's go-to presenter in San Diego, but I was thrilled beyond words about her full-flowered emergence into the mainstream after decades of sharing her art with a loyal, but modest following. It gave a lot of us music lifers hope that maybe the business was on the verge of "getting it right" again.

I attended several of Bonnie's "bigger" concerts, and at each one of them, when she addressed the audience, she asked, "Did any of you ever see me at Humphrey's?" Thousands of people roared, even though she had only played there three times. "I miss that place!"

She finally made it back to Humphrey's in 2010, sharing a blues show with Taj Mahal. It had been twenty-five years since I'd been enlisted as her late-night guitar porter and thirty-eight years since I couldn't persuade her to wake up for a morning radio interview.

JOAN BAEZ

Based on my initial impression of Joan Baez when she played Humphrey's for the first time in 1987, I would have predicted that she'd end up among the divas. She was forty minutes late for her sound-check and no one knew where she was.

Martha, her friendly but demanding tour manager, nervously paced around the empty venue, looking at her watch a few times a minute. "This is *so* unlike Joanie," she said. "She's the most punctual person I've ever worked with."

No one thought to look for her in her hotel suite until I suggested it. Joan answered after one knock and waved us in. She quickly returned to the living room and sat on the floor next to a shoebox.

"This sparrow flew into the picture window," she said softly. "I'm trying to nurse her back to health."

On the table was a first-aid kit that included an eyedropper Joan was using to feed the bird. She slowly administered one drop of water into the sparrow's responsive beak. Within minutes, the tiny bird's senses had revived, and Joan placed the box on the veranda. The sparrow flew toward the bay.

"Time to soundcheck," Martha said, prodding her gently.

Joan looked at me, extended her hand, and said, "I'm Joan."

What do you say when an icon you've followed for twenty-five years introduces herself to you?

Her concert was an artistic triumph, her range as broad as when she first recorded "Scarlet Ribbons" in 1958. I closed my eyes and was transported back to the '60s—the Newport Folk Festival and the Dow Chemical protests in Madison. When she launched into her Bob Dylan impressions, the audience laughed through an entire rendering of "It Ain't Me Babe."

Midway through the concert, Martha tracked me down in the audience and asked me to come backstage with her. There was an urgency in her voice. I had a reflexive dread when approached by tour managers.

Upon reaching Joan's dressing room, Martha pointed to a huge bouquet of roses. "I want you to walk out onstage at the end of her show and give them to Joanie."

I was slightly befuddled, nonetheless amused. "I hadn't planned on staying until the very end of the show," I said, relieved that the situation wasn't dire. "Let my production director do it."

"Joan really likes it when her presenter gives her the flowers. It *has* to be you."

I flashed on how silly this was. A preconceived gesture intended to seem genuine. Of course I said nothing, cradled the roses, and took my position at the side of the stage. My instructions: wait until the final note of "The Night They Drove Old Dixie Down," give the audience about twenty seconds of applause, walk out onstage, hand her the flowers, and exit stage right.

As Joan was soaking up the applause and bowing for the third time, I walked toward her. She knew I was coming yet still seemed surprised to see me. I handed her the bouquet and then deviated slightly from the script when I threw my arms around her and kissed her on the cheek. The crowd ate that up and Joan graciously went along with my spontaneous smooch. At that moment, I felt as if I could soar like the sparrow Joan had saved that afternoon.

Joan returned to Humphrey's five more times. Her 2006 performance was especially significant to me because it marked the final night of my career as a concert producer. As we watched her handpicked opening act from her dressing room balcony, I thanked her for all she had done for the world in general and our concert series specifically. She didn't kiss me goodbye, but thanked me for being so supportive over the past twenty years.

When I drove home from Humphrey's for the last time, my inner glow burned brightly when I realized that my career as a concert producer was bookended by Miles Davis and Joan Baez.

LEONARD COHEN

When I got the unexpected opportunity to present Leonard Cohen in concert in July 1993, I immediately flashed back to the day I threatened my radio listeners with nonstop Leonard until I found a place to live. It might have been just a coincidence that I invoked the name of Leonard Cohen, moved into a new home the next day, and met my future wife weeks later. Then again, maybe not.

I gave him his reasonable asking price of $10,000 without doing any market research or negotiating. I had no idea if he'd sell tickets in San Diego. I just needed to tell him that he was responsible for my lifelong hookup with Helen.

Using official Humphrey's stationery, I composed a long-winded, over-detailed dramatization of the events leading up to the final resolution of my housing dilemma. In between personal anecdotes, I wrote glowingly about my affection for his entire musical canon, especially his most recent album *The Future*, which included instant classics like "Democracy," "Waiting for the Miracle," "Anthem," and the title track.

As the band filed in for their late-afternoon soundcheck, I introduced myself to the tour manager, handed him an envelope, and asked him to make sure he delivered it to Leonard.

"Yeah, yeah," he said, stuffing my heartfelt ramblings into his inside jacket pocket.

The concert itself was magnificent, one of the five best of the 2,000 shows I produced in San Diego. For someone who toured irregularly, we sold a respectable but modest 1,091 tickets (mostly to chain-smoking Canadians). Cohen's show was seamlessly well rehearsed, down to his choreographed pliés and between-song patter. Song after song elicited "he wrote that *too*?" awe: "Hello, Marianne," "First We Take Manhattan," "Tower of Song," "Hallelujah," "Bird on a Wire," "Sisters of Mercy," and, of course, "Suzanne."

The one spontaneous part of his show came when he addressed

the audience after the fourth song. "I want to thank all of you for coming to see us tonight," he began in his deep, almost-Shakespearean, raspy, gentlemanly voice. "Thank you for all the lavish gifts that were waiting for me in the hotel room."

He paused for fifteen seconds. "Actually, there weren't any gifts, but I so much appreciated all the flowers, cards, and letters!"

Another pause.

"There was none of that either." Titters of nervous laughter from the audience.

"But thank you for the note."

After the show, I took Helen backstage to meet Leonard. She hated hanging backstage and usually drove herself home from the

venue to avoid the after-party schmoozing. But Leonard Cohen was one of the few artists she was eager to meet.

Unlike most stars who retreat to private dressing rooms, Leonard shared his hotel suite with his band members. When Helen and I were waved into his room, he was sitting on the couch between his gorgeous backup singers, Julie Christensen and Perla Betalla. I introduced him to Helen and asked if the "note" he referred to onstage was the one I had written to him.

"It was," he said softly with a smile.

"I hope you didn't think I was disparaging you by threatening my audience to force-feed them your music. I love everything you've ever done."

Then Helen chimed in. "Your new album blows me away!" she said, rattling off the titles of three of her favorite songs. It was completely out of character for her to be starstruck and she seemed to be on the verge of hyperventilating and fainting.

Amused, Leonard looked Helen straight in the eye and said those magic words every woman wants to hear, "Would you like some popcorn?"

So we pulled up some chairs, poured ourselves two glasses of red wine, and noshed on popcorn with Leonard Cohen.

A few months after his Humphrey's performance, Leonard Cohen literally disappeared from the music business. He moved to the Mount Baldy Zen Center outside Los Angeles to live a monastic life and study with Joshu Sasaki Roshi. He stayed there for five years.

When he returned to his home in LA in 1999, Leonard discovered that his longtime manager and former paramour had emptied his retirement savings of some $5 million. It isn't clear if Leonard Cohen would have ever returned to the concert stage, but suddenly he had no choice—he was nearly broke.

I began submitting offers. I figured since I'd paid him $10,000 in 1993 and he had been away from touring so long, the curiosity factor would be high enough that I could offer $25,000 and raise the ticket price from $23 to $35. His agent said he wasn't quite ready to work, but when he was, he'd be taking only lucrative offers from Europe and Japan.

The next time he played in San Diego was April 7, 2009, in the intimate confines (2,200 seats) of Copley Symphony Hall. Tickets were priced from $250 for orchestra seats down to $89 for the far reaches of the balcony. Soon after that, Leonard Cohen was traveling around the world playing 15,000-seat arenas, often earning more than $500,000 a performance. The shows exceeded three hours in length and usually included four multisong encores.

His music career nearly an afterthought when he entered Mount Baldy, Leonard Cohen, today in his seventies, was having paydays usually reserved for the likes of U2, the Rolling Stones, and Bruce Springsteen.

A comeback story for the ages, dwarfing anything else in rock 'n' roll history? Absolutely.

LYLE LOVETT

I was fortunate that in the twenty-three years I spent in the trenches producing concerts, my roster was filled with more than enough harmonic convergence to counterbalance any dissonant mayhem.

One singer-songwriter responsible for a bit of both—although clearly an angel—was Lyle Lovett. I was swept away by his 1986 debut album, which included instant classics like "God Will," "You Can't Resist It," "If I Were the Man You Wanted," and "This Old Porch." When I put him on the Bonnie Raitt show in 1987, I paid him $750 and he appeared in acoustic-duo format with cellist John Hagen. Due to time constraints, he performed only four songs, but I was floored by his voice, his words, and his deft guitar picking.

Promoters who do favors for unknown artists always hope that the act will remember them down the road if they should become famous. More often than not, the favor isn't repaid. I didn't immediately get to test Lyle's loyalty quotient, because he won the "Best Male Country Vocal" in 1989 and started touring with multi-act packages (including Bonnie Raitt) accompanied by his seventeen-piece Large Band.

When Lyle finally returned to Humphrey's for a two-night stint on July 27 and 28, 1993, he brought his bride of one month with him. I remember vividly how beautiful Julia Roberts looked in jeans, a T-shirt, and no makeup. She was sweet and unassuming, but Lyle's tour managers enforced a long list of Roberts Regulations, insisting we hire four security guards and block off half our VIP balcony to give Julia her own private viewing area. The green room, which usually housed our sponsor parties, was off-limits to everyone for two nights. And when Lyle's needlessly paranoid management team noticed that all the boats in the Shelter Island Marina could see the stage as well as Julia Roberts's cordoned-off balcony area, they asked about the feasibility of erecting a fence to obstruct the freeloaders' view. We nixed that idea with only a modicum of pushback from the beleaguered Lovett crew.

Backstage, the Lovett-Roberts honeymoon continued to flourish. Lyle had sent a limo to LA to bring down an all-black, five-piece, a cappella/doo-wop vocal group to serenade Julia. While the Large Band had dinner before the show, the nattily dressed quintet crooned in a semicircle engulfing Julia and Lyle. "In the Still of the Night" segued nicely into "Earth Angel," which in turn gave way to "Ten Commandments of Love." I felt like a voyeur as I watched Julia beam and blush.

Alas, the Lovett-Roberts union was short-lived. When Lyle returned again to Humphrey's in 1997 supporting his *Road to Ensenada* CD, he had time for a south-of-the-border excursion to Ensenada, where he pursued his passion for dirt biking. After a dusty desert ride,

Lyle recruited an all-string mariachi band (eleven acoustic guitars and a guitarrón), stuffed the ensemble into his tour bus, and drove them to San Diego as an unannounced support act. He paid them out of his own pocket.

My initial concern that Lyle Lovett might not remember my $750 favor from 1987 was unfounded. He performed at Humphrey's thirteen times during my tenure, and he continues to play there to this day. When he first returned as a headliner in 1993, I asked him if he had remembered his one prior appearance at Humphrey's. Without hesitating, he said, "Sure. It was in '87 and I opened for Bonnie."

Most artists I dealt with didn't even know the name of the city they were in at the moment.

I was certain that Lyle Lovett's sold-out show on July 8, 2002, would be canceled. Three months earlier, Lovett's pet bull, Cotton, had charged at Lyle's uncle at the family ranch in Texas. When Lyle shooed the angry bull away with his cap, saving his uncle's life, the bull turned on his master, pinning Lyle to the wall and shattering his shinbone. Lyle was sentenced to six months of rest and rehab. The doctors advised him to cancel all scheduled tour dates until the fall of 2002.

With seventeen pins in his leg and an intricate clamp holding all the pieces in place, Lovett climbed the stairs of the Humphrey's stage and stood for the duration of his two-hour performance. He didn't cancel a single show on his tour. I don't recall him even wincing.

PART 5

Hard Lessons

34.

music
without boundaries

WHEN I DID MY FIRST radio show in 1971 at age twenty-three, I discovered what a "mighty cloud of joy" was. I was walking on one.

But then radio changed and my enthusiasm for the medium started to wane. After six years of reveling in being a freeform DJ in Boulder, playing whatever I wanted at KRNW, my new bosses at KBCO instituted a conservative, card-catalogued format with a limited playlist. Progressive radio as we knew it was categorically being eliminated from coast to coast.

I tried to adapt but failed miserably at my full-time audition. Every time I would intentionally deviate from the format and play a song of my choice, the Big Brother program director would call me from home or race down the hallway from his office to insist that I follow the rules. I couldn't, so in late 1977, they exiled me to Sunday nights, where I happily presented a six-hour show I called *Hot off the Press* that afforded me the programming freedom I'd been used to.

Six months later, when I was recruited to be a cofounder of Boulder's first public radio station KGNU, it was the closest I'd ever come to being born again. I envisioned a world of complete artistic freedom *and* no commercials! Alas, the station hadn't been on the air for a week before I got called on the carpet for my questionable song selection.

After one of my afternoon shows, the program director, development director, and general manager requested a formal powwow with me. "Don't take this the wrong way," the PD said, "but you play far too much rock 'n' roll. Rock music has no place on public radio. In fact, nothing in 4/4 time should be on our airwaves. I think you should be playing a lot more jazz and classical music."

The development director, whose job was to procure national grants and local business contributors, was less subtle. "I can't attract underwriters to a station that plays Bruce Springsteen and the Sex Pistols!"

Although the GM (RIP Glen Gerberg) had been well aware of my rock 'n' roll pedigree when I was at KRNW and KBCO and ostensibly hired me because of my trendsetting reputation, it was his job to quash any dissension and he asked me to tone it down a little. The four of us had a heated but constructive debate. I was the oldest person in the room at age thirty, but it felt like my parents were castigating me.

The next day I began my show with Lou Reed's "Street Hassle," an X-rated symphonic rock opus with depraved lyrics and a somewhat cacophonous mélange of classical cellos, doo-wop sha-la-las, and an uncredited spoken-word cameo from public-radio enemy number one, Bruce Springsteen. It's an eleven-minute masterpiece, and by the time it reached the halfway mark, my flustered colleagues had surrounded me at the console. They insisted that I segue immediately into something more palatable like Ellington's "Take the 'A' Train." I refused, and our disagreements intensified.

Somehow I managed to hold on to my air shift (on my own terms) for the next five years, although I gradually lessened my load from five days a week to a single Friday afternoon music/talk show called *Fear of Fridays*. When I moved to San Diego at the end of '83, I assumed that my twelve-year journey as a radio guy was over.

It *was* over—but not forever.

A decade later, in July 1993, during my tenth year as a concert promoter, I got a call from KiFM program director Bob O'Connor, one of my more simpatico pals. We shared East Coast roots, loved the San Diego Chargers, and had a mutually beneficial working relationship. KiFM was San Diego's first and only "smooth jazz" station (referred to as "lite" or "contemporary" jazz at the time). It was modern-day elevator music with little soul or substance, but San Diego equated that music with its affluent, sailboat-steering, chardonnay-and-brie lifestyle, and I presented the cream of the smooth-jazz crop in concert at Humphrey's: Spyro Gyra, Kenny G, Lee Ritenour, Hiroshima, Acoustic Alchemy, the Rippingtons, David Benoit, Grover Washington, Jr.

"Would you ever consider doing a radio show again?" Bob asked me backstage at a Larry Carlton concert.

As much as I enjoyed my camaraderie with KiFM's employees who came to all of our concerts, I couldn't possibly envision myself working there. Even though it was the top-rated station in the San Diego market, the music was monotonous and the announcing styles were friendly, but antiseptic. Bob O' needed a knowledgeable music person to replace Ron Galon, a jazzbo who had helmed the station's token straight-ahead show on Sunday nights for many years. Instead of the normal low-cal, no-protein fare of Chuck Mangione and Earl Klugh, Galon dished out meatier entrees like Art Blakey, John Coltrane, and Charles Mingus. He was on the air for only two hours a week, but the show succeeded in mollifying traditional jazz aficionados (disparagingly called "jazzholes" by station management), who loudly derided KiFM for using the word "jazz" to describe the confections that dominated the format.

I was flattered that Bob O'Connor offered me the slot and eager to see if hosting a radio show after such a lengthy hiatus would be like riding a bike or if I'd be tongue-tied and monosyllabic. But jazz wasn't my area of expertise and I was leery of being compared to an icon like Ron Galon.

I suggested a compromise. "What if I include a healthy portion of straight-ahead jazz in a broader mix of world music, R&B, blues, rock, and intelligent singer-songwriters? I'll be sure to get in enough Miles, Ella, and Bird and toss in young lions like Joshua Redman, Wynton Marsalis, and Roy Hargrove—but I'll also play music that was derived from jazz, whether it's Otis Redding, Gilberto Gil, or Baaba Maal. Give me your blessings to mix in some Spirit, Howlin' Wolf, Joni Mitchell, and Solomon Burke, and I'd love to do it."

If Bob O' had any trepidation about my proposal, it was outweighed by the fact that he had to act fast and find a replacement show within two weeks. "Let's go for it," he said with his characteristic enthusiasm.

I couldn't believe it. Here was a radio programmer in 1993 hiring me to do a freeform show, in essence giving me license to deviate entirely from the station's predictable repertoire—as long as I satisfied Ron Galon's former listeners.

Music Without Boundaries was launched on Sunday, August 1, 1993, at 10 p.m. The two-hour program remained at KiFM for the next three years (149 original episodes). I not only pacified the "jazzholes," but also brought a new audience to the radio station.

During my maiden voyage, I played it relatively safe, cooking up an aural gumbo that mixed Muddy Waters, Sarah Vaughan, and Louis Jordan with the world music spices of Khaled, Johnny Clegg, and Zap Mama.

By the fifteenth week, I was mixing in Dead Can Dance with Big Joe Turner, John Prine with David Murray, and Chinese eccentrics the Guo Brothers with Wilson Pickett. *Music Without Boundaries* was off to the races in a big way. The San Diego radio audience had never heard anything like this, even dating back to the halcyon days of progressive radio in the late '60s and early '70s that focused entirely on rock 'n' roll. Amazingly, *MWB* was consistently rated in the top three in its time slot, thanks in part to Art Good's popular *Jazz Trax* preceding me.

In 1996, with radio consolidation wreaking havoc on adventurous radio, KiFM was sold to Jefferson Pilot, an insurance company with a growing appetite for radio properties. JP owned a country station in San Diego and, after axing Bob O'Connor for no apparent reason, brought in one of their country programmers, Cowboy Dick, to consult with their "smooth jazz" acquisition. It was akin to bringing in a potato farmer to harvest strawberries, but that's the direction commercial radio had taken.

It's easy to guess who was the first casualty. To be fair, Cowboy Dick called me on the phone and admitted that he didn't "get" *Music Without Boundaries* and wondered what it was doing on KiFM in the first place. It didn't matter that the show had developed a large and loyal audience. It was atypical and didn't belong. Cowboy Dick, attempting to be diplomatic, adopted a stance that by today's radio standards was beneficent. He said I was welcome to remain at the station, but he was moving the show from 10 p.m. to midnight and eliminating my $75 weekly stipend.

I thought about it for a week. As much as I wanted to continue showcasing music you couldn't hear anywhere else, I didn't want to work for a myopic suit. Spoiled by Bob O'Connor's open-minded encouragement, I refused to relive my brief stint at KBCO when Big Brother monitored my every move. Losing my pittance of a salary didn't bother me, except when I remembered that Jefferson Pilot had just spent $30 million to acquire the KiFM frequency. Why budget $75 a week on a locally produced specialty show when they could throw on a syndicated show for nothing?

I broadcast my final show at KiFM on August 12, 1996. It was rife with song lyrics that decried the state of the radio and emphasized my inability to fit into a cookie-cutter format—short, sharp screeds like Elvis Costello's "Radio Radio" and Tom Petty's "I Won't Back

Down." The final playlist contained no jazz, a healthy dose of world music, prophetic singer-songwriters, and plenty of rock 'n' roll—not to mention five consecutive songs by my muse, Otis Redding.

During my final sign-off, I heaped kudos on Bob O'Connor and thanked him for his belief in the show. I filled the audience in on Cowboy Dick's feelings about *MWB* and said farewell. I collected addresses, assuring the listeners I'd contact them if the show resurfaced elsewhere. My final musical bursts were the Animals' "We Gotta Get Out of This Place" and Roy Orbison's "It's Over."

I didn't think I'd return to the airwaves in San Diego. Visionary program directors were an endangered species, and the city had no format compatible with the breadth of *Music Without Boundaries*.

Just the same, I reached out to a radio veteran I had never met before, and a month after *MWB*'s demise on KiFM, I was doing Sunday mornings at KUPR.

35.

station hopping

Very few people call him Mike. His listeners know him by his surname—Halloran.

A radio maverick, Halloran is revered among music fans for his decade (1986–1996) of breaking alternative rock acts at San Diego's 91X. The pride of Detroit, he is more Stooges than Temptations. In the '80s, he championed emerging British bands like the Smiths and the Cure. Today, he continues to support unsigned artists by playing their music on the radio and helping them get record deals. Six foot two and papa bearish, he seems to change his appearance weekly, ranging from full beard/bushy hair to clean shaven/spiky do.

When Jacor Communications bought 91X in 1996, Halloran's days were numbered. He wasn't enough of a corporate yes-man to accompany the regime change. He ended up getting a program director/afternoon drive gig at KUPR, a small, independent station located in a quaint old house in a semirural section of Carlsbad, an affluent community thirty-five miles north of San Diego.

It was the era before email and MP3s, so I sent Halloran a package containing a cover letter, sample playlists, an edited cassette of my announcing style and segues, and an article from the *San Diego Union* that named *Music Without Boundaries* the best radio show in San Diego, "perhaps in the country."

In the end, Halloran's decision to hire me came down to one thing. "You play Patti Smith!" he said during our first meeting. "There's a lot of great stuff on your playlists, but *that's* fucking cool. Can you start next Sunday?"

Not only did he hire me, but he also moved my show from the late-night-radio dead zone to a prime-time Sunday morning slot and expanded the show to three hours (nine to noon). He encouraged me to take calls from listeners, play as many genres as possible, and continue to be myself. During my three years at KiFM, I had been prodded to keep jazz as the focal point of the show and not veer too abrasively into rock 'n' roll, but Halloran wanted me to live up to the show's title. So I did.

During my debut at KUPR, I played South African protest music, an ethereal Finnish folk song, a screaming guitar trio instrumental, an a cappella song from the Belgian Congo, a reggae song about a bandit, a jazzy hip-hop ditty about casual sex and HIV, a Mexican lament, a Haitian chant, an American gospel song from 1938, and some jump-swing from the '40s. And that was just the first hour.

If I had felt somewhat deflated about going from the number-one-rated station in the city to a low-powered frequency in North County, those feelings evaporated after one show. The phones rang for three hours, the majority of the callers expressing elation that this kind of program was on commercial radio.

I was always prepared for negative bombshells and I got those too. The ones that stung most came from listeners chastising me for playing so many songs not in English. I patiently asked them to keep an open mind and give *MWB* another try the following week. That type of call disappeared entirely during the fourth week of the show. Now the audience was prepared for each song to be a surprise, understanding that 30 percent of the singing would be in foreign tongues.

Halloran admitted he didn't like every selection, yet he was 100 percent behind the concept of the show and appreciated my conversational and informative delivery. In all my years in radio, I never worked for such a supportive PD. As we got to know each other better, Halloran, ten years my junior, would say things like, "Whenever I worry about losing my edge as I get older, I look at you and I don't worry anymore." I'm pretty sure that was a compliment.

But my stint at KUPR ended after just ten weeks when consolidation once again reared its ugly head. Nationwide Insurance, another company looking to diversify, bought the station, fired everyone without notice, and switched from the existing "adult rock" format to automated (no disc jockeys) country music. I heard about it for the first time while pulling into the Tower Records parking lot as Chris Isaak segued into Garth Brooks with no explanation.

The staff was shocked, although that had become radio's modus operandi. New ownership begat new formats begat wholesale firings. I was glad that radio had become a hobby and I wasn't dependent on it as my livelihood. I sympathized with the full-timers who had to start from scratch again and again.

Once more, I figured my radio days were over and I made a note that November 17, 1996, was the official end of my rejuvenated radio life. Halloran moved to LA to program another emerging station, but his time there proved to be only slightly longer than his brief tenure at KUPR.

Then a year later, I got a manic call from him on his car phone, somewhere on I-5 South between San Juan Capistrano and Oceanside. "Hey! I'm moving back to San Diego and taking over what used to be called the Flash," he said, proceeding to tell me about his marketing strategies for 92.5 (XHRM-FM) that would revitalize the floundering alternative rock station. "I want you to be my first new hire and do Sunday mornings starting on January 4."

Music Without Boundaries had been off the air for about a year, so this was an unexpected New Year's gift. I was introduced at a staff meeting and got a standing ovation from my new colleagues. At forty-eight, I was nearly twice the age of everyone in the room and their reverential respect made me feel like Alice Cooper wincing at the "I'm not worthy" huzzahs of Wayne and Garth in *Wayne's World*. I was already an elder statesman.

Heading home from my orientation, I marveled at *MWB*'s evolution: The show had been a part of three distinctly different formats (smooth jazz, adult rock, and alternative rock) in three different sections of San Diego. I had spent three years in the swank environs of a La Jolla high rise office building and ten weeks at a pastoral split level in residential Carlsbad, and now I would be airing my show from a nondescript strip mall in between a Denny's and an In-N-Out Burger in National City, less than ten miles from the U.S.-Mexico border. Overall, it was an enjoyable road trip for this eclectic specialty program.

It felt like 92.5 was gaining momentum and I would be set for a long time. Halloran continued to support *MWB*'s diversity and anarchy. A sample playlist from February '98 reveals an aural hodgepodge that included acoustic guitar tapper Michael Hedges, Chinese chanteuse Yungchen Lhamo, Venice Beach street singer Ted Hawkins, '60s folk icon Odetta, bombastic British rockers Barclay James Harvest, French provocateur Serge Gainsbourg, and seminal R&B powerhouses Dyke & the Blazers. My primary goals were to entertain and educate, but it was also mandatory that I crack myself up on a regular basis.

Eight months later, my 92.5 experience came to a crashing halt. To eliminate their competition, Jacor Communications gobbled up the 92.5 FM frequency, fired everyone, and changed the format to old-school R&B. While they wouldn't admit it, they bought the station primarily to get Halloran out of their hair. He was a more adventurous programmer than anyone in their camp and eventually would have eroded and surpassed their ratings at 91X.

Within days, Halloran was negotiating to become program director of the AAA (adult album alternative) station KXST, which operated under the moniker Sets 102.

"I'm not taking the job. There's not enough money," he told me several weeks later. "But I told Bob he should pick up your show."

Making money has never been my motivation in radio, so I met with owner/general manager Bob Hughes, who had occasionally listened to *MWB* during all three incarnations. After sharing some dim sum at a sparsely populated Chinese restaurant, he offered me Sunday nights from eight to eleven.

I started on November 8, 1998, less than three months after the hostile takeover of 92.5. The new station was in another peculiar part of town: the historic, somewhat ramshackle KCBQ building in downtown Santee, twenty-one miles east of my Point Loma home. I was warned by a few East County residents not to eat at the neighborhood Jack in the Box where the local anti-Semitic skinheads congregated.

Sets 102, which changed its call letters to KPRI in 2002, was independently owned and operated, an anomaly on the landscape of radio consolidation in San Diego. When Bob Hughes introduced me on the air during his afternoon-drive show, the entire staff gathered around me in the studio and applauded my arrival. As flattered as I was by this gesture, I predicted another short run for *MWB*.

"This is my fourth stop on the San Diego radio dial," I said. "The first three stations have been sold. So the one thing I can guarantee you, Bob, is that you're going to get your asking price."

Much to my utter surprise, I spent six and a half years (304 episodes) at KPRI, my longest affiliation with any of the eight stations I worked for. I honed *MWB*'s identity there, developing assorted featurettes I relied on until they had run their respective courses.

"The Byrds Dropping of the Week" paid tribute to the innovation of the Byrds. While I wasn't too proud to play hits like "Mr. Tambourine Man" and "Turn! Turn! Turn!," I spent more time giving airplay to obscurities like "One Hundred Years from Now," "Bugler," and "Old John Robertson."

"The Spirit Offering of the Week" showcased a different track each week from one of my all-time favorite bands, rock-fusion pioneers Spirit. I played every song from their first four albums with repetitive nods going to "Dream Within a Dream," "Give a Life, Take a Life," and "Mechanical World."

"The Tex Tile of the Week" featured the musical mosaic of the late Joe Tex, the original rapper. Even before seeing him open a benefit for Aretha Franklin, the Young Rascals, and Sonny and Cher at Madison Square Garden in 1968, I'd been a huge fan. It was the least I could do to preserve his legacy by introducing my listeners to songs like "I Believe I'm Gonna Make It," "Buying a Book," and "The Love You Save (May Be Your Own)."

"The N'awlins Nugget" explored seventy-five years of historic music from the Crescent City. Although preferring icons like Fats Domino, Louis Armstrong, and Professor Longhair, I also gave lots of airtime to regional treasures like Snooks Eaglin, Irma Thomas, and Sonny Landreth. The well of music that comes out of New Orleans will never run dry.

The "Foolish Pleasures" segment offered back-to-back chestnuts, often silly reminiscences of days gone by. My three most oft-repeated foolish pleasures were the Jarmels' "A Little Bit of Soap," Skeeter Davis's "The End of the World," and the Browns' "The Three Bells." Unlike normal commercial radio, however, heavy rotation of a "hit" song on *MWB* was twice a year as opposed to six times a day. During this part of the show, you'd hear Spike Jones, Iron Butterfly, the Kingston Trio, and the Monkees—novelty songs or music I should have been embarrassed to admit that I liked.

MWB continued to focus on international music and singer-songwriters at KPRI. The ratings were strong enough to warrant my lobbying for and getting a Saturday morning time slot, which had five times the Sunday evening audience.

From 2002 to 2005, *MWB* was broadcast twice a weekend and I was quietly content. I'd drive to the station on Tuesday mornings, record my show, schmooze with the morning show dudes and the sales and promotion staffs, and then be on my way. Everything went smoothly until March '03, the week after the United States invaded Iraq. I had just concluded my weekly tribute to singer-songwriters and was back announcing what I had played. "We kicked things off with 'Wuthering Heights' by Kate Bush, no relation to the warmonger." It was a spontaneous quip, delivered matter-of-factly with no pregnant pauses or dramatic emphasis of any kind.

The next day, I was called on the carpet. An internal email went out to the entire staff saying (I'm paraphrasing) "one of our announcers referred to President Bush as a warmonger. We are a radio station that plays music. We are not talk radio. Political statements of any kind will not be tolerated."

Of course, everyone knew who the announcer was, and for the next month, I was no longer greeted with smiles by a majority of the business staff. One major sponsor had threatened to cancel his account with the station if I wasn't fired. The sales rep handling that account asked me what kind of trouble I was going to cause on next week's show. A female rep who had been openly flirtatious with me during the two months she had been working at KPRI now looked down at her Jimmy Choos when I tried making eye contact.

Determining I needed to be proactive, I approached the sales manager and asked him if he wanted me to call the offended sponsor and smooth things over.

"No, I did that already. It's under control." He assured me he had put out the fire, but when I ran into him at an AC/DC concert a few days later, the always-gregarious salesman nodded in my direction and headed away as quickly as possible.

Management let me off the hook with a mild wrist slap but asked me to avoid any further political commentary. I bit my lip, sat on my hands, adhered to their directives, and said nothing. I let the music reflect my feelings instead. Here's a partial list of the songs I played on the next show:

	Dolly Parton	Peace Train
	Dire Straits	Brothers in Arms
	The Byrds	Turn! Turn! Turn!
	Leonard Cohen	Democracy
	Bob Dylan	Talking World War III Blues
	Buffalo Springfield	For What It's Worth
	Edwin Starr	War
	The Beatles	All You Need Is Love
	Luka Bloom	I Am Not at War with Anyone
	John Lennon	Give Peace a Chance

No memos went out to the staff, and when I showed up the following Tuesday, a few of the closet liberals gave me knowing smiles.

The ill will that certain KPRI personnel had toward me disappeared when the next Arbitron ratings book revealed that *Music Without Boundaries* was the third-highest-rated show in San Diego during its time slot. This was unprecedented in station history, due to a mediocre antenna site and a signal that effectively covered only certain portions of the city. A memo was distributed trumpeting *MWB*'s stellar ratings with a cryptic message: "Who knew?"

I also became the only person in station history to win a San Diego Radio Broadcasters Association Award for Best Weekend Specialty Show. So my otherwise positive persona at KPRI survived its pothole encounter and all was well—until I made the mistake of informally polling the staff (off the air) a few months before the 2004 elections regarding their presidential candidate of choice. I was shocked that most of the people hoped for a Bush reelection, the majority singling out the fact that we hadn't been attacked since 9/11 and that the Iraq War was a justifiable response to terrorism. One of the head honchos at the station cited that Bush would not raise taxes and that was all he cared about.

I was appalled. I wasn't naïve enough to forget that San Diego was the most conservative large city in the otherwise blue state of California. But I was working for a rock 'n' roll radio station that played Bruce Springsteen, John Mellencamp, REM, U2, and other politically progressive artists in heavy rotation. There wasn't anything close to Ted Nugent or Toby Keith on KPRI's airwaves. Stationed at my home computer, I engaged in email warfare, sending *New York Times* columns and op-ed pieces to the station brass. In return, they'd send me editorials from the *Wall Street Journal* and the *National Review.* When the production director started quoting Rush Limbaugh and Sean Hannity over lunch that I was treating him to, I knew I was fighting a losing battle.

Despite the unspoken truce following my "no relation to the warmonger" comment at the onset of the Iraq occupation, I again lost my grip during my show on October 30, 2004, three days before Election Day. Without directly imploring my audience to vote for John Kerry, I peppered my intros and outros with "vote for change this Tuesday," which was the moniker of the rock 'n' roll tour that had barnstormed through the swing states hoping to get the Democrats back in the White House. Snippets from my set list:

Patti Smith	People Have the Power
Curtis Mayfield & the Impressions	This Is My Country
The Rascals	People Got to Be Free
John Fogerty	Déjà Vu (All Over Again)
Spirit	Soldier
Southside Johnny	Better Days
Bruce Springsteen	We Shall Overcome

Alas, Dubya was reelected on November 2. When I walked into the station the next morning, it was business as usual, but I made a point of extending an olive branch to every Republican. Handshakes all around and let's talk about something else.

Even though I made solid contributions there for six years, my involvement with KPRI would end five months later. A new program director, who never knew my nickname for him was St. Louis Slick, was hired to retool the station. He slashed the playlist, replacing the intelligentsia of Lyle Lovett, Lucinda Williams, and Steve Earle with heavy doses of generica like Coldplay, Gavin Rossdale, Jack Johnson, and John Mayer. He played the Rolling Stones' "Start Me Up" and Supertramp's "Breakfast in America" with enough frequency that you'd think they were current hits. The soul of the station had vanished.

Needless to say, Slick wasn't a big fan of *MWB*. He went through the motions of sending out a press release when I did my three hundredth show at the station and even budgeted a few bucks to buy an "anniversary" cake from the local supermarket. Four weeks after this pseudo pomp and circumstance, he had his hapless assistant inform me that my show was being discontinued on Saturday mornings.

"Why didn't Slick tell me himself?" I asked her.

"He wanted to give me practice handling uncomfortable personnel situations," she said meekly.

Admittedly, I was blood-pumping angry and should have doused myself with ice water and walked around the parking lot for fifteen minutes before marching into Slick's office unannounced. He'd fired dozens of people during his lengthy radio career so this was nothing new or strenuous for him. He listened impassively to my objections.

"We paid a huge fee to a consulting company and I'd be irresponsible if I didn't follow their advice," he said, adding that I could continue on Sunday nights if I wanted to. "*MWB* attracts listeners who tune in for your show only and tune out when it's over. That ultimately hurts the radio station."

Later I found out from a station mole that the consulting report never mentioned *Music Without Boundaries* at all, positively or negatively. Slick had used the report as an excuse to move the show out of prime time and back to specialty-show isolation. Corporate commercial radio mentality had infected this mom-and-pop station and I couldn't stomach working for the new regime.

Feeling that I had given the station too much for too little over the past six years, I quit on the spot (although we reached a conciliatory agreement that they would run *The Best of MWB* on Sunday nights until one of us gave the other thirty days' notice). When looking back on what I didn't know would be my final playlist at the station, I laugh at my last three selections:

	Bessie Smith	Mistreating Daddy
	The Ramones	Gimme Gimme Shock Treatment
	Solomon Burke	What Good Am I?

36.

the final episode

I NEVER IMAGINED I'D END UP at 91X. A legendary alternative rock station, it built a massive following in the '80s championing emerging British acts like Culture Club, Duran Duran, Depeche Mode, and Tears for Fears, playing them alongside their American counterparts Oingo Boingo, Jane's Addiction, and the B-52's.

In the early 2000s, 91X suffered an identity crisis, undoubtedly brought on by the rule of Clear Channel, its monolithic new owners. The station lost its way and its audience. In 2005, Clear Channel divested itself of 91X and two other San Diego frequencies, selling the three holdings to a locally owned company called Finest City Broadcasting, headed up by San Diego radio veteran Mike Glickenhaus.

Mike and I had a history dating back to my first year at Humphrey's in 1984 when he was our sales rep at 91X. While we didn't do much business together, we shared East Coast Jewish backgrounds and became fast friends. We met for lunch once a month, and there was never a lull in our conversation.

Over a steak sandwich and a beer at Black Angus in late '86, I sought out Glickenhaus's negotiating advice regarding my evolving situation at Humphrey's. After Brent folded up Southland Concerts and I began working directly for Richard Bartell, Brent told Bartell that my salary was $45,000. This irked me because I had planned to ask my new boss for at least $50K.

"Why don't you ask for a back-end deal?" Glickenhaus suggested.

I cut deals like that with artists all the time: I provided them a guarantee but also a percentage of the profits ("back end") if they surpassed a certain gross dollar amount at the box office. Could an employee cut a deal like that with his boss?

Mike helped me construct a proposal, which called for me to get 10 percent of the first $125,000 in profits and 33 percent of everything above that. Since Southland Concerts hadn't made more than $90,000 in its three years of producing the Humphrey's series, Bartell readily agreed to my terms. Coincidentally or not, the concert series took off in '87 and netted more than $250,000. My year-end bonus came to $58,000, $13K more than my salary. For the first time in my life, I had ventured into the six-figure zone and my paycheck kept escalating during my remaining twenty years as a concert producer.

Needless to say, I have never forgotten Glickenhaus's input. He even picked up the check at lunch that day. We remained friends, and when I launched *Music Without Boundaries* on KiFM in 1993, he was one of the first to call and congratulate me.

Still, I was surprised when he invited me to bring *MWB* to 91X after my departure from KPRI. At the time, 91X's target audience was twenty-four-year-old males, and I was fifty-seven with an audience strongest among men and women thirty-five to sixty-four.

Despite my expressed concerns that 91X might not be the right fit for *MWB*, I graciously accepted his offer. I laughed when I realized that my radio career had begun in 1971 at KRNW with a 1,000-watt signal and now my similarly exotic mix of musical selections would be beamed from a 100,000-watt transmitter, entertaining listeners in Mexico to the south and as far north as Santa Barbara (on a clear day).

The first staff meeting was surreal. I walked into a room teeming with multicolored tattoos and wince-inducing body piercings. Other than the iconic British DJ Steve West, a holdover from the original 91X staff in the '80s, I was at least fifteen years older than everyone else there. In fact, I was the oldest DJ in the station's history. Yet my reputation as a radio maverick had preceded me, and I was greeted warmly.

For my debut 91X show on December 3, 2005, while still emphasizing world music and singer-songwriters, I rocked a little bit harder in deference to the younger audience joining the fans who followed me from station to station. I played crunchers from the Dead 60s and Amy Rigby side by side with Rodney Crowell and Ry Cooder. Algerian expatriate Khaled segued into multicultural lounge lizards Pink Martini. I satisfied the bizarre quotient with Tom Waits's "What's He Building?" and interspersed modern-day storytellers like Sufjan Stevens and Coco Mbassi with Roy Orbison and Richard Thompson.

My weekly recording sessions at 91X consistently felt good and I continued to have fun, exposing my audience to a mixture of excavated gems and profound discoveries. Upstairs in the executive offices, however, discordant chaos reigned. The coterie of investors, who had paid far too much (an estimated $107 million) for their three-station cluster, grew impatient as sales targets were not being met. They put pressure on Glickenhaus to make changes and one of my strongest supporters, program director Kevin Stapleford, became the first scapegoat.

How many times had I lost an ally in radio? Bob O'Connor, Mike Halloran, and, now, Kevin Stapleford. The moment I met the new PD—whom I'll call Pocket Protector—and his gaze avoided mine throughout our ninety-second interaction, I knew I was a dead man walking. I looked down at his desk and noticed a legal pad filled with capital letters: *A, B, A, B, C, A, B, D, A, A, B, E, A, B.* Music had become a science of categories broken down into letters and numbers. Before you play a *C*, you have to play at least two *As* and two *Bs*.

Less than two months later, I was toast. Pocket Protector didn't even give me a courtesy call. My friend Mike Glickenhaus, who was responsible for my hiring, made it easy on Mr. Protector by dishing out my verbal pink slip over the phone. He was matter-of-fact about the whole thing (this *is* radio, after all), saying he had hired the new PD from Seattle and a new consultant from LA and was paying them big money. It was prudent to abide by their recommendations. I'd heard it all before.

MWB was the first casualty of the Pocket Protector era. Over the next nine months, nearly every full- and part-time personality got the axe, replaced by vapid voices in search of the skateboarding male demo. Two months after *MWB*'s demise, Mike Glickenhaus was fired from the stations he created, managed, and partially owned. And when ratings and revenues remained below expectations, Pocket Protector also got the boot, less than a year after he had relocated his wife and two kids from Seattle to San Diego. At last sighting, he was the henchman for another faceless station in Phoenix.

Commercial radio has become a soulless, brutal business, no longer the go-to necessity it was for a music lover. When consolidation ran amok during the '90s, and stations in San Diego, Cincinnati, and Colorado Springs were being dictated to and programmed from corporate headquarters in San Antonio, the local essence of what radio used to be—when it *mattered*—was lost.

Mike Glickenhaus respected our common heritage in San Diego enough to let me say goodbye to the listeners. That's unheard of in radio or in most bottom-line businesses. Once you're fired, management changes the locks and bans you from the building. Since *MWB* was taped in advance, there was no danger I would go on the air live and tear Pocket Protector a new asshole, but I managed to convey that the new management thought a show like *MWB* was not aligned with the desired target audience. Listeners could expect to return to a predictably repetitious onslaught of grunge and drone delivered by a roster of the same thirty artists—over and over and over again.

As always, I let the music passionately express my strong feelings. I ended the show with the same song I played when Boulder's KRNW was sold in 1977: "We'll Meet Again" by the Byrds. Here's the playlist from the final episode on February 24, 2007:

Johnny Cash	Hurt
Johnny Clegg & Savuka	Asimbonanga
Spirit	Give a Life, Take a Life
The Byrds	Turn! Turn! Turn!
Loituma	Levan Polkka
Love	Andmoreagain
Andy Palacio	Baba
Otis Redding	Pain in My Heart
Roy Orbison	A Love So Beautiful
Cat Stevens	Tea for the Tillerman
Ismaël Lo	Aiwa

Soul Clan	Soul Meeting
Iron City Houserockers	Don't Let Them Push You Around
Rodney Crowell	Don't Get Me Started
Bruce Springsteen	Darkness on the Edge of Town
Tom Waits	Step Right Up
Harry Nilsson	Spaceman
Steve Earle	The Revolution Starts Now
Skeeter Davis	The End of the World
The Everly Brothers	Crying in the Rain
Emmylou Harris	Goodbye
Southside Johnny	I Don't Want to Go Home
The Animals	We Gotta Get Out of This Place
The Byrds	We'll Meet Again

Music Without Boundaries had been aired on five different San Diego radio stations over a fourteen-year span. After speaking to a few other program directors who professed interest in the show but lacked the creative fire I needed in a leader, I decided to give the show a rest.

37.

playing the game

Thoughts about leaving my job began as early as my first year at Southland Concerts. Relocating from Boulder to San Diego had been difficult enough, but working in an environment where my main responsibility was to mediate staff arguments that threatened to explode into fistfights was not my idea of a good time. Before long, though, I got through boot camp, the majority of the objectionable players disappeared, and I was running the show.

I learned how to play the game but grimaced at most of the lessons. I witnessed more despicable behavior in my first year as a concert producer than I'd seen during my entire twelve years as a DJ, journalist, and musician in Boulder. I saw agents and managers being bribed with drugs, lavish gifts, hookers, paid vacations, and blowout dinners. I saw promoters create phony expense documents to cheat the act during settlements, add seats to the venue that weren't on the computerized capacity manifest, and take kickbacks from everyone from Ticketmaster to the equipment rental company to pad their profits (or minimize their losses). I was privy to outrageous bidding wars between promoters whose goal was to get the show at all costs, quash the competition, and create a monopoly if possible. Greed and deception were the norm in the concert industry. All sides expected to be cheated, yet everyone coexisted amid a curious mixture of smiles and screams.

After the demise of Southland Concerts, my shift from working with an unpredictable dilettante like Brent to becoming a profit-sharing employee of a straightforward businessman like Richard Bartell was akin to a carnivore switching to a diet of kale and Brussels sprouts. The jarring transition was a godsend on many crucial levels and a soul squelcher on others.

On the positive side, Richard was a respected hotelier whose family empire included seven properties and a thousand employees. He admittedly knew nothing about the concert business, so he relied on me to book the shows, hire the office and production staffs, and run the operation. He was meticulous and honest and had seemingly bottomless pockets. Deposits went out like clockwork, vendors got paid on the day of the show, and he agreed with my recommendation that he pour a small fortune into upgrading the venue, doubling its capacity in the process.

On the flip side, Richard viewed music solely as a commodity. Whereas Brent and I spent countless hours devising strategies to give exposure to deserving, unknown artists and I prided myself in creating two- and three-act packages, Richard agreed to take on this business only if it was commercially successful. "Just book the winners" was his oft-repeated credo, as if the concert business were a laboratory science. "I want the big names, not the acts you *think* will be big one day."

From the outset of our partnership, Richard made it clear that to him, "art" was a four-letter word. He scoffed at the concept of artist development and tried to reel me in when he felt the "artiste" in me was interfering with a strict business decision. We had ongoing philosophical differences, and I have little doubt he would have fired me if we hadn't been making so much money.

Richard also rolled his eyes whenever I'd book a world music act. If it wasn't a blockbuster like Hootie & the Blowfish, Ringo Starr's All-Star Band, or Diana Ross, he wasn't interested. I would adorn the schedule with acts like Hawaiian crooner Keali'i Reichel, Senegalese superstar Youssou N'Dour, and South African vocal group Ladysmith Black Mambazo, and he'd say in mock derision, "I don't want you booking any acts whose names I can't pronounce."

Our tug-of-war reached a peak in 2001 when I worked my ass off to secure a rare booking with Buena Vista Social Club, a band of Cuban musicians in their seventies, eighties, and nineties who had been lifted from obscurity by Ry Cooder and an Academy Award–nominated documentary by Wim Wenders. Richard had never heard of them and I spent fifteen minutes effusively describing how lucky we were that Ibrahim Ferrer, Compay Segundo, Rubén González, Omara Portuondo, and Eliades Ochoa would be gracing our stage.

Richard was the antithesis of impressed. He urged me to cancel the show before it went on sale.

"The series is going on sale this weekend," I told him, "and Buena Vista Social Club is part of our lineup. Our word is our bond with these agents. I refuse to cancel a confirmed show."

"See if you can get out of it."

"I can't."

"Try."

"No."

Ultimately it was a fight that Richard was happy to have lost. The show sold out in an hour, the quickest sellout of our seventy-five-show season. That night, as part of our annual tradition, I went over the on-sale numbers with Richard. I didn't rub it in (too much) when I came to Buena Vista Social Club. He no longer wanted me to cancel the show.

"Can we get a second night?" he asked.

Richard's essence can be summed up by his own self-assessment. The day after a 2000 Democratic fund-raiser that a friend insisted he attend, Richard described his meet-and-greet with Al Gore and San Diego's political elite: "I was in a room with all these people who were trying to save the world. All I cared about was waking up the next day and figuring out how to make more money." He said it with a smile. That's who he is.

No one would deny Richard Bartell's charisma. Somewhat short in stature, but with Hollywood actor good looks, he engenders tremendous loyalty and respect from his workforce. He considers the concert series nothing more than an adjunct to his hotel business, albeit a profitable and glamorous one. Richard would use the series to his advantage, wining and dining San Diego's most prominent bankers, business moguls, and politicos with complimentary tickets and meals at the upscale Humphrey's Restaurant. It's one thing to oversee a multimillion-dollar group of hotels, but the real "glitz" and "sizzle," two of Richard's favorite words, come from his being the executive producer of the most prestigious concert series in San Diego.

Richard and I disagreed not only about artistic matters, but about business practices as well. Early on in our working relationship, I learned that he was unwilling to adopt certain time-honored behaviors inherent in the concert industry. Although I tried to persuade him otherwise, he adamantly opposed showering the artists, agents, and managers with gifts and bonuses as all our competitors did. "We're giving them a good payday and a beautiful place to play. That's more than enough," he said.

I ran down numerous examples of what our rivals had done to curry favor with influential agents. Airline tickets. Free golf and time-share accommodations in Maui. Private rooms at Spago. Envelopes stuffed with C-notes. A partridge in a pear tree.

Nothing I said would change Richard's mind. Fearing for the future of our concert series, I took matters into my own hands.

I began to casually give our box office manager a small stack of unused comp tickets before each show and told her to sell those to the walk-up crowd (night-of-show ticket buyers). When the show was over, I'd separate the comps revenue from the overall take and add it to a special account for taking care of the big boys.

In November, after the concert season ended, I'd go to LA bearing gifts to significant agents and managers. It wasn't a coincidence that I was combining my Santa Claus impressions with making offers for the following season's lineup. I filled Christmas stockings with computers, televisions, golf clubs, gift certificates to resorts in Big Sur and Aspen, and expensive software programs. On top of that, I bonused my Humphrey's coworkers with Richard Bartell's money. I never second-guessed that this was what I needed to do to stay competitive, justifying all my actions in my own mind. Each ensuing year, we'd reap record-breaking profits, and I could point to dozens of shows we presented that most likely had been sold to us as a result of my misguided largesse.

I was a fucking moron to think I wouldn't get caught. It took a few years of investigation, but the crackerjack Bartell Hotels accountant called me at my office on a muggy July afternoon in 1991 to tell me he had uncovered some chicanery emanating from our box office. He said that Grace's receipts didn't jibe with the amount of tickets being pulled off the computer and that hundreds of complimentary tickets were unaccounted for.

"Grace is the most trustworthy person I've ever known," I said honestly, quivering in my sandals at my own dishonesty. "She'd *never* do anything that wasn't kosher."

"I think she's trying to bring you down," said Crackerjack. "Hang tight. We'll know more on Monday."

I was leaving town with Helen for a romantic weekend in the mountains outside Idyllwild to celebrate our fourteenth wedding anniversary. We'd be back by Monday for two sold-out Tony Bennett shows at Humphrey's. Needless to say, I was a nervous wreck for forty-eight hours, couldn't make love with my wife, couldn't enjoy our bottle of Veuve Clicquot, and sweated profusely despite the chilly night air. Making matters worse, I hadn't shared any of this with Helen and told her I was feeling fluish when she asked me what was wrong.

When I got to work on Monday, Mitzi told me that Richard had called and sounded agitated. I tended to all my other calls before returning Richard's a couple of hours later. There was none of our customary Monday morning schmoozing about last week's episode of *Dallas* or comparing notes about trendy new restaurants.

"Come on over. We need to talk," he said, offering no further explanation.

"I'll be right there."

Bartell Hotels' lavishly appointed corporate offices are on the fifth floor of the Holiday Inn across the street from the concert office, located in a spartan, second-story walk-up at Driscoll's Wharf. We had a primo view but had to endure the rank odor coming from a wholesale fish market below.

Shoulders slouched, I marched to my execution, entirely drained of confidence and dignity. I was ready to take my medicine.

Sitting alone at a conference table that could accommodate sixteen people, I stared at a pile of folders and awaited Richard's arrival. When he walked into the room, he handed me a one-page summary of the past several years of box office discrepancies.

"How do you explain this?" he asked. I hallucinated frosty clouds of smoke coming out of his mouth.

I flashed back to being a spectator at settlements during arena shows in 1984, my first year on the job. Ballbusting tour accountants would grill Jerry Mack about every expense, demanding itemized receipts for every dollar spent. If we claimed to have paid three bucks for a box of pushpins to put up posters, we had to prove it. The sweat on Mack's mustachioed lip started dripping and his voice cracked with every lie. I couldn't imagine sitting in that chair.

I came clean immediately. I didn't come prepared with a master list of gift recipients or receipts for products purchased, but I rattled off the accounting from memory.

He either didn't believe me or didn't care. "You just wanted to make an extra 10 percent for yourself."

"I didn't spend a dime on myself, except if you count a few dinners with agents at Chinois on Main," I said, trying to make eye contact without bursting into tears. "We scored dozens of shows we wouldn't have gotten otherwise, like—"

"What about your bonuses to the staff? We talked to everyone. Some said you gave them a hundred, others two hundred. Who do you think you are? *Robin Hood*? Robbing from the rich and giving to the poor?"

My explanations weren't helping me. Nor was readily admitting my guilt. "So where do we go from here?"

"Well, first of all, you're fired! And I want restitution for every dollar you spent."

I got up, weak in the knees, and walked out of his office mumbling an incoherent apology. By the time I returned to my office across the street, Richard's assistant had already gathered all my files and called a locksmith. Mitzi was sobbing uncontrollably. I had kept all of this from her as well.

I gathered my personal belongings. Autographed promo photos, Helen's larger-than-life-size painting of a twenty-four-year-old me, my bulging Rolodex, two boxes of CDs. I drove home slowly, talking aloud to myself. "I blew it. What the fuck have I done? I blew it." It was time to tell Helen about all of this too.

As has been the case throughout our forty-plus years together, Helen was unconditionally supportive. In between my bouts of crying and wheezing, we discussed pragmatics ranging from if we could afford to keep up payments on our house to whether I should hire an attorney. After making a few calls, we made an appointment with one of the most prominent criminal lawyers in San Diego.

By the next morning, the phone was ringing off the hook at our house. Every agent who had done business with Humphrey's had received a FedEx letter from Bartell announcing that I had been "terminated" and that Humphrey's would continue to thrive thanks to the financial backing of Bartell Hotels. Mercifully, he provided no further details.

I kept my composure and shared the truth with some of my closest compatriots, like Marc Geiger, John Harrington, Clint Mitchell, and Chuck Morris. I told the others that my firing was justified, for I had crossed the lines in my employer-employee relationship. I encouraged them all to continue to do business with Humphrey's and thanked them for their support. After each phone call, I'd drench my pillow with tears. I was unraveling.

Later that day, I found out that the agents had begun calling one another and rallying on my behalf. Humphrey's was ultimately a minor part of their universe, but a tasteful and consistently appealing summer stop on many of their artists' itineraries. Among themselves, they devised a plan to call Bartell one after the other. Some would scream. Some would be mild-mannered yet firm. The tirades ranged from "I'll never put another fucking show into your piece-of-shit venue again!" to "I hope you're not going to lose Kenny to the competition, because we'll all follow him."

Flustered by this onslaught, Bartell called me at home. Incredulously, he asked me to drive with him to LA and introduce him to the agents and managers, tell them why I was fired, and urge them to continue doing business with Humphrey's. I nixed that plan, explaining that I had spoken with all the agents individually and told them I deserved to be fired.

I cut our conversation short and took off for my appointment with the criminal lawyer. After a one-hour consultation, I ended up not adhering to one piece of his advice. He told me to immediately suspend all communication with Richard Bartell, avoid offering him anything that might be construed as an apology, and by no means should I put *anything* in writing. A few hours later, I wrote a six-page letter to Richard accounting for every dollar I had taken, detailing every purchase I had made (without identifying the recipients of the gifts) and the profit his company had made from the agencies, managers, and acts that probably returned to Humphrey's because of this preferred treatment. I apologized as well and hoped that Richard would remember the successes we had shared over the previous seven years. I gave the letter to a Holiday Inn bellhop who hand-delivered it to Richard's desk.

Less than two days after I was fired and less than one day after my termination had been reported to the industry, Richard called me at home and asked me to meet him at my former office. He gave Mitzi the afternoon off and told me he'd be waiting for me there. Showing up in my customary jeans and T-shirt, I was greeted by my boss in a custom-made suit, dress shirt with monogrammed cuffs, and silk designer tie.

Sitting at the desk, Richard motioned for me to sit across from him. He acknowledged reading my letter and sharing it with his father, Lee, the much-loved patriarch of the Bartell family.

"My father feels sorry for you," he said, before launching into a monologue I'd heard many times before about how all decisions should be made for the well-being of the business. Neglecting to mention being tag-teamed by the agents, he said that he had decided that his business would be best served if I booked the series and, astonishingly, offered me my job back. He would deduct the total of my slush fund from my year-end bonus.

I had poured my heart and soul into the development of Humphrey's. Much to my surprise, it had become my identity. Although I hadn't slept in a week, fretting about my future and visualizing life after Humphrey's, at that moment I had the mental clarity to realize I wasn't ready to move on.

Richard and I shook hands. He handed me a new set of office keys, and my life as a concert producer resumed.

Even though my relationship with Richard was plagued by philosophical head butts, I have never worked for a more reliable person. He didn't have to give me a second chance, but he did. Whenever this nerve-shredding incident came up in conversation over the years, Richard brushed it off and reminded me that our successful working relationship hadn't missed a beat.

I remained at Humphrey's for another fifteen years before leaving it all behind.

38.

denouement

FRIENDS AND COWORKERS WERE STUNNED when I voluntarily walked away from my lucrative job and well-connected professional life. To them, I had it all. A hefty paycheck, semiannual bonuses, a grab bag of perks, a five-minute commute, and no time clock to punch.

Why would I abandon the golden goose? Had I lost my marbles?

I blame it on the chickadee that landed on my fingertips and ate birdseed off my palm in Beech Forest outside Provincetown, Massachusetts. That was my epiphany. It was May 24, 2006, and I announced to anyone who would listen that I was going to quit my job as soon as we got back to San Diego.

We had been in Northampton, Massachusetts, attending the graduation of our granddaughter, Shira, from Smith College. Witnessing a horde of optimistic young women tossing their caps in the air and subsequently musing about their wide-open futures made me yearn for a similar kind of freedom I hadn't had in a long time. The Smithies had their whole lives in front of them to go wherever their hearts directed them. A few days later, as I gazed into the eyes of a chickadee just inches from my face, I felt an intense need to awaken my dormant free spirit.

That all-consuming feeling reminded me of when I failed my draft physical in 1970 and exhaled a lifetime of relief. It reminded me of when I quit or got fired from four part-time jobs in 1980 and, when gifted with an abundance of time, decided to put my first band together. It reminded me of when I cast my fate to the wind, changed careers, and moved to San Diego in 1983. On all those occasions, I heard my heart singing, felt my blood pumping and surging in mystical ways, pondered the enormity of the void that awaited me, and envisioned filling that void with buckets of creativity.

I no longer relished the safety and comfort of my job, no matter how big the paycheck was. The power, perks, and prestige that were part of my daily routine for so long had become irrelevant. My soul needed to dance again.

The thrill of being in the concert business had evaporated years before I finally had the guts to leave. I originally entered the worlds of radio, journalism, and concert producing because music was my passion. By the time my long run ended, I had witnessed firsthand all my chosen fields being crippled by relentless greed and decay while struggling to hold on to relevance and profitability.

Music radio stations have narrowed their playlists to belt-tightening extremes. Music-loving programmers have been exterminated, replaced by focus groups and market researchers. With the onset of deregulation, the concept of local radio has virtually disappeared as corporations swoop in to buy blocks of stations in small markets and program them from afar. The few remaining independent stations have become afraid of their own shadows.

Newspapers, on the endangered species list as I write this, have savaged their staffs with layoffs as advertising dollars dry up or head in the direction of new media. Writers previously encouraged to flesh out their stories with wit, personality, opinion, and tangential sidebars are now given a strict word count and nudged toward the sensational.

Despite the emergence of MTV and YouTube, nothing will replace the excitement and chills provided by the live music experience. But going to concerts has become a chore, increasingly generic and not worth the effort, as ticket prices have soared irrationally and promoters have forgotten how to accommodate and pamper their clientele. The average customer used to be able to line up the day a show went on sale with a solid chance of getting a front-row seat. Today, that same customer, who logs on to Ticketmaster the exact second the on-sale begins, will be lucky to get a pair of seats in the first thirty rows due to sponsor holds, venue holds, fan club holds, presales to American Express cardholders, and inside relationships between promoters and scalpers. Even fan club members, who have spent hundreds of dollars for the "privilege" of buying tickets before they go on sale to the public, get shitty seats.

In 1969 I saw a free Rolling Stones concert in Hyde Park and three years later paid an obscenely high (at the time) $14 for my third-row Rolling Stones/Stevie Wonder ticket at the Denver Coliseum. When the Stones hit Madison Square Garden in 2006, my childhood friend Elliot and I were willing to pay $450 a ticket to see this celebrated band from the '60s whose members were now all *in* their sixties (I got comped as an industry favor, but I *would have* paid the price as thousands of others did that night). For the Stones' fiftieth-anniversary tour in 2013, tickets maxed out at $600 a pop, before service charges and venue fees.

Even at a midsize venue like Humphrey's, prices have risen much more sharply than the cost of living. When I began in 1984, our average ticket cost $13. When I exited in 2006, the norm was $56. The average Humphrey's ticket is now in the $65 range, and to get a front-row seat, you have to buy dinner and stay in a hotel suite, even if you live just a few blocks away. The closest you can get to the stage without buying a dinner show or hotel package is the ninth row. Two front-row seats to the 2012 Ringo Starr concert (with dinner and hotel suite) would have set you back $759, excluding Ticketmaster fees.

The elitism that now rules the concert business is by no means limited to Humphrey's, but it was a major impetus in pushing me toward the exit. You can't get a good ticket to a show unless you're rich or well connected. I hated that I was working for a company perpetuating that equation.

Toward the end of my tenure at Humphrey's, neighboring casinos had begun sprouting like dandelions, and the mentality of the artists, agents, and managers shifted again. The casino buyers raided the Humphrey's talent roster by offering our high-caliber acts two to three times their market value. We were paying Bill Cosby his asking price of $105K for two shows. Viejas Casino offered him $150K. We never saw Mr. Cosby again.

We had nurtured acts like Chris Issak and Lyle Lovett to a healthy $50K-payday level. Suddenly Viejas Casino was offering them $100K a night and we had to match the offer to keep the artist. In playing that game, from one year to the next, the cost of a ticket to see Isaak or Lovett at Humphrey's rose from $45 to $95. How do you explain that to a loyal customer?

Ultimately it comes back to greed. No one *ever* made enough money. I got dragged into the gutter more often than I want to remember. I cheated. I lied. I became someone I disliked. Every time I confessed my sins to a close confidant in the business, the response was the same: "Get over it. Everyone does it. You fuck them. They fuck you. What's the big deal?" My favorite colleagues were all willing participants in the ongoing scam.

I found a legal pad the other day from 2006 with pages of late-night ramblings filled with the pros and cons of my job, self-loathing snippets, and random assessments and overviews of my lot in life. One line was circled, highlighted, and underlined: TWO DECADES OF COMPROMISE AND ADVILS!

Compromise is fine if you're a politician in a two-party system and need to figure out ways to jam your legislation through, but it's a trait I tried to sidestep as long as possible.

I never compromised during my life on the radio. If I didn't personally love a song, I didn't play it. My only audition to work within the context of a format was an utter failure as I kept inserting my own selections, much to the chagrin of my program director who was counting on me to be a team player. "This just isn't working, Kenny," he said, sighing. I didn't argue with him.

When *Denver Post* columnist G. Brown singled me out as the best disc jockey in the Denver/Boulder metro area in 1978, he gushed, "Weissberg has made a career of having his own way on the radio. He is one of the only people in Colorado to showcase all sorts of music and is well-versed in everything from reggae to punk to country rock." Translation: *no compromise.*

When I was a journalist in Colorado, I served as my own assignment editor. In a state that worshipped John Denver and the Nitty Gritty Dirt Band, I wrote instead about the emergence of glam rock, posing for accompanying photos in face powder and mascara while wearing Helen's leggings and feathered boa. When my editor at the *Boulder Daily Camera* urged me to cover the disco phenomenon, I refused and turned my readers on to new artists like Devo, Joan Armatrading, Southside Johnny, Rockpile, and Garland Jeffreys. Translation: *no compromise.*

In my three and a half years orchestrating and fronting Kenny & the Kritix, I scoffed at the advice of my seasoned band members to give the audience what they wanted, meaning familiar songs by the Eagles, Led Zeppelin, Fleetwood Mac, and Jimmy Buffett. I peppered my set lists with obscure gems from the Iron City Houserockers, Wreckless Eric, Ducks Deluxe, and Mink DeVille, sprinkling in non-hit album cuts from recognizable artists like Springsteen, the Cars, David Bowie, and Jerry Lee Lewis. Translation: *no compromise.*

My transition to concert producer, where I was responsible for someone else's financial investment, was rife with compromise from the beginning. I could no longer present or recommend music according to my own daring, off-kilter taste. I *had* to give the people what they wanted, even if they demanded mediocrity. When I confirmed the first booking of my career—Chuck Mangione—I can't even begin to describe the shame I felt signing that contract. Not only was his music the aural equivalent of corn syrup, but he was needlessly arrogant to boot. At the end of a show bereft of meaning, though, I had to take into account that we netted $12,000. I booked him again and again.

We made money for years on acts like Kenny G, Air Supply, Spyro Gyra, Chicago, the Rippingtons, Christopher Cross, Earl Klugh, and Dave Koz, none of whose music I've ever played on the radio, written about, or emulated as a performer. All of them were consistent box office smashes at Humphrey's. Translation: *compromise with benefits.*

When I returned to San Diego from Shira's graduation at the end of May 2006, I called Richard Bartell to set up a private meeting. We met at the same conference table where he had fired me fifteen years before.

I was nervous and stammered uncharacteristically. "I . . . want to thank you for all you've done for me and my family over the past twenty years. Working for you at Humphrey's . . . is the best thing that has ever happened to us. It's been a great, great ride. But I'm leaving at the end of the season. I'll do whatever I can to help you find a replacement—if you want me to—but I've reached the end of the line. Again, thank you for everything."

Richard sat in stunned silence. "Is this about money?" he finally asked. I had given notice once before only to be lured back into the fold with a substantial raise.

"No. This is about self-preservation. It's about avoiding burnout." Rather than admit that I was finished with his micromanaging and my in-house battles with various members of his support staff, and had recurring nightmares about Humphrey's plastic chairs and overbearing security guards, I blamed it on my pressing need to process Helen's emergency surgery and eleven-day hospitalization in April and to mourn my mother who had died the previous year.

In the past, Richard had acquiesced to my occasional demands in order to preserve our continuity and not rock the boat. This time, he seemed sincerely relieved that I was leaving. "Are you sure?"

"Very."

And that was it. I composed an email to every agent, manager, and artist who had been instrumental in Humphrey's success. I hit Send without sleeping on it. I refused to give myself another chance to hold on. This is what I had to say:

After a glorious twenty-three-year run as producer/talent buyer of the Humphrey's Concerts by the Bay series in San Diego, I will be moving on at the end of the current season. My decision is my own and my departure is completely amicable. Richard Bartell, Humphrey's owner, has often told me that our handshake deal was "for life" if I wanted it. Having spent nearly 40 percent of my life at this job, I almost took him up on his offer.

I leave with my head held high, extremely proud of what this concert series has meant to San Diego and the patrons who have flown in from all around the world to see their favorite artists in such an idyllic setting. Highlights are too numerous to mention in this email . . .

Humphrey's Concerts celebrates its twenty-fifth anniversary this year. We've remained proudly independent throughout that time, defying all the odds and rampant consolidation that has inextricably changed the music business all of us fell in love with at an early age. My sincere thanks to Richard Bartell, who has approached this wacky extremity of his hotel business with solid and consistent backing, putting up with his eccentric talent buyer all these years. Richard and I will carefully work together

to choose my successor and continue to bring the best entertain-
ment to San Diego for years to come.

I also never would have made it this far without my loyal
and undyingly supportive assistant, Mitzi Stone, who has stood
by me and kept me sane and organized for the past nineteen
years. She will remain at Humphrey's and doubtlessly continue
to be the glue that holds it all together.

Finally, my gratitude goes out to all of you who sold me
shows, encouraged me to continue on a job that I've been "quit-
ting" for the past fifteen years, and offered advice when I most
needed it and suggestions that I may never have come up with
on my own. "Symbiotic relationship" has become a cliché, but
that's what we've had and I will never forget the collaborative
spirit that has made Humphrey's so successful and enabled me
and my family to thrive as a result.

Thanks for accompanying me on this wonderful, amaz-
ing ride. While I will miss this phase of my lifelong devotion to
music, I eagerly look forward to new adventures that await me
down the road.

With passion, respect, and much affection,
Kenny Weissberg

Bartell called a meeting of the concert staff on the following Monday. We went over a dozen potential people or corporations to replace me as talent buyer/producer. They ranged from a few of my independent-minded colleagues in Orange County and Santa Cruz to monoliths like Live Nation, AEG, and Nederlander.

"I know I have no say in this," I said in soft, respectful tones, "but whatever you do, don't hire a casino buyer, especially the guys at Viejas Casino."

"I won't even take a meeting with them," Bartell said.

You can guess the punch line.

Bartell hired the buyers from Viejas Casino. I was probably the last to know, having found out from several agents the day before Richard revealed his choice to the concert staff. I was outraged but then I had to laugh. After working with me for more than two decades, Richard couldn't wait to work with the anti-Kenny, a corporate entity that shared his dispassionate approach to the business of music. Within a year, the Viejas team was absorbed by the gigantic AEG Live. Humphrey's has become one of the hundreds of venues that AEG books worldwide.

In essence, Richard's decision made it easier for me to let go. I dutifully saw the 2006 season through to its conclusion, showing up at every concert to say farewell to all the artists who had fallen in love with Humphrey's and become regulars on our lineup. Warm embraces and onstage acknowledgements abounded from the likes of George Carlin, Ringo Starr, Joan Baez, Lyle Lovett, Chris Isaak, Richard Thompson (who actually announced my "retirement" to the audience as he was changing a broken guitar string), Southside Johnny, Etta James, Randy Newman, Dave Brubeck, and Emmylou Harris.

I sipped champagne with Helen, Mitzi, Bartell, and the concert staff backstage at the October 18 Joan Baez show. It was the end of my era at Humphrey's and I was the last person to leave the venue that night. I stood wistfully by myself on the balcony overlooking the crowd heading toward the exits and watched the crew break down the stage one last time. I waved at the "boat people" on their yachts in adjacent San Diego Bay and tried to estimate how many people I had provided free entertainment to over the past twenty-three years.

The party was over.

39.

what's next?

I SPENT MY FIRST DAYS IN the void coming to grips with numerical adjustments. When I was active as a concert producer, my average daily dosage of communiqués (phone calls, emails, faxes, texts, taps on the shoulder) was two hundred. After I left the building, that count dwindled to two. No exaggeration—two hundred to two. Also noticeable was a less encumbered keychain. When I was a promoter, my pocket bulged like a building superintendent's. An assortment of fifteen color-coded keys to a double-locked office, two post office boxes, safety deposit boxes, hotel dressing rooms, equipment lockers, and briefcases. I'm now down to a single key to my house and a smart key for my Lexus.

I felt disoriented most of 2007. My DayMinder went from a thick forest of miniature, scrawled appointment data to an oasis of blank space. Without a timetable to follow, I started staying up until two in the morning watching movies, lurking on Facebook, and reading *Mojo* magazine. Yet my body clock continued to wake me at 7 a.m. even though I had no agenda or deadlines sparking my engine.

Most days, I walked up and down the stairs of our two-story

home hoping that a vibration or a tingle would spur me into action. I didn't miss Humphrey's, and when *Music Without Boundaries* ended in February, I actually felt a modicum of relief not having to prepare for a weekly radio show for the first time in fourteen years. But I clearly was going through withdrawal from my addictions to stress, productivity, and constant interaction with other people.

To compensate for my lack of structure, I started each morning leafing through the *New York Times*, *LA Times*, and *San Diego Union-Tribune*. I took leisurely shits, did a few crossword puzzles, and walked on Shelter Island or Sunset Cliffs, stopping to photograph pelicans. Although I had never drunk coffee during my twelve-hour workdays, I made a ritual of walking to my neighborhood Peet's four times a week for a medium mocha with whole milk, hold the whipped cream. I can't explain my sudden craving for chocolate-flavored caffeine. I was under no pressure to stay awake and run a multimillion-dollar company anymore.

I did set up a consultancy. Business was anything but brisk as I quoted a fee of $300 an hour and did no outreach or self-promotion. My only paying customer was an endodontist who had dreams of being a major concert promoter. After paying me $600 for a two-hour introductory overview, I agreed to trade all future consults for root canals.

When I turned down a huge offer to book and manage a brand-new $6 million nightclub in the Little Italy section of San Diego (after a lengthy courtship), I had officially dropped out of the business. I have never contacted or been approached by anyone about working in the music business again.

The main benefit of being invisible is not having to fake it on any level. I no longer had to make witty small talk on the phone with sexist, racist, money-exalting, Republican, yacht-club assholes. I no longer had to listen to long-winded Monday morning conversations about golf, NASCAR, strip clubs, and Porsche Carrera GTs. I no longer had to endure the refrain "Get the money *up!*" Although I valued every professional relationship I made during my concert career, I remain in touch with only a select few of the thousands who crossed my path.

When you're in the void, you're your own boss. There are no clocks, no deadlines, no bosses, no paychecks, no itemized tax deductions, no excuses. The only pressure is self-inflicted. Am I contributing anything to society? Am I watching too much TV? Am I living within my means? Am I a blessing or a curse to Helen now that I'm spending so much time at home? Am I eating enough fiber?

I traveled back in time to when my marriage was in chaos during the mid-'80s. To save it, I determined I needed to find a marriage counselor, quit doing drugs, and join a health club. That combo platter of self-improvement worked wonders then, so I set out on a similar course to keep my body and mind from atrophying into irreparable mush. I went into therapy to deal with loss (of job, income, identity, daily routine, power) and forged a relationship with a personal trainer who constructively beats the shit out of me twice a week. I flew to various parts of the country to spend quality time with my father, sister, brother, stepchildren, and grandchildren.

It's been a rock 'n' roll life for me. If you don't count the day I spent making crunchy granola, every post-college job I've had related to music. I worked retail in two record stores. I talked into a microphone, spun records, and interviewed pop-culture icons at eight radio stations. I wrote music criticism and features for seventeen publications (including creating/publishing a monthly arts-and-culture magazine called *Cake Eaters* in 1974, which lasted for thirteen glorious issues). I was a disco DJ at two major hotel nightclubs. I hosted a rock video TV show in Denver. I designed and booked a live music venue in Boulder. I fronted my own rock band for three and a half years. I managed the fledgling career of Jim Croce's young son, A. J., for twenty-one months. And I capped it all off with twenty-three years of producing concerts at Humphrey's.

Amid all the professional mayhem and merriment, I managed to keep a marriage together for forty years, raise two stepchildren, play an important role in the lives of three grandchildren, and travel the six-thousand-mile round trip between San Diego and New Jersey two dozen times over a five-year period to care for and honor my elderly parents at the end of their lives. As my mother lay dying in 2005, her body weakened and shriveled, but her mind as lucid as a forty-year-old in full force, her last words to me were, "So when are you going to write your book?" Busting my balls until the very end, although the smile on her face implied a touch of sarcasm.

My father, who worked as a stockbroker for Smith Barney for forty-one years until unceremoniously being laid off at age eighty-eight, lived for another five years after my mother died. My mother had instructed him to mourn her for six months and then pursue one of the acceptable widows on a list she'd given him. He ended up happily "going steady" with one of my mother's dearest friends for the rest of his life.

In March of 2009, racked by a combination of lung malfunctions, blood clots, a bowel obstruction, and congestive heart failure, my dad was told he had a week to live unless he had major surgery. He declined that option and was at peace with his decision, so Helen and I raced to the East Coast to spend his final days by his side. His dire conditions self-corrected within two days of his death sentence and he lived for another sixteen months.

I'm laughing as I head down the homestretch of this tome. To paraphrase two different songs by the Kinks and the Kingston Trio, "Where have all the bookstores gone?" I wonder if my time might have been better spent scaling fish on the Ocean Beach Pier or learning dressage. Writing a book seems so mid-twentieth century.

I think back on all the changes I've lived through: 45s begat LPs, which morphed into CDs, which gave way to digital downloads. We went from mono to stereo to quadrophonic sound before reverting to muddled sonic compression. From jukeboxes to iTunes. From speakers the size of silos to earbuds that can fit into a thimble. The joy of finding new records at E. J. Korvettes, Victor Music, or dozens of Tower Records has been taken away from us, replaced by one-click shopping at Amazon.

My portable Olympia (a bottle of Liquid Paper always at hand) was soon replaced by a used IBM Selectric II with lift-off tape. That served me well for ten years until I moved to San Diego and upgraded to an Apple II with an Epson printer. I've been a Mac guy ever since.

Most of the periodicals I wrote for have gone to newsprint heaven, and my dinosaur status will be further enhanced when these words appear on carefully chosen paper stock entombed in a hardcover binder. I'm a little late to that party. My hope is that you somehow absorb the content, likely on your Kindle or iPad, or have it read to you aloud by Siri on your iPhone as you walk across a crowded intersection while texting your cousin about tonight's Hulu marathon.

I've spent my entire life being a magnet for crazy.

So what's next? What else? I've got a few years left. It's time to close my eyes and fabricate some sort of impossible dream. Something completely unattainable.

And then tell everyone I know.

acknowledgments

I've been gifted in this lifetime with an extraordinary cast of supporting characters who have made my adventures thrilling, tantalizing, and twisted.

First and foremost, I'm down on my knees thanking my lucky stars for the day I spotted Helen Redman across the backyard fence. Helen, you are my soul mate, my muse, my conscience, and my wife. Thank you for your art that enriches my life every day. You make my heart sing.

I cherish my wonderfully diverse and quirky family: Nicole and Kevin, Paul and Kathryn, Shira, Issac, Ethan, Ellen and Lewis, Roger and Stephanie, Elizabeth, Ted, and Nik—a soulful and selfless tribe.

Hugs and squeezes to my caring readers, opinionated editors, and gentle prodders, without whom this book would still be in a box gathering mold and housing silverfish: Sandra Jonas, Ange Takats (the girl from Oz), G. Brown, Anne Marie Welsh, and John D'Agostino. Much appreciation to Phel Steinmetz for making the photos come alive, some of them wrinkled snapshots. And special thanks to the editors who believed in me when I was a twenty-something in Boulder with an Olympia typewriter: Wayne Robins, Stephen Foehr, and Barbralu Cohen.

Sincere thanks to my radio colleagues who embraced my persona and trusted what I did from 1971 to 2007: Glen Gerberg, Bob O'Connor, Michael Halloran, Robert Hughes, Mike Glickenhaus, Kevin Stapleford, Jason Sherman, Peter Lengsfelder, Peter Rodman, Bob Skutelsky, Jon Steele, Bob Wells, Dennis Constantine, and Robert Neil Wilkinson.

The Kritix. How could I have been so fortunate to attract such brilliant and supportive musicians to make my dream come true? I will remember every one of them. Thank you, Mark Andes, Sam Broussard, Jamie Kibben, Michael Reese, Milt Muth, Brian Brown, Chip McCarthy, David Muse, Greg Overton, Jeffrey Wood, Hawk Hawkins, Peter Roos, Jamie Polisher, Dennis "Dr. Roc" Durakovich, Craig Skinner, Judy Rudin, Tim Duffy, and Jim Waddell.

My favorite agents, who always got me to spend five to ten thousand dollars too much, but whose faith in me and our venue helped make Humphrey's Concerts by the Bay one of the longest running concert series in the United States. Thank you, John Harrington, Clint Mitchell, Guy Richard, Jim Gosnell, Fred Bohlander, Paul Goldman, Brett Steinberg, Steve Levine, Rick Farrell, Chyna Chuan, Jeff Allen, Rod Essig, David Fishof, Wayne Forte, Chris Goldsmith, Dave Hart, Steve Hauser, Josh Humiston, Paul LaMonica, Jack Randall, Frank Riley, Richard Rosenberg, Peter Sheils, Steve Smith, Nanci Stevens, Warren Wyatt, and Dick Alen.

The body and mind workers who have kept me sane, fit, relaxed, and whole: Susan Carabello, Joan Maresca, Gita Morena, Michael Scott, Greg Sterner, Lynette Triere, and Nancy Ursuliak.

Richard Bartell, both a boss and a collaborator, who gave me the freedom to create a colorful palette of performers. His loyalty and steadfast approach to business were crucial to Humphrey's unqualified success. Our twenty-plus years of camaraderie and conflict gave the concert series a winning combination of art and commerce.

Mitzi Stone, my assistant for my final nineteen years at Humphrey's. I could *never* have done it without you, Mitzi. All who know you feel that you're their best friend, including me.

Chuck Morris, my friend, confidant, advisor, and Jew-ru from my first day on the radio in 1971 through my last day at Humphrey's in 2006 . . . and beyond.

Marc Geiger, my mentor in the concert business when he was a twenty-one-year-old college kid. Although we worked together for only six months at Humphrey's in 1984, Geigs continued to be there for me throughout my career, even after ascending to super-agent status. I've had vicarious pleasure watching him be a pathfinder in the tech revolution, cofound the iconic Lollapalooza, and develop an impressive stable of artists and agents with his progressive, visionary approach to the business of music.

The boys: Kenny Weinberg, Sam Goldberg, Elliot Satsky, and John Lee.

In closing, I give eternal gratitude to my parents, Snooks Weissberg (1920–2005) and Ned Weissberg (1918–2010). Mom and Dad, you didn't always approve of my chosen paths, but you never turned your backs on me for a second. I learned so much from you and will love you both forever.

about the author

Kenny Weissberg has worn nearly every hat in the music industry. He produced and hosted twenty-five hundred radio shows for eight stations from 1971 to 2007, cofounded Boulder's KGNU in 1978, and programmed and hosted the award-winning *Music Without Boundaries* for fourteen years. As a music critic, he wrote a thousand newspaper and magazine articles for seventeen publications, including the *Denver Post, Boulder Daily Camera, Creem, Rocky Mountain Magazine*, and *Cake Eaters*. From 1980 to 1983, he fronted his own rock band, Kenny & the Kritix, and for the next twenty-three years, he produced the internationally acclaimed Humphrey's Concerts by the Bay series in San Diego, presenting two thousand concerts.

Kenny lives in San Diego with his wife, artist Helen Redman.